Writing as Social Action

Writing
as
Social Action

Marilyn M. Cooper
Michigan Technological University

and

Michael Holzman

BOYNTON/COOK PUBLISHERS
HEINEMANN
PORTSMOUTH, NH

Boynton/Cook Publishers
A Division of
Heinemann Educational Books, Inc.
70 Court Street   Portsmouth, NH 03801
Offices and agents throughout the world

The following has generously given permission to use material in this book:

"Voyage in the Blue," *Self-Portrait in a Convex Mirror* by John Ashbery. Copyright © 1972 by John Ashbery. All rights reserved. Reprinted by permission of Viking Penguin Inc. Originally appeared in *The New Yorker*.

Versions of some of the essays have been published previously:

"The Ecology of Writing," *College English*, 48 (1986), 364–75. Copyright © 1986 by the National Council of Teachers of English. Reprinted by permission of the publisher.

"A Post-Freirean Model for Adult Literacy Education," *College English*, 50 (1988), 177–89. Copyright © 1988 by the National Council of Teachers of English. Reprinted by permission of the publisher.

"Evaluation in Adult Literacy Programs," *The Writing Instructor*, 7 (1987), 8–20.

"Talking About Protocols," *College Composition and Communication*, 34 (1983), 288–93. Copyright © 1983 by the National Council of Teachers of English. Reprinted by permission of the publisher.

"More Talk About Protocols" (reply to Flower and Hayes), *College Composition and Communication*, 36 (1985), 97–100. Copyright © 1985 by the National Council of Teachers of English. Reprinted by permission of the publisher.

"Context as Vehicle: Implicatures in Writing," in *What Writers Know: The Language, Process, and Structure of Written Discourse*, ed. Martin Nystrand (New York: Academic Press, 1982), pp. 105–28. Copyright © 1982 by the Academic Press.

"The Social Context of Literacy Education," *College English*, 48 (1986), 27–33. Copyright © 1986 by the National Council of Teachers of English. Reprinted by permission of the publisher.

"Teaching Is Remembering," *College English*, 46 (1984), 229–38. Copyright © 1984 by the National Council of Teachers of English. Reprinted by permission of the publisher.

We thank NCTE, *The Writing Instructor*, and Academic Press for permission to use them here.

Library of Congress Cataloging-in-Publication Data
Cooper, Marilyn M.
    Writing as social action / Marilyn M. Cooper and Michael Holzman.
      p. cm.
    Bibliography: p.
    ISBN 0-86709-244-0
    1. Elementary education of adults. 2. Functional literacy.
    3. Rhetoric—Social aspects. I. Holzman, Michael. II. Title.
    LC5219.C62 1989
    374'.012—dc19   88-31483
                                              CIP

Designed by Vic Schwarz.
Printed in the United States of America.
93 92 91 90 89 9 8 7 6 5 4 3 2 1

Contents

Introduction

The scene of writing is often conceived in terms of the ideologically loaded image of the individual writer sitting at a desk in a garret, searching her own soul for inspiration in order to write for some individual reader, equally isolated in her curtained window-seat (cf. Brodkey 1987, 396). But as writing teachers and researchers, we have found that the actual scene of writing is much more open: the classroom crowded with other writers, the computer lab, the writing center, or perhaps the archetype of all of these, the newspaper editorial office in which individuals embodying the different parts of the writing process compose, edit, revise, and proofread in a noisy and exuberant enactment of literacy. Neither image, of course, is meant to describe all writing in all times and places. The image is where we begin thinking about writing, an encapsulation of what we think is important to consider.

As we remember our school experience, the dominant form of writing was not anything our teachers assigned (though in those days, of course, much writing was assigned), but rather the notes passed hand to hand, hidden in desks to avoid the teacher's eyes. Much of this writing was dyadic in mode, the "come to my place after school" variety. But some of this writing involved larger social groups, and sometimes the entire class participated. One of us remembers a fourth grade class in particular in which a good part of several weeks was spent writing serial stories: each student wrote a sentence before passing the story on to the next. An especially good contribution was one that left the next writer with an impossible situation to resolve or explain. By the time the story returned to you, the characters and plot line had usually changed radically. Students expressed themselves—and more particularly their relation to the rest of the class—in what they wrote. Some attempted to restore unity in the story while others delighted in creating the wildest imaginable scenes; some defended rules of decorum while others strove to go beyond the consensus of what should be written in the stories; some frequently initiated new stories while others frequently skipped their turn or repeated what others had written. We knew each other by our writing; we created a particular kind of social group in our stories. They ended when the teacher found one, not because she was upset by it (she wasn't really), but because just her knowing about the stories changed the way we wrote them.

The argument of the following pages is that writing is a social activity. In the composition classroom, in the writing research laboratory, in the basic education or adult literacy class, teacher and learner, researcher and subject bring with them entire communities whenever they are engaged with writing. When, either in our research or in our teaching, we ignore these communities, we ignore the complexities of social structure and dynamic that characterize writing. Researchers might argue that simplification is essential in some kinds of experimental inquiry, but, with writing, results derived from individuals in a laboratory setting must always be measured against what happens in the real—and not so simple—world. Likewise, a familiar way of thinking about teaching writing is in terms of the interactions between the individual teacher and learner, but there are few actual situations in which this occurs: usually learners are plural and they often interact with each other more than they do with the teacher, circumstances that can be made contributory to learning if they are not ignored.

Increasingly, writing researchers have found that "elegant" methods of studying writing are reductive, producing results that have no bearing on what writers—either beginning or expert—do. The common view of the natural science paradigm of research—the bracketing of variables so that a single one can be studied in isolation—is fundamentally inapplicable in the human sciences. No variables in human behavior are isolable. Thus, the mode of our research in this book is more interpretive than experimental: we offer analyses, stories, arguments, meditations, but no quantifiable data.

It is difficult to sufficiently appreciate the density of everyday life. Whether we are considering the question of why a particular student in a particular class cannot seem to organize his argument on a particular subject or the question of the effect of the mode of writing on what is written and by whom, there is no single determining factor. There is peer pressure and there is writing anxiety and there is ideology and there is institutionalized alienation; there is Gutenberg and there is Petrarch and there is the proletariat and there is the microchip. Culture, as we were taught by Althusser, who learned it from Freud (who may have learned it from Marx), is overdetermined. Politics and sexuality, economics and technology, MTV and advertising interpenetrate as a great nexus of causality so that all interpretation is a constant call for yet more mediations as we strive to avoid, on the one hand, reductionism, and, on the other hand, the perpetual play of interpretation that is finally a defense of the status quo.

From theorists such as Vygotsky and his American students, we have recently learned to think that language and learning themselves are in the first instance social activities, that what we had thought—in Piagetian terms—to be natural stages of maturation are actually culturally conditioned *activities* by means of which small groups of individuals in each generation reconstruct the social world. That the social nature of thought and its representation has been overlooked is not surprising; our culture places a great emphasis on individualism, on a Cartesian idea of the self. But even ideas that have ideological motivations as strong as those of individualism can eventually be modified by lack of success in application. Many teachers in schools and colleges, as well as adult education practitioners, have found that the Romantic paradigm of the isolated writer thinking individualized thoughts simply does not work as the basis for writing instruction. In addition to being an artificial and inefficient way to write—when, other than in school, are writers forbidden to enlist help from anyone handy?—the content of the writing that is produced under these circumstances is likely to be inauthentic. Asking students to write something based on their own ideas results in students writing what they have been told—by their parents, their peers, the media. Asking them to look into their souls results in their remembering conversations they have heard. As Bruffee has said, "reflective thought is public or social conversation internalized" (Bruffee 1984, 639). To pretend otherwise, as we all too often do, is at best hypocrisy, at worst a form of indoctrination.

These social aspects of writing have increasingly received attention within our profession, particularly in the last several years. But the meaning of "social" in all of this work is not always the same. Thus, we wish to be very clear about what we mean when we say that writing is a *social activity*—and we wish to emphasize both parts of this term.

First, perhaps, what we don't mean by social. We don't mean that writing is social in the sense that Saussure said that language is social. Saussure used the term in order to emphasize that language is a communal product, not the original creation of individuals as they strive to express themselves. Those who study language, he argued, should focus not on the individual act of speaking but rather on "the social fact" of the system of language, "the instrument created by a collectivity" (Saussure 1966, 13, 11). This might at first seem close to a theory rooted in the world of talk and labor, but, on the contrary, it is only a short step from Saussure's concept of language as "a grammatical system that has a potential existence in each brain, or, more specifically, in the brains of a group of individuals" (13–14) to Chomsky's socially agnostic specification of language as a cognitive ability to produce and understand correct syntactic structures. For us, writing is not merely a common system through which individual minds can communicate—an abstract telephone network in the brains of a group of individuals—but rather a real interaction among social groups and individuals.

Similarly, in saying that writing is social, we don't simply wish to emphasize that writing necessarily involves an audience—readers. The work on social cognition, the ways writers do and/or should think about their readers when writing, converts a social reality into a cognitive category. The writer is still isolated in this view; the absent reader—an ideal, always a fiction—must be reconstructed by the writer. In contrast, if we think of writing as a social activity, readers are always present to writers—real people we know and talk with and do other things with. Writing is not fundamentally a cognitive process, though of course thinking is involved. Writing is a way of interacting with others—a social activity.

What we do mean by social is that writing is located in the social world and, thus, is fundamentally structured by the shape of that environment. Our sense of the term is closer to that employed by Humboldt, who defined language as an activity and argued that "language develops only in social intercourse" (Humboldt 1971, 27, 36). And to Halliday, who says,

> Language is as it is because of the functions it has evolved to serve in people's lives; it is to be expected that linguistic structures could be understood in functional terms. But in order to understand them in this way we have to proceed from the outside inwards, interpreting language by reference to its place in the social process. This is not the same thing as taking an isolated sentence and planting it out in some hothouse that we call a social context. It involves the difficult task of focusing attention simultaneously on the actual and the potential, interpreting both discourse and the linguistic system that lies behind it in terms of the infinitely complex network of meaning potential that is what we call the culture. (Halliday 1978, 4–5)

Like Halliday, we think that we cannot begin with the isolated writer and then add on social factors. To understand what writing is we must first and primarily understand its place in the social process.

In turning from product to process, composition theory and research nevertheless remained safely within an idealist framework. Just as we once analyzed and taught an ideal essay form even though it never existed purely in any real essay, we discovered an ideal writing process, even while recognizing that it would never actually be realized in the writing of any individual or on any particular occasion. In both cases the object of inquiry and imitation is the uniform ideal, from which all realities are divergent, defective, troublesome in the way that Shakespeare was to Dr. Johnson. Though this sometimes seems an apt way to look at student writing, we have learned from Shaughnessy and others that "defective" writing and "divergent" writers have a logic of their own that cannot be understood simply by noting their distance from the ideal. Nor can the writing of such students be "improved" simply by changing the way they think while writing (as if that were even possible). As Bakhtin said about another social activity, "we are most inclined to imagine ideological creation as some inner process of understanding, comprehension, and perception, and do not notice that it in fact unfolds externally, for the eye, the ear, the hand. It is not within us, but between us" (Medvedev/ Bakhtin 1978, 8). Writing happens where we can see and hear and touch it: a fourth-grade student composes an intricate plot turn to confound her classmate, whose turn it is to write next; in Parma, Petrarch notes the death of Laura in his copy of Virgil. If we wish to change writing activities within our society, we must look not at what we think happens within our students' heads but rather at what happens between our students and us, between our students and other social groups with which they interact.

Still another way to distinguish our approach is that we assert the primacy of the social over that of the technological. One of us was asked, recently, to observe a Level One adult basic education class to monitor the teacher's effectiveness. This can be an intensely distasteful activity, with its associations of Matthew Arnold, Yeats, and the police, but there seemed at the time little choice but to do it. The class was taking place in a room where each of the students had their own computer, each seemingly quite comfortable using the machines as writing instruments. One of the students, a gentleman in his mid-twenties, spent most of the class session writing a sentence. He would key in the letters of a word, turn to the teacher, ask the spelling of the next word, key those in, and so forth. The interest of this is that he was doing precisely what Shaughnessy describes in *Errors and Expectations* as hypercorrection, although Shaughnessy's description involves a pencil and much erasing, not an Apple IIe and the Bank Street Writer. Everything had changed, but everything was much the same. The quantitative transformation of the technology had no effect at all on the activity, which had its roots not in the archaic nature of pencils, as we once thought, but in the enduring character of the organization of our system of education—its highly successful function in limiting learning opportunities for perhaps half our people, and nearly eliminating them for millions. Computers will not end illiteracy. Literacy is not a technology that can be freely transferred from one culture to another, or acquired like an appliance. Writing is not a technique.

Writing is a form of social action. It is part of the way in which some people live in the world. Thus, when thinking about writing, we must also think about the way that people live in the world. Over the last few years we have been thinking in these terms about our teaching, about research in composition, and about literacy programs in the schools and in other institutions. The essays in this volume represent some of that thinking.

1

The Ecology of Writing

I wrote this essay in response to the chain of events narrated in the final essay in this collection. Though I was not directly involved in the literacy project that was developed for the California Conservation Corps in 1982, I did spend a lot of time talking about the pedagogical and theoretical implications of what was going on with my colleagues who were working in the project. In these discussions—in seminar rooms, in offices, in restaurants, on front and back stoops—I began to see how to ground the ideas I had been developing about writing as social action (drawing, for the most part, on sociolinguistic and speech act theories of language) in the actuality of social structures. Aspects of language use that function as discrete abstractions in these theories—Grice's background knowledge, Brown and Gilman's power and solidarity, for example—appeared in these discussions as operational facts, completely enmeshed not just in the immediate conversational context but in a whole web of social systems that had been built up over time. When one of my middle-class students in a linguistics class responded with disdain to an approach from one of the uniformed corps members in the halls of our building, I began to see the inadequacy of describing such encounters as infelicitous because of an imbalance in power and the lack of sufficient solidarity. For both Michael and myself, the literacy project served as a catalyst to bring together theory and practice. But as he increasingly turned his attention to the problem of teaching writing in workplace settings, I took up the problem of seeing college writing classrooms as also part of the social world.

Since its publication in *College English* in 1986 this essay has been much commented on. I respond to one interpretation of it in the essay on discourse communities later in this collection. Here I wish only to say that what seems most important to me in the way of thinking about writing I propose in this essay is the idea of dynamic, interacting systems.

I make no argument for the explanatory power of the particular five systems I distinguish; they are meant to serve merely as a heuristic, not as a taxonomy in any sense.

☐   ☐   ☐

The idea that writing is a process and that the writing process is a recursive cognitive activity involving certain universal stages (prewriting, writing, revising) seemed quite revolutionary not so many years ago. In 1982, Maxine Hairston hailed "the move to a process-centered theory of teaching writing" as the first sign of a paradigm shift in composition theory (77). But even by then "process, not product" was the slogan of numerous college textbooks, large and small, validated by enclosure within brightly-colored covers with the imprimatur of Harper & Row, Macmillan, Harcourt Brace Jovanovich, Scott, Foresman. So revolution dwindles to dogma. Now, perhaps, the time has come for some assessment of the benefits and limitations of thinking of writing as essentially—and simply—a cognitive process.

Motivation for the paradigm shift in writing theory came first perhaps from writing teachers increasingly disenchanted with red-inking errors, delivering lectures on comma splices or on the two ways to organize a comparison-contrast essay, and reading alienated and alienating essays written from a list of topic sentences or in the five-paragraph format. Reacting against pedagogy that seemed completely ineffective, we developed methods that required students to concentrate less on form and more on content, that required them to think. We decided to talk about ideas rather than forms in the classroom and sent students off to do various kinds of free writing and writing using heuristics in order to find out what they thought about a topic—best of all, we found we didn't have to read any of this essential but private and exploratory prewriting. We told students they had primary responsibility for the purpose of their writing: only they could decide what was important to them to write about, only they could tell whether what they intended was actually fulfilled in the writing they produced. We decided to be friendly readers rather than crabby Miss Fidditches; we said things like, "You have lots of ideas," and, with Pirsig's Phaedrus, "You know quality in thought and statement when you see it," instead of "Your essay does not clearly develop a point," and "You have made many usage errors here."

These ideas were in the air—and in print. We developed them in talking with colleagues, in reading the advice of fellow teachers Peter Elbow and Donald Murray. We found further support for them in similar ideas being developed by literary theorists, educational psychologists, and linguists—some of whom were also writing teachers. In literary theory the shift from a New Critical emphasis on the text to a post-structural emphasis on the reader paralleled the shift from product to process in writing theory. As Jonathan Culler and Stanley Fish adapted the nouvelle French notions to American tastes, the complementarity between reading and writing in terms of their both being mental processes became clear. Culler states that readers possess "literary competence," that they make sense of texts by applying various conventions that explain how one is to interpret the cues on the page. Writers, ideally, possess the same literary competence. Fish states that readers are guided by interpretive strategies, that these strategies are constitutive of interpretive communities, and that the strategies originate with writers. Culler's conventions, Fish's strategies, are not present in the text; rather, they are part of the mental equipment of writers and readers, and only by examining this mental equipment can we explain how writers and readers communicate.

In the fields of educational psychology and linguistics, research on how readers process texts also revealed an active reader who used strategies to recreate meaning from the cues on the page. These strategies implied certain expected structures in texts. When adopted by writing teachers, readers' expectations became a new way of explaining "errors" in student writing and a new rationale for instruction on matters of form. George Dillon, expanding David Olson's analysis, attributes much of the incomprehensibility of his students' writing to their inability to shift from the conventions of utterance to the conventions of text, conventions that enjoin explicitness, correctness, novelty, logical consistency, and so forth. Linda Flower and Joseph Williams explain how readers link new information to old information in order to comprehend texts, and they advise students, consequently, to supply context and to clearly mark old and new information in sentence structure.

Gradually, as interest in writing theory increased, a model of writing as a cognitive process was codified, and the unified perspective the model offered in turn allowed us to redefine other vexing problems: the relation between grammar and writing, the function of revision. These were all undoubtedly beneficial changes. But theoretical models even as they stimulate new insights blind us to some aspects of the phenomena we are studying. The problem with the cognitive process model of writing has nothing to do with its specifics: it describes something of what writers do and goes some way toward explaining how writers, texts, and readers are related. But the belief on which it is based—that writing is thinking and, thus, essentially a cognitive process—obscures many aspects of writing we have come to see as not peripheral.

Like all theoretical models, the cognitive process model projects an ideal image, in this case an image of a writer that, transmitted through writing pedagogy, influences our attitudes and the attitudes of our students toward writing. The ideal writer the cognitive process model projects is isolated from the social world, a writer I will call the solitary author. The solitary author works alone, within the privacy of his own mind. He uses free writing exercises and heuristics to find out what he knows about a subject and to find something he wants to say to others; he uses his analytic skills to discover a purpose, to imagine an audience, to decide on strategies, to organize content; and he simulates how his text will be read by reading it over himself, making the final revisions necessary to assure its success when he abandons it to the world of which he is not a part. The isolation of the solitary author from the social world leads him to see ideas and goals as originating primarily within himself and directed at an unknown and largely hostile other. Writing becomes a form of parthenogenesis, the author producing propositional and pragmatic structures, Athena-like, full grown and complete, out of his brow. Thus, the solitary author perceives the functions that writing might serve in limited and abstract terms. All four of the major pedagogical theories James Berlin describes assume that the function of writing is solely cognitive, a matter of discovering the truth and communicating it: the solitary author can express his feelings, pass on information, persuade others to believe as he does, or charm others with his exquisite phrases (cf. Kinneavy's taxonomy of the aims of writing). Finally, the solitary author sees his writing as a goal-directed piece of work, the process of producing a text.

Such images of the solitary author inspire a great deal of what goes on in writing classes today—and more of what is recommended in composition textbooks, especially those that depend on the latest theory. But many classes still escape its tyranny, classes in which students engage in group work, activities such as collaborative brainstorming on a topic, discussions and debates of topics or readings, writers reading their texts aloud to others, writers editing other writers' texts. Some teachers eschew setting writing assignments (even writing assignments that are "rhetorically based") in favor of letting writing emerge from the life situations of their students, whether this writing takes the form of papers that fulfill requirements for other courses, letters written for employment or business purposes, journals kept as personal records, reports of projects completed or in progress. And in some classes, students even use writing to interact with one another: they write suggestions to their teacher and to other students; they produce class newspapers full of interviews, jokes, personal stories, advice, information.

Such changes in writing pedagogy indicate that the perspective allowed by the dominant model has again become too confining. I suggest that what goes on in these classes signals a growing awareness that language and texts are not simply the means by which individuals discover and communicate information, but are essentially social activities, dependent on social structures and processes not only in their interpretive but also in their constructive phases. I am not, of course, the only—or even the first—writing theorist to notice this. In 1981, for example, Kenneth Bruffee argued that "writing is not an inherently private act but is a displaced social act we perform in private for the sake of convenience" (1981, 745). And, more recently, James A. Reither, summarizing the work of four other prominent theorists, comes to the same conclusions I have as the beginning point of his attempt to redefine the writing process:

> the issues [Larson, Odell, Bizzell, and Gage] raise should lead us to wonder if our thinking is not being severely limited by a concept of process that explains only the cognitive processes that occur as people write. Their questions and observations remind us that writing is not merely a process that occurs within contexts. That is, writing and what writers do during writing cannot be artificially separated from the social-rhetorical situations in which writing gets done, from the conditions that enable writers to do what they do, and from the motives writers have for doing what they do. (1985, 621)

The idea that language use is essentially social also underlies much current work in literary theory and sociolinguistics. David Bleich proposes a literature classroom in which students transform their initial responses to a text into communally negotiated and thus valid interpretations: "although the resymbolization of a text is usually a fully private affair, it is always done in reference to some communal effort" (1978, 137). Fredric Jameson, perhaps the foremost of the neo-Marxist theorists, argues that interpretation "must take place within three concentric frameworks, which mark a widening out of the sense of the social ground of a text" (1981, 75). Among linguists, William Labov is renowned for his demonstrations that the so-called verbal deprivation of children in ghetto schools is an artifact of the means of data collection, face-to-face interviews of black children by white adult investigators, and that "the consistency of certain grammatical rules [of black English vernacular] is a fine-grained index of membership in the street culture" (1972a, 255). And in *Ways with Words*, a book already nearly as influential as Labov's *Language in the Inner City*, Shirley Brice Heath delineates the complex relationship between children's differential acquisition of reading and the uses of and attitudes toward texts in their home communities.

Just as such research calls for new models of the interpretation of literature and of language use, so too do the intuitively developed methods we are now beginning to use in writing classes and in literacy programs call for a new model of writing. Describing such a model explicitly will lend coherence to these intuitions by bringing out the assumptions on which they are based, illuminating aspects of writing that we have perceived but dimly heretofore through the gaps in the cognitive process model.

What I would like to propose is an ecological model of writing, whose fundamental tenet is that writing is an activity through which a person is continually engaged with a variety of socially constituted systems. Ecology, the science of natural environments, has been recently mentioned by writing researchers such as Greg Myers, who, in his analysis of the social construction of two biologists' proposals, concludes: "Like ethologists, we should not only observe and categorize the behavior of individuals, we should also consider the evolution of this behavior in its ecological context" (1985, 240). The term *ecological* is not, however, simply the newest way to say "contextual"; it points up important differences between the model I am proposing and other contextual models such as Kenneth Burke's dramatistic pentad.

Such models, oddly, abstract writing from the social context in much the way that the cognitive process model does; they perceive the context in which a piece of writing is done as unique, unconnected with other situations. Kenneth Burke's is perhaps the best contextual model that is applied to writing; Burke develops a heuristic for interrogating the immediate situation in order to impute motives for individual language acts. The terms of his pentad are conceived of as formal or transcendent, and Burke tellingly labels his description of them a "grammar," a model of "the purely internal relationships which the five terms bear to one another" (1969, xvi). Actual statements about motives utilize these "grammatical resources," but the grammar determines the statements only in a formal sense, much as syntactic rules predict the occurrence of certain structures in sentences. One's perspective, or "philosophy," crucially guides how the terms will be applied, and, since Burke proposes no link between the grammar and the perspective, what perspective is chosen appears to be arbitrary, and perhaps trivial: "War may be treated as an Agency, insofar as it is a means to an end; as a collective Act, subdivisible into many individual acts; as a Purpose, in schemes proclaiming a cult of war" (xx). Thus, though the grammar allows one to assign labels to important aspects of a situation, it does not enable one to explain how the situation is causally related to other situations. Burke is perhaps more aware of the limitations of his model than are some of his disciples. The description of linguistic forms the pentad enables is, in his opinion, "preparatory": "the study of linguistic action is but beginning" (319).

In contrast, an ecology of writing encompasses much more than the individual writer and her immediate context. An ecologist explores how writers interact to form systems: all the characteristics of any in-dividual writer or piece of writing both determine and are determined by the characteristics of all the other writers and writings in the systems. An important characteristic of ecological systems is that they are inher-ently dynamic; though their structures and contents can be specified at a given moment, in real time they are constantly changing, limited only by parameters that are themselves subject to change over longer spans of time. In their critique of sociobiology, R. C. Lewontin, Rose, and Kamin describe how such systems operate:

> all organisms—but especially human beings—are not simply the results but are also the causes of their own environments. . . . While it may be true that at some instant the environment poses a problem or challenge to the organism, in the process of response to that challenge the organism alters the terms of its relation to the outer world and recreates the relevant aspects of that world. The relation between organism and environment is not simply one of interaction of internal and external factors, but of a dialectical development of organism and milieu in response to each other. (1984, 275)

In place of the static and limited categories of contextual models, the ecological model postulates dynamic interlocking systems that structure the social activity of writing.

The systems are not given, not limitations on writers; instead they are made and remade by writers in the act of writing. It is in this sense that writing changes social reality and not only, as Lloyd Bitzer argues, in response to exigence. A historian writes a letter of appreciation to an anthropologist whose article she has read and connects with a new writer with whom she can exchange ideas and articles. A college president who decides to write a Christmas letter to his faculty creates a new textual form that will affect his other communications and at the same time alters, slightly, the administrative structure of his institution.

Furthermore, the systems are concrete. They are structures that can be investigated, described, altered; they are not postulated mental en-tities, not generalizations. Every individual writer is necessarily involved in these systems: for each writer and each instance of writing one can specify the domain of ideas activated and supplemented, the purposes that stimulated the writing and that resulted from it, the interactions that took place as part of the writing, the cultural norms and textual forms that enabled and resulted from the writing.

One can abstractly distinguish different systems that operate in writing, just as one can distinguish investment patterns from consumer spending patterns from hiring patterns in a nation's economy. But in the actual activity of writing—as in the economy—the systems are entirely interwoven in their effects and manner of operation. The systems reflect the various ways writers connect with one another through writing: through systems of ideas, of purposes, of interpersonal interactions, of cultural norms, of textual forms.

The system of ideas is the means by which writers comprehend their world, to turn individual experiences and observations into knowledge. From this perspective ideas result from contact, whether face-to-face or mediated through texts. Ideas are also always continuations, as they arise within and modify particular fields of discourse. One does not begin to write about bird behavior, say, without observing birds, talking with other observers, and reading widely in the literature of animal behavior in general. One does not even begin to have ideas about a topic, even a relatively simple one, until a considerable body of already structured observations and experiences has been mastered. Even in writing where the focus is not on the development of knowledge, a writer must connect with the relevant idea system. If one is recommending ways to increase the efficiency of a particular department of a publishing firm, one must understand what the department does and how it fits into the firm as a whole.

The system of purposes is the means by which writers coordinate their actions. Arguments attempt to set agendas; promises attempt to set schedules and relationships. Purposes, like ideas, arise out of interaction, and individual purposes are modified by the larger purposes of groups; in fact, an individual impulse or need only becomes a purpose when it is recognized as such by others. A contributor to a company newspaper writes about his interest in paleontology; his individual purpose is to express himself, to gain attention, purposes we all recognize; but within the context of the company newspaper, his purpose is also to deepen his relationship with other employees.

The system of interpersonal interactions is the means by which writers regulate their access to one another. Two determinants of the nature of a writer's interactions with others are intimacy, a measure of closeness based on any similarity seen to be relevant—kinship, religion, occupation; and power, a measure of the degree to which a writer can control the action of others (for a particularly detailed discussion of these factors, see Brown and Levinson 1978). Writers may play a number of different roles in relation to one another: editor, co-writer, or addressee, for instance. Writers signal how they view their relationship with other writers through conventional forms and strategies, but they can also change their relationship—or even initiate or terminate relationships— through the use of these conventions if others accept the new relationship that is implied.

The system of cultural norms is the means by which writers structure the larger groups of which they are members. One always writes out of a group; the notion of what role a writer takes on in a particular piece of writing derives from this fact. I write here as a member of the writing theory group, and as I write I express the attitudes and institutional arrangements of this group—and I attempt to alter some of them.

The system of textual forms is, obviously, the means by which writers communicate. Textual forms, like language forms in general, are at the same time conservative, repositories of tradition, and revolutionary, instruments of new forms of action. A textual form is a balancing act: conventional enough to be comprehensible and flexible enough to serve the changing purposes of writing. Thus, new forms usually arise by a kind of cross-breeding, or by analogy, as older forms are taken apart and recombined or modified in a wholesale fashion.

The metaphor for writing suggested by the ecological model is that of a web, in which anything that affects one strand of the web vibrates throughout the whole. To reiterate, models are ways of thinking about, or ways of seeing, complex situations. If we look at, for example, a particularly vexed problem in current writing theory, the question of audience, from the perspective of this model, we may be able to reformulate the question in a way that helps us to find new answers. Though I cannot attempt a complete analysis of the concept of audience here, I would like to outline briefly how such an analysis might proceed.

The discussion of how authors should deal with their audience has in recent years focused on the opposition between those who argue that authors must analyze the characteristics of a real audience and those who argue that authors always imagine, or create, their audience in their writing. The opposition, of course, has classical roots: in the *Phaedrus* Plato suggests that the rhetorician classify types of audiences and consider which type of speech best suits each; while, at the other extreme, epideictic rhetoric sometimes took the form of a contest in which speakers imagined an audience. Lisa Ede and Andrea Lunsford characterize "the two central perspectives on audience in composition" as "audience addressed and audience invoked" (1984, 156). Douglas Park identifies the conception of audience "as something readily identifiable and external" with Lloyd Bitzer, and the opposite conception of audience as represented to consciousness, or invented, with Walter Ong (Park 1982, 248).

I would like to draw attention, however, to what unites both these perspectives: whether the writer is urged to analyze or invent the audience, the audience is always considered to be a construct in the writer's mind. Park specifies four meanings of audience, then argues that "the last two meanings are obviously the most important for teachers or for anyone interested in forms of discourse": "the set of conceptions or awareness in the writer's consciousness," and "an ideal conception shadowed forth in the way the discourse defines and creates contexts" (1982,

250). Park concludes, "Any systematic answers to these important questions will depend upon keeping in constant view the essential abstractness of the concept of audience" (250).

The internalization of the audience, making it into a mental construct often labeled the "general audience," is inescapable within the perspective of the cognitive process model. By focusing our attention on what goes on in an author's mind, it forces us to conceive all significant aspects of writing in terms of mental entities. Even Fred Pfister and Joanne Petrick, often cited as proponents of the idea of real audiences, begin by conceding that for writers the "audience is unseen, a phantom. . . . Students, like all writers, must fictionalize their audience. But they must construct in the imagination an audience that is as nearly a replica as is possible of those many readers who actually exist in the world of reality and who are reading the writer's words" (1980, 213–14). Less surprisingly, in her textbook Linda Flower labels one of her "problem-solving strategies for writing" "talk to your reader," but she actually recommends that the writer play both roles in the conversation (1981, 73).

Barry Kroll, who breaks down approaches to audience into three perspectives—the rhetorical, the informational, and the social—demonstrates, in his definition of the third perspective, how pervasive the tendency to internalize all aspects of writing is: "writing for readers is, like all human communication, a fundamentally social activity, entailing processes of inferring the thoughts and feelings of the other persons involved in an act of communication" (1984, 179). The redefinition of social activity as a cognitive process is even more striking here in that it is unmarked, mentioned as an afterthought in the gerundive phrase. Kroll goes on to conclude, "From [the social] view, the process of writing for readers inevitably involves social thinking—or 'social cognition' " (1984, 182–83). In a more recent discussion of studies of the relation between social-cognitive abilities and writing performance, Kroll more clearly advocates the social-cognitive approach to audience: "It seems reasonable that individuals who can think in more complex ways about how other people think ought to be better writers" (1985, 304). But, as he also admits, "successful performance (in terms of creating texts that are adapted to readers' needs) may not always reflect social-cognitive competence, because writers probably learn to employ many of the linguistic and rhetorical devices of audience-adapted writing without needing to consider their readers' characteristics, perspectives, or responses" (1985, 304).

As should be obvious, the perspective of the ecological model offers a salutary correction of vision on the question of audience. By focusing our attention on the real social context of writing, it enables us to see that writers not only analyze or invent audiences, they, more significantly, communicate with and know their audiences. They learn to employ the devices of audience-adapted writing by handing their texts to colleagues to read and respond to, by revising articles or memos or reports guided by comments from editors or superiors, by reading others' summaries or critiques of their own writing. Just as the ecological model transforms authors (people who have produced texts) into writers (people engaged in writing), it transforms the abstract "general audience" into real readers (for an insightful discussion of the use of "audience" versus "reader," see Park 1982, 249–50).

These real readers do appear in discussions of audience dominated by the cognitive process model, if only in glimpses. Ruth Mitchell and Mary Taylor point out that "the audience not only judges writing, it also motivates it. A writer answers a challenge, consciously or unconsciously. The conscious challenges are assignments, demands for reports, memos, proposals, letters" (1979, 250–51). Ede and Lunsford criticize Mitchell and Taylor's model from the familiar cognitive process perspective: "no matter how much feedback writers may receive after they have written something (or in breaks while they write), as they compose writers must rely in large part upon their own vision of the reader, which they create . . . according to their own experiences and expectations" (1984, 158). But in their account of the readers of their own article, it is the real readers who are obviously most important: "a small, close-knit seminar group"; each other; Richard Larson, who "responded in writing with questions, criticisms, and suggestions, some of which we had, of course, failed to anticipate"; and readers of *College Composition and Communication*, pictured as "members of our own departments, a diverse group of individuals with widely varying degrees of interest in and knowledge of composition" (167–68). Ede and Lunsford know their readers through real social encounters; the cognitive act of analyzing them or creating them is superfluous. As Park suggests, "as a general rule it is only in highly structured situations or at particular times that writers consciously focus on audience as a discrete entity" (1982, 254).

The focus on readers as real social beings opens up new vistas for research on audience and for classroom methods. Questions we might seek answers to include: What kind of interactions do writers and readers engage in? What is the nature of the various roles readers play in the activity of writing? What institutional arrangements encourage writer-reader interaction? How do writers find readers to work with? How do writers and readers develop ideas together? How do writers and readers alter textual forms together?

In the classroom, we can enable our students to see each other as real readers, not as stand-ins for a general audience. Students learn about how to deal with their readers not "by internalizing and generalizing the reactions of a number of specific readers" and thereby developing a "sense of audience" (Kroll 1984, 181), but by developing the habits and skills involved in finding readers and making use of their responses. Students, like all writers, need to find out what kind of readers best help them in the role of editor, how to work with co-writers, how to interpret criticisms, how to enter into dialogue with their addressees.

In contrast, then, to the solitary author projected by the cognitive process model, the ideal image the ecological model projects is of an infinitely extended group of people who interact through writing, who are connected by the various systems that constitute the activity of writing. For these "engaged writers" ideas are not so much fixed constructs to be transferred from one mind to the page and thence to another mind; instead, ideas are out there in the world, a landscape that is always being modified by ongoing human discourse. They "find ideas" in writing because they thus enter the field of discourse, finding in the exchange of language certain structures that they modify to suit their purposes. Nor for them do purposes arise solely out of individual desires, but rather arise out of the interaction between their needs and the needs of the various groups that structure their society. As Dell Hymes says about purposes in speaking, "Ultimately, the functions served . . . must be derived directly from the purposes and needs of human persons engaged in social action, and are what they are: talking [or writing] to seduce, to stay awake, to avoid a war" (1972, 70). The various roles people take on in writing also arise out of this social structure: through interacting with others, in writing and speaking, they learn the functions and textual forms of impersonal reporting, effective instruction, irony, story-telling. In the same way, they learn the attitudes toward these roles and toward purposes and ideas held by the various groups they interact with, and they come to understand how these interactions are themselves partly structured by institutional procedures and arrangements. These attitudes, procedures, and arrangements make up a system of cultural norms that are, however, neither stable nor uniform throughout a culture. People move from group to group, bringing along with them different complexes of ideas, purposes, and norms, different ways of interacting, different interpersonal roles and textual forms. Writing, thus, is seen to be both constituted by and constitutive of these ever-changing systems, systems through which people relate as complete, social beings, rather than imagining each other as remote images: an author, an audience.

It is important to remember that the image the ecological model projects is again an ideal one. In reality, these systems are often resistent to change and not easily accessible. Whenever ideas are seen as commodities they are not shared; whenever individual and group purposes cannot be negotiated someone is shut out; differences in status, or power, or intimacy curtail interpersonal interactions; cultural institutions and attitudes discourage writing as often as they encourage it; textual forms are just as easily used as barriers to discourse as they are used as means of discourse. A further value of the ecological model is that it can be used to diagnose and analyze such situations, and it encourages us to direct our corrective energies away from the characteristics of the individual writer and toward imbalances in social systems that prevent good writing; one such analysis by my colleague Michael Holzman appears later in this collection ("The Social Context of Literacy Education").

Writing is one of the activities by which we locate ourselves in the enmeshed systems that make up the social world. It is not simply a way of thinking but more fundamentally a way of acting. As Wilhelm von Humboldt says of language, it "is not work (*ergon*) but activity (*energia*)" (1971, 27), an activity through which we become most truly human. By looking at writing ecologically we understand better how important writing is—and just how hard it is to teach.

Marilyn M. Cooper

2

A Post-Freirean Model for Adult Literacy Education

A request from the Conrad N. Hilton Foundation for a report on possible opportunities for program development in Third World literacy gave me the chance to talk with many people who have worked in the field and to consider the current state of work and thought on the issue. It is difficult to think of a more literal way that writing is social action than in literacy campaigns and in the programs of "grassroots development" now promoted by a bewildering variety of organizations. There are "First World" classroom implications here, also; not only for adult educators but for college composition instructors. Each can learn much by asking the question central to the critique of the Experimental World Literacy Program: What is it that we are teaching by *how* we teach?

It seems that literacy education is best founded on the needs and desires of those seeking it—a highly variable combination. In the vocabulary of "The Ecology of Writing" (Chapter 1), learning to read and write always takes place within ongoing social systems. Attempts by providers of literacy tuition to ignore these systems limit their chance for success.

> Far too often there is a contradiction between the values stated and the way we go about sharing them. . . . We . . . need to be involved in strategies for transformation which start from the bottom up, growing out of the expressed needs of the people. (Hope and Timmel 1984, I.5)

There are many ways to get to Maryknoll. The way I took was to ride the Metro-North railroad to Ossining. At Ossining there were three or four cabs waiting for the train. Each accepted three or four passengers, and we all went off together, not, as it turned out, to Maryknoll, but to Sing Sing, which molders down along the railroad tracks, newer sections and older sections heaped together in what I gather must be the style of the region, in this case depicting an image of a century or more of industrialized punishment. After my fellow passengers left the cab with their gifts and visiting hour stories, the driver circled back to town, up the usual steep main street and out into a residential area on top of the bluffs overlooking the river. We passed the Chinese Imperial style residence of the Maryknoll priests, the retirement and nursing homes, then reached the center used by the Maryknoll sisters, a large complex of buildings that had once included a college. There are fewer Maryknoll sisters than there once were. Their colleges and hospitals have been closing not only in Ossining, but all over the world. Partly, this is simply because fewer women are joining the order. Partly, it is a matter of policy. The order no longer wishes to run institutions for people; it wishes to help people run their own institutions.

All the rest of the day I sat in a small room near their library and listened to the nuns tell me stories of their years spent "accompanying" communities in the Third World. I was there to hear about their literacy work; they each told about how they went about it, about an educator they admired named Paulo Freire. All the stories were similar, though each had local particularities. In Panama, for instance, they had had a radio station that coordinated the schedules of literacy classes in a number of villages. They had to leave when a priest was killed and the local bishop decided the sisters were in danger. In Tanzania they had helped women compile a cookbook, which was also a reading text. Now, of course, many of the recipes cannot be used, as the foods named in them are unavailable. In El Salvador . . .

Those conversations at Maryknoll, and conversations with other international adult education practitioners over the next few months, acquainted me with the recent emergence of a new standard approach in the field. This is not only a new way of teaching reading and writing; it is also a new attitude toward teaching and learning—and toward teachers and learners themselves. I believe that the appearance of this model, and the remarkable consensus among adult educators in the field of international education in its favor, is an event of major significance for that discipline, one that also has implications for many levels of education in this country.

In the more economically developed countries education is primarily based on systems of state-supported, universal primary education. Debates in these countries concerning the amount of investment in education necessary for further economic development or for the full participation of more individuals in cultural and decision-making roles take this structure for granted. No matter how concerned those in the economically developed countries might be about adults who are illiterate or about adolescents who leave school early without sufficient education to allow full participation in their national economies, they assume that improvements in education must be based in the first instance on reform of the schools. It is only then that they consider supplementary measures necessary for those who reach adulthood having been schooled but not adequately educated. And although this latter group is numerically large, such studies as the recent National Assessment of Educational Progress report on the literacy of young adults in the United States show that it is far from being a large enough group to be taken as characteristic of the nation (Kirsch and Jungeblut 1986). In the industrially developed countries the problems of this group are serious, but they do not affect the educational system as a whole.

However, in many countries that are not economically developed this situation is reversed. In most of these countries primary education is not universal; even where schools are widely available, children leave them early at rates so high as to produce an absolute increase each year in the number of illiterate adults worldwide. At this point quantity becomes quality: those overwhelming numbers of inadequately educated adults are a significant negative influence on efforts to provide education for their children. In the first place, poorly educated parents frequently need the full-time work of their school-age children for economic survival; and, in the second, parents who are themselves uneducated tend not to value education for their children.[1]

In some of the more economically developed countries further *increases* in the rate of development are threatened by the deficiencies of the educational system (and what may be called cultural development has turned retrograde). In many of the less economically developed countries, the very social fabric is threatened by the merely peripheral role of education in the everyday lives of large numbers of their people. In these countries cultural and media resources remain in the hands of elites who may believe themselves to have little in common with the rural and urban poor, and the effective size of the work force in the more developed sectors of the economy is limited by widespread illiteracy. Both these factors serve to exacerbate the divisions between rich and poor, between people who live in the countryside and those who live in the city, divisions that are crucial issues often affecting national stability in the Third World.

It was once possible to argue that education—like economic development itself—could be *elective*, that a country or group could so isolate itself as to be able to maintain its traditional way of life without reference to the requirements of the dominant forces in the rest of the world. As many countries that are now economically developed became so while large parts of their populations were illiterate, so many countries have developed their culture under similar circumstances. But it is now rarely possible to find defenders of a hegemony of cultural elites, and it is equally difficult now even to conceive of a process of economic development with an uneducated population. Furthermore, as we have seen in the years since the "development decade," countries that are not developing are in danger of "undeveloping," of becoming poorer and less stable (Rodney 1981). For these and similar reasons, education in terms of a more or less universal standard is becoming recognized as a worldwide necessity.

Some argue that in these circumstances economic realism dictates that investments in education should be focused on primary education. This seems reasonable and has strong historical precedents. However, there is an enormous existing uneducated population in the developing countries that cannot be simply written off—condemned to a life outside much of the cultural and economic life of their countries. The relevant arguments are not only economic; they are political and cultural as well. Politically and culturally the education of adults is often a necessary stage in the transformation of national culture. In addition to benefiting the adults in question, it facilitates the education of their children. The education of women, in particular, contributes to a home environment that values education, which influences decisions as to how long, or whether, children remain in school. From all these points of view, while national investments in primary schooling are essential, a sustained effort for adult education is also necessary. And while the establishment of systems of primary education requires investments in buildings and teacher training on a scale usually only possible for comparatively wealthy governments, the costs of adult education are more modest and may be undertaken locally by nongovernmental organizations.

Large-scale attempts to encourage the spread of literacy by educating adults are for the most part a phenomenon of this century, attributable to ideological motives or religious motives or to the belief that since those nations that are economically developed are also those with nearly universal literacy, general literacy must be achieved as a prerequisite for development. Historically, these various motives have had associated with them characteristic approaches to promoting literacy among adults. *Literacy campaigns* may mobilize much of the literate population of a country to act as tutors for the illiterate during the relatively short period of the campaign, usually a matter of a few months, or they may be undertaken repeatedly in various sectors of a country that have particularly high illiteracy rates, using school teachers and other educated segments of the population as instructors. *Literacy projects* that are founded on the concept of development tend to be even more incremental, relying on experts—often foreign nationals—and focusing on particular population groups and regions: fruit growers in a hill district of Iran, say, or cotton farmers in Tanzania. In some cases—notably that of Tanzania—the motives and techniques have been combined. There is yet another category of expert-centered literacy efforts formed by those instances in which a country that is unevenly developed uses the typical methods of state educational ministries to serve the needs of its less developed sectors. This has been the case with India, Indonesia, Thailand, Nepal, and Brazil, among others. These latter efforts bear certain resemblances to contemporary adult education programs in the more industrially developed nations, and perhaps also some to the process by which formal educational systems were extended in Europe and elsewhere in the decades around 1900.

The methodologies of adult literacy instruction in this century at first evolved mainly from those used to teach children to read and write. In those programs influenced by the Soviet and Cuban examples, there has also been considerable emphasis on using materials with a highly charged political content. Until the late 1960s, the most widespread *specific* technique for adult literacy tuition was the well-known system developed by Dr. Frank Laubach, who had acquired his interest in adult literacy instruction while serving as an American Protestant missionary in the Philippines. The Laubach method, which has been used throughout the world (including developed nations such as the United States), moves from the presentation of iconic mnemonic devices to phonemic exercises designed to give the learner rapid command of a practical, if small, vocabulary concerning familiar items. In addition to the technical details of chart and phonemic exercises, the identifying characteristic of the Laubach method is its well-known slogan of "Each One Teach One." Every new literate is meant to become an additional teacher until the community achieves complete literacy. The underlying belief system of emphasis on the individual, self-help, and the importance of disinterested "works" is evident.

Adult literacy programs outside the Soviet Union and China tended to be localized and semiprivate initiatives, such as Laubach's and those growing out of Literacy House in India, until the founding of UNESCO, where they became matters of continuing international interest and debate. Cuba, just after its revolution, pioneered in adopting adult literacy education as a central, highly publicized objective of a new regime. Although in retrospect this seems a normal procedure for a revolutionary government, it was not as clear then. In 1959 the Soviet literacy campaigns of the 1920s had been nearly forgotten, and the similar efforts in China were too remote both geographically and culturally to serve as viable models. The Cuban campaign, then, appeared dramatically innovative. It mobilized large numbers of school teachers, students, and other educated people, primarily urban, and placed them in the countryside for months as literacy tutors for peasants. Despite the progressive ideology invoked, the organization and the form of the literacy methodology of the Cuban program reflected the actual mixed conditions of the country at the time, emphasizing, on the one hand, individualist values, and, on the other, the dependence of individuals on the state or the revolutionary group. Thus, it is not surprising that the techniques used in the Cuban literacy campaign were quite similar to the Laubach method, which, with its roots in Protestant theological considerations, was readily adaptable to this purpose.[2]

The primary methodological innovation in adult literacy projects since the Cuban campaign has been that associated with Paulo Freire, who as a community organizer in the 1960s in the poverty stricken northeast of Brazil had extended what had begun as a community organizing technique to a method for adult literacy education. Although Freire's work is well-known, it is not generally appreciated that his method has two distinct aspects, a division reflecting the history of its development. First, it facilitates the organization of otherwise powerless groups of people by raising to consciousness their desires and needs and giving them tools for achieving some improvement in their lives. And it is a method for teaching reading and writing *per se*. Freire himself unites these two strands conceptually in his contention that the poor remain poor partly because they are habituated to intellectual as well as economic dependence on wealthier people. He sees the conventional educational system as being as much an instrument of domination as some systems of land ownership—teachers possessing knowledge as landlords possess the land. Teachers treat their students as having no knowledge of value, as "empty vessels" that must be "filled" with (approved) items of knowledge. Thus even when educated, Freire argues, the poor are habituated to dependence on the rich (or on their representatives) for their access to knowledge and further education. It follows then for Freire that if his primary goal of a change in social relations is to be achieved in the educational sphere, the knowledge actually held by the poor must be validated and made capable of extension.

Once we realize that Freire's method of education has purposes not strictly educational, we may begin to see other methods in a similar light. School-based methods for adult literacy education, as seen from this perspective, might similarly have a dual "purpose": to have adults receive the education they would have had if they had completed (or been successful at) school as children, and to do so in such a way as to habituate them to the education structures and forms of the state. The Laubach method, as has already been observed, might be said to have the educational purpose of achieving basic literacy skills and the social purpose of emphasizing individual—rather than community—values. By directing our attention to the manner, effects, and implicit wider goals of educational methods Freire has made a significant contribution to the formation of education theory.

In contrast to those of the Laubach or schools tradition, the typical

Freirean procedure is to gather people into study groups where an "animator" leads discussions of the conditions of their everyday lives. As in the Laubach method, pictures are used as stimuli for discussion, but the Freirean method differs from Laubach in that the picture is not taken as neutral; it is selected specifically to spark a discussion of social inequities. For example, if the animator displays a sketch of a house, it will deliberately be a sketch of a common house of the people themselves and, therefore, conspicuously lacking in luxuries, or even some necessities. The structure of the subsequent discussion used by Freireans again differs from the Laubach procedure in that it is conducted in such a way that the group of students are asked to use their own knowledge not only to describe but to evaluate the reality depicted in the sketch.

The Freirean animator's role is meant to be restricted to the asking of questions: whether the house depicted in the sketch is adequate, how it could be improved, what is standing in the way of improving it—lack of access to pure water, high rent, the like. After a series of such discussions, which are intended to lead the group to validate their own knowledge and intellectual abilities (demonstrating, for example, that they need not be dependent on a teacher), the lists of social needs developed from the discussions are arranged in a hierarchy from the broadest to those more particular. Only then will literacy acquisition itself begin with the inscription of the name of the picture, *casa*, for instance, followed by a Laubach-like process of phonetic analysis and recombination—new words from the lists of needs being formed out of the syllables of the others until a basic vocabulary is achieved from these "generative words."[3]

The Laubach method prefers a single teacher and a single student. (One remembers also those romantic images of the Cuban campaign— the isolated peasant hut, the small circle of kerosene lamplight within which the young volunteer from the city patiently works with the middle-aged *campesino*.) The Freirean method takes the group as its basic unit, and dialogue, rather than instruction or interrogation, as its mode of communication. The dialogic method is appropriate to Freire's teaching that the community, by definition, holds within it the knowledge necessary for its survival. This fact is often obscured by the circumstance that knowledge is usually distributed within the community. (It is no accident that people do not normally live alone.) When people are brought together to share their knowledge, each becomes intellectually whole, rather than a dependent victim of fragmentary knowledge, and the entire group realizes its strength—as a group. It is easy to see that this process could have certain political implications.

Freire's work in Brazil was cut short by the military coup there, and his subsequent stay in Chile was similarly ended, but since then his method has become a favored basis for adult literacy education, particularly in developing countries whose governments wish to be viewed as socially progressive. Although the Freirean method could be seen as being in large part an elaboration and systematization of certain (minority) elements found in the Soviet and Cuban literacy campaigns and is usually associated with revolutionary groups or those sympathetic to such groups, it has also been adapted for community literacy work in the United States by organizations without such aims. In Brazil itself some of its techniques were used by the military government's literacy agency MOBRAL—in isolation from the method's social organizing component, to be sure. This has been possible because of the distinctive nature of the two phases of Freire's method. The de-centered organization of the group and the relatively passive role of the animator are properly political; the technical means through which these are applied to the task of literacy acquisition are not. Generative words need not be socially destabilizing. They can be references to mainstream economic goals in a framework that reinforces rather than challenges existing social relations, or they can be religious, or they can be references to family life or patriotic sentiments. It is particularly piquant—and telling—that the literacy program of the military government that briefly imprisoned Freire himself was based on such an adaptation of his principles.

The model for adult education I have referred to as a new standard is used by widely disparate groups. The Maryknoll sisters have evolved a version of it; practitioners associated with a different religious organization, The Grail, have a version of it; and I have also heard it described by people associated with World Education, Inc. and The Inter-American Foundation. The latter is a United States government agency; the former is a private consulting firm. These are strange enough bedfellows to find in agreement with one another on an issue as complex as this, strange enough that their agreement is itself an indication of the scale of the failure of the previous models and the degree of hope felt for the new. This contemporary consensus of opinion concerning literacy work focuses on those furthest from the centers of global power, a focus then particularly on women in rural and poor urban areas of the Third World as exemplary, a focus on their judgments of their own hierarchies of needs.

On the day I visited the Maryknoll Center, a nun who had gone out to the Philippines in 1947 told me stories that began as stories about literacy, but gradually became stories about community organizing. She said that when she first arrived in the Philippines the public schools were good, education was free and nearly universal. For instance, most people could not only speak English, but could read and write it too. After Marcos came to power, things became difficult. People were forced off their land because of the "Communist threat" or because the land was needed by multinationals or by friends of Marcos. They were told they would be resettled, but they weren't. They were just driven to the slums of the nearest city. Now, she said, when you visit them there, you find many generations of a family packed into an ugly, little room. The old people are literate in English and Tagalog; their children can read a little Tagalog; the others are illiterate.

In the 1970s this nun began "accompanying" groups of women who lived in urban slums, facilitating the organization of sewing groups, finding local funding sources for loans to set up a marketing effort, and organizing literacy and numeracy instruction necessary to meet the conditions of those loans. All of this was done on a very small scale, with minimal direction from the "intermediary organization"—the nun—and all the goal-setting was done by the local women themselves. This Maryknoll sister lived in the community. Like any other member of the community, if there was a need she could meet, she attempted to do so. If one of those needs was literacy instruction, she provided that, if asked.

I was struck by the contrast between this mode of behavior and those sponsored by the Experimental World Literacy Program, or by the literacy campaigns of Cuba and Nicaragua. There was no more or less abstract talk of development, none of the "needs of the people." At Maryknoll, no one talked of national economies, only of household budgets. No one thought in terms of "people," only in terms of this person or that, of this village or that barrio. There was a remarkable singularity of aim. Well, as Kierkegaard put it, "purity of heart is to wish one thing." I left Ossining a little bit in love with the order, I suppose, pleased to have met so many good people, but not at all sure whether I had learned something about education or just something about Maryknoll. Later, when I had listened to practitioners from other organizations, I realized that the approach I had first learned about in Ossining was not specific to the practice of the Maryknoll sisters, but was exactly the current consensus, what has become the nearly unanimous orthodoxy of the most thoughtful people in the field of international adult education.

The current consensus about the appropriate method for adult literacy education endorses the use of *both* phases of the Freirean method, with a preference for going a step further in applying the method by making the local community members of the group from which animators are drawn and the central decision-makers concerning the method's use. In this way adult literacy education becomes a process of discovery, not one of instruction, and may then become integral to the achievement of broader educational and community goals. These matters of *who* determines the structure of the learning process and *what* it includes require some emphasis. This is not simply an issue of theoretical purity. Historically, even progressive educators have often allowed themselves to translate their pedagogical authority into forms of inadvertent paternalism. In Cuba, in Nicaragua, in many of the literacy projects using some

Freirean techniques in the United States, the crucial decision-making role all too often has been taken by experts and facilitators from outside the community, who decide what programs are to be offered and what they might include. This would be bad enough in itself, but it is made worse by the fact that the programs determined in this way are often designed without sufficient consideration for the felt needs of the local community or, to move to the global scale in the case of international programs, for the goals of individual nations.

It is consistent with this new consensus concerning techniques of adult education that many practitioners today believe that what is needed in a country or community is best decided by those in need, not by those with one of another set of resources or skills that they may wish to make available to meet certain needs. UNESCO's development-linked literacy projects were typical of approaches used by international agencies and analogous institutions of the industrialized world that sought to effect what they believed to be positive change in the less economically developed nations through infusions of expertise and capital. The use of conventionally trained primary school teachers in politically inspired literacy campaigns—and the extraordinary funding for those campaigns —has been a little-remarked parallel technique used by revolutionary regimes in their campaigns for enhancing literacy. Thus when Seth Spaulding and Arthur Gillette, in their *Critical Assessment* of UNESCO's Experimental World Literacy Program, explicitly challenged the role of international experts, they also implicitly called into question much of the methodology of the Russian, Cuban, and Nicaraguan literacy campaigns (Spaulding and Gillette 1976). Just as national projects may not need "expert" planners and the related resources and burdens these imply, local or individual adult literacy work does not necessarily require "expert" teachers, especially those with backgrounds in conventional—or even special—education systems. Those who endorse the new standard methodology for adult education believe that, given certain necessary conditions, communities can generate from their own people much of what is required and can define rather narrowly what is necessary to acquire from outside.

To pick the example readiest to hand, experts often decide (without consulting the community) that what a particular community needs is basic literacy classes, as there is a tradition among educators—and governments and nongovernmental funders—that literacy can be isolated as the most fundamental educational need. And yet literacy instruction, *per se*, may not be of as much interest to its intended individual or community beneficiaries themselves as a broader approach, one including literacy education, but also including education in health, farming, and manufacturing methods, community organizing techniques, and the like. In this area politics and education theory intersect. It may be seen as a

political question—whether formally educated experts will determine
the learning process—or it may be seen as a question of theory—that
adults have different learning requirements than do children. (We remember in this regard the stories about the Vai told by Sylvia Scribner
and Michael Cole: the children in that culture require schools and teachers to learn English or Arabic literacy skills, but young adults who wish
to become literate in Vai itself learn from one another.)

From an international policy point of view, Spaulding and Gillette
observe that a

> crucial lesson of EWLP seems, then, to be the need to avoid viewing
> or designing literacy as an overwhelmingly technical solution to
> problems that are only partly technical. A broad, multidimensional
> approach to both development and literacy is required. Indeed, it
> would seem that literacy program can only be fully functional—
> and development contexts can only be fully conducive to literacy
> —if they accord importance to social, cultural and political change
> as well as economic growth. (1976, 122)

The debate about literacy and development has included a growing awareness of the chauvinism inherent in a concern for development that so
takes for granted the cultural and political framework of economic development in the industrialized countries that it believes economic development (or educational "development") can be promoted with little
reference to the analogous frameworks in countries that are not yet as
industrialized. Those administering development and education projects
often tended to follow the usual practice of many types of projects in
industrialized societies—specialization and the isolation of issues and
problems—while it now appears to be the case that this is an inappropriate way of going about things for nonindustrialized countries and
groups, which hold different values. Indeed, some people are beginning
to wonder whether this approach is always a good one in the developed
countries themselves. These various critics of the traditional approach
would place considerations of economic development in the individual
political and cultural frameworks of each country. This would obviously
apply also to literacy programs either linked to development in the large
sense of "the development decade," or on some more modest scale appropriate to individual groups and communities.

The conclusions of the Spaulding-Gillette analysis of the Experimental World Literacy Program and similar critiques have been generally
accepted by practitioners, theorists, and some Third World ministries of
education. There is little faith now in top-down, development-linked
programs, either as engines for development or even simply as vehicles
for eradicating illiteracy. Much of the very terminology (epidemiological

and military) used by the EWLP international experts has been discredited. The special conditions necessary for literacy campaigns, their problematic motivations and effects, are beginning to throw that alternative into question, also. In general, there is a growing distrust of centralized planning, of initiatives from outside the local community (whether from ministries of education or international agencies), and of the isolation (and treatment) of any single factor in the socioeconomic life of a community as the key to that community's transformation into something judged as better by those outside the community. Few concerned with these matters are advocates of new "crusades" or the recruitment of "armies" of literacy volunteers from the urban middle class. Crusades are inspiring for the crusaders, less so for those crusaded against. Leading an army of volunteers may be gratifying, participating in a campaign may be inspiring for the members of the literacy brigades, but what does it mean to take armies as the model in educational and community development matters? Who is the enemy? Are these even the metaphors, much less the actions, of a civilized society?

If the EWLP considered matters from a global perspective, current thought seeks the most local of viewpoints; if the planners of politicized literacy campaigns sought to transform the values of the rural population, the contemporary consensus attempts to facilitate the articulation of their own values by small groups—fisherman's collectives, women's marketing associations; if it seems that both of the hegemonic traditions often sought to *appear* to do something dramatic *for* these people, the contemporary consensus is that activities *by* these groups themselves are what is important, no matter how trivial these activities might appear from the perspective of Geneva, New York, or Havana. Today we find an emerging awareness that frequently the first priority of people in the Third World is not literacy itself, but the organization of their local communities for their own betterment. Issues that arise in the course of such organization most commonly include basic economics and health education, farming and manufacturing techniques at an appropriate level of technology—and literacy education as needed to effect these ends. It is now believed that outside support for these efforts is best provided on a small scale and in a decentralized manner. Intermediary organizations now often tend to conceive of their role as supplementary to those of local community groups. Here we might invoke the term the Maryknoll sisters use to describe their work—they wish to "accompany" members of local communities who are engaged in attempting to improve their own lives.

The field of international adult literacy education is highly complex, controversial, and deeply involved with issues including, on the one hand, broad questions of development and national identity and, on the other, technical matters concerning the relationship of adult literacy programs to adult education in general and to formal school institutions.

All these are involved with the issues of the methodological choices to be made in terms of mode of instruction, language, teacher training, delivery vehicles, and so forth. Nonetheless, there is this emerging agreement on many of these latter points, an agreement so widespread that it might be appropriately referred to as the current standard adult education methodology.

This preferred technique for literacy education today is that of self-instruction by small groups of people voluntarily assembled, assisted by representatives of intermediary organizations as necessary, but always in such a way that the mode of education furthers the end—that is, self-reliance and improved living conditions visibly achieved through the efforts of the people themselves. This method of organizing education stands in stark contrast to most of the EWLP projects and to the extremely centralized procedures of the Cuban and Nicaraguan campaigns. People value what they have achieved themselves. As local groups in many areas achieve better lives, in part through improved literacy, they may come to value literacy for themselves and their children. In the long run it is this that will produce a climate of opinion valuing education, enhancing support for schooling, increasing the efforts made to keep children in school. It is because of this process that it can be said that, ultimately, universal primary education and locally initiated adult education programs are both essential for bringing into being a world in which adult illiteracy is no longer an issue.

There are other lessons to be drawn from those stories told in a quiet room in Maryknoll, in an office near Boston's Chinatown, at a restaurant in Georgetown—lessons applicable to adult education in the United States and lessons applicable perhaps more widely in our educational institutions. The history of international adult education teaches us that where educational institutions and traditions have been tested under the most extreme conditions, they have broken on the issues of specialization and outside authority. This implies that "the truth of education" is to be found in a rejection of specialization and outside authority, that an education that is holistic and democratic is not only desirable, it is the only education practical for the most oppressed. Upon reflection, one also asks why anyone, anywhere, should be given an education that is not holistic, not democratic?

Michael Holzman

Notes

1. Thomas G. Sticht points out, "There is a significant relationship among parents' education levels, the persistence of their children in school, and their achievement in school. This suggests that a more intensive effort to educate youth and adults who are present or future parents may produce an 'intergenerational transfer' of literacy that will better prepare preschool children for school" (Thomas G. Sticht, "Foreword," in Kirsch and Jungeblut 1986, vii).
2. The information on the Cuban literacy campaigns is voluminous and usually quite committed. See, for example, Kozol (1978).
3. This technique is probably quite natural in Romance languages. In English it is rather artificial, the hallmark of a certain sectarianism.

The research upon which this essay is based was supported in part by the Conrad N. Hilton Foundation. Interviews were conducted with representatives of Maryknoll, World Education, Inc., the Inter-American Foundation, and individuals including Valerie Miller, Seth Spaulding, and Carman St. John Hunter. The Grail, World Education, Carman Hunter, and Seth Spaulding provided materials and publications which would otherwise have been difficult of access. Needless to say, all these have my gratitude and none are responsible for my opinions and errors.

3

Unhappy Consciousness in First-Year English

How to Figure Things Out for Yourself

If we are to conceive of writing as social action, we must also submit our own teaching of writing to a similar analysis. What are we doing to students in the writing classroom, and why? In this essay I argue that our central purpose in a first-year writing class is to convince students of the value of using writing to criticize and change their social world. The fact that we often express this purpose by claiming to be introducing students to the conventions of the academic discourse community is significant.

This essay might be considered a case study, for it focuses on a particular writing class I taught when I came to Michigan Technological University. However, my purpose in discussing this class is not just to develop new data but also to examine current theories of collaborative learning and discourse communities. Thus, the beginning of the essay is a story, a genre that is often used to redefine beliefs and expectations within a community (cf. "The Social Context of Literacy Education," p. 133). I then attempt to interpret the story in terms of current theories, and, finally, I explain the inadequacy I see in these theories.

☐　　☐　　☐

This is a story I have been telling people about what I consider to have been a successful writing class.

I had been away from teaching first-year English for some time when I began teaching it again at Michigan Technological University.

I was not terribly satisfied with the first-quarter course I taught, which focuses on the personal essay, and as I prepared to teach the second-quarter research writing course, I decided I had to do some serious thinking about teaching writing. I knew I could not bear to teach citation styles, where to find things in the library (or not find them), how to write summaries; I dreaded reading essays consisting of partially digested information on Star Wars or AIDS. From my experience of the first-quarter course, I knew that even if I encouraged my students to examine the ideas they encountered in their research, many would simply reproduce the views of their communities and would, in this particular case, produce infuriatingly smug statements of the importance of self-help, a strong defense, economic stability, and patriotism. While the clichés of liberalism produced by other students are somehow less infuriating, I had for some time been struggling to find a way to get students to use research writing as a method of inquiry rather than as an occasion to reaffirm traditional beliefs. So I thought about what research means to me.

Like all writing, research is essentially collaborative, or communal: it has not much to do with solitary searches in a library for authoritative information[1] and a lot to do with reading and writing and talking about a complex set of ideas with peers. It gets exciting when a new way of thinking about ideas of concern is discovered and this new way of thinking is explored with the help of others. I decided to build my course on these thoughts; I decided to confront students with a new way of thinking about something that concerned them and that would force them to think and talk and write together to explore the ideas that resulted.

At this stage, I had no very explicit ideas about the theories or practices I would use to carry out this plan. I had instead more of an image, or a dream—a dream of students talking together in groups as they referred to books and notes, occasionally calling on me to answer a question when they got stuck. In this dream, the students had taken the central question I had posed and converted it into their own project, something they needed to answer for themselves, not just because I had asked it, not just to pass the course. I referred to this dream image by saying that students would form a discourse community in the class, by which I meant nothing more precise than that the students would be engaged in a common project: they would investigate a single question using research methods that relied heavily on reading and writing.

Later, as I began planning the course in earnest, I made decisions about what question to center the research on, how I wanted the students to interact with each other and with me, and what work I would require them to do.[2] The most difficult part was finding a central question that would be so compelling to the students that they could not regard it as just an assignment. By this stage in their educational careers, many students' intellectual curiosity and willingness to examine ideas has been fairly effectively suppressed by assignments that stress finding the correct answers to questions that have no relation to students' "real life" experiences. Somehow this training in obedience and alienation had to be counteracted.[3] I thought of setting a common topic, a well-known and useful way to center writing courses, but I concluded that even in investigating a topic most students found interesting too many of them would merely summarize and rearrange information from the articles they read, perhaps venturing to say they agreed or disagreed but that was only their opinion. I decided instead to give my students a book that proposed an argument with which they would initially disagree, that was based on a theory they would have to come to understand before they could express their disagreement, and that employed forms of argument they would have to master if they were to deal with the claims the author made.[4]

After thinking about the particular experiences and aspirations of my students, I decided to have them work with Herbert Marcuse's *One-Dimensional Man*. Marcuse argues that technology is a system whose only purpose is to reproduce itself and that it achieves this goal by eliminating the appearance of contradiction in society so that the only rational choice for an individual is to accept, happily, what technology has to offer. I figured that my students, who are planning careers in the creation and implementation of technology, could not be indifferent to an argument that technology, rather than enhancing life, perverts social values and denies to individuals the freedom to choose their own goals. Moreover, I was fairly certain that most would not immediately understand the theory Marcuse's argument was based on and would find it necessary to read some of the writing Marcuse referred to—Marx, Freud, Sartre—and to discuss his claims at some length before they could understand how he could possibly say what he seemed to be saying. And, finally, in discussing, and perhaps arguing with, Marcuse's claims, they would have to adopt at least some of the conventions of his type of discourse: the assumptions that claims are not based on personal opinion but rather on theories whose tenets must be explained, that claims must be backed up with observation and analysis, that claims must be related to what others have said about the question under investigation.

I also realized that if I wanted students to make the project of understanding and arguing about Marcuse's critique of the technological society their own, I would have to emphasize the value of their own insights and explanations and of their discussions with each other and deemphasize my role as an interpreter of the readings and as an evaluator of their ideas. This involved some decisions about class structure and evaluation procedures. Lectures—about Marcuse, about research theory and methodology, even about writing strategies—were out of the question. I decided that when we met in the classroom, students would work in small, stable groups of three to five students each. I also decided to use the department's Center for Computer Assisted Language Instruction

(CCLI) for some class meetings, for the center is designed as a writing workshop for students. In both these environments, I would be on the outside, with students' attention directed toward each other and toward their research and their writing. I decided that I could ask them questions and could direct their attention to passages in the readings to get discussions going, and that I would be willing to answer specific questions that came up as the groups worked together. In commenting on their writing I planned to respond primarily to their ideas, again often asking questions and directing their attention to passages. In these activities, I would still be obviously guiding discussions in directions I thought were profitable, but the emphasis would be on their developing a dialogue with Marcuse, learning how to address the questions he raised, rather than on divining the "correct" interpretation of the book.

Forsaking the standard of correct interpretation required me to find another way to evaluate their work. I explained to them that I would evaluate exploratory writing on the basis of sincere effort to engage the questions raised in the materials of the course, and in evaluating the formal essays I would add to that standard an ability to use explanations of theory, accounts of observation, analysis, and citations to back up claims. In order to emphasize the value of their own insights and explanations, I told them I would weight the exploratory writing in journals equally with the more finished writing in essays. Most importantly, I arranged for the grading of the final drafts of their essays to be done by another writing instructor (in return, I graded his classes' essays), so that I could, I hoped, respond to my students' writing more as a reader than as an evaluator. While grading the essays, my colleague and I repeatedly reminded each other that, though we alerted students to passages in Marcuse that contradicted their interpretations of his ideas, we were not requiring them to make sense of the book in the same way we did.

I organized the work of the course so that students would learn research methods that depended heavily on reading and writing and peer discussion. They read, by the end of the quarter, most of *One-Dimensional Man* (omitting only the two chapters on philosophy). As they progressed through the book, I asked them to find and read background material in the library, such as biographical information on Marcuse, definitions of specialized terms, and excerpts from the writings of Hegel, Freud, Sartre, and Marx. In the classroom, students discussed the readings in their groups. I also asked them to discuss as a class what they were finding out by reading and writing weekly in a common file on the "Marcuse Disk," which was kept in the CCLI.[5] I asked them to relate Marcuse's theory to the theme of *The Terminator*, a popular film featuring Arnold Swartzenegger we viewed in class; I asked them to test Marcuse's claim that technology creates an illusion of freedom of choice by researching, in their groups, the differences among the brands of a single product;

and I asked them to research a topic related to technology using materials I put on reserve in the library—and they discussed these things in their groups in class and on the Marcuse Disk. They individually explained, applied, and critiqued Marcuse's claims in three formal essays and in journal entries twice a week. The class met periodically in the CCLI to critique and respond to drafts of papers using the net linking the PC's, and they wrote replies to their classmates' formal essays in short papers.

Much of their interaction, which was the center of the course, was not available to me in any systematic way. Though I joined individual group discussions sometimes (and usually checked in with any group that fell silent for a while), I have only a few notes on things I overheard from these in-class discussions. When they worked in the CCLI critiquing each other's papers, groups sitting together, they discussed what they were reading on the screen with each other, often making small changes in the text with the writer's approval. I could see these interactions happening, but as I did not join in, I have no notes on what they said to one another. But what they wrote on the drafts I saw as I commented on the drafts after they finished their work in the CCLI. And their entries on the Marcuse Disk gave me a notion of how they were inter-acting in this particular forum.[6] I also kept copies of some individual journal entries and all the final drafts of papers.

Their initial reaction to Marcuse was far from positive. Many were angry and upset at having to read someone whose views so contradicted their own. Robert wrote that he found it ironic that at a technological university we were reading someone who hated technology. (I have used pseudonyms for all students.) This, of course, was just the reaction I was looking for, the kind of cognitive unease that begins an inquiry.[7] All the students found Marcuse's vocabulary unfamiliar, and most knew little or nothing about the other theories Marcuse refers to in weaving his own. (Unfortunately, they also had a lot of trouble with his Germanic style, which was not as productive a difficulty, although it did allow me to make the points that styles of writing vary with cultural and language differences and that not all published writing is equally good.) Nor did they find the background theories much more accessible, though one student commented that after reading Sartre and Hegel, Freud was pretty easy. Of course, some students dropped the course. But those who stayed were, if not exactly eager for the challenge of understanding Marcuse, at least curious and willing to work at it.

Especially early in the course, most students understood Marcuse in terms of views and positions they were familiar with. This phenomenon is familiar to reading reseachers; readers at all levels impute intentions to writers and fill the "gaps" in texts with bridging assumptions based on their own beliefs and values (cf. Tannen). A particularly obvious example of this is Mark's entry on the Marcuse Disk in which he explained

Freud's notion of sublimation in terms of the virtues of hard work and self-denial:

> I think Freud is trying to say that [when] a person has to do without something he is better off.[8] This forces one to suppress ones desire for pleasure, and appreciate things more when one aquires them. If everything is handed to a person and he doesn't have to strive to aquire them, he will not appreciate them. Therefore, through this denile the person can come to appreciate the fruits of his labor.

Many students tried at first to align Marcuse with communism, for to them socialism is synonymous with communism (and communism is evil by definition). But, as he critiques both capitalist and communist uses of technology, Marcuse's theory proved immune to simple dismissal as un-American, and as their understanding of his claims developed, these essentially conservative young people began noting, with some uneasiness, that they agreed with some of his ideas. In a journal entry, Robin explained Marcuse's argument that in our advanced technological society "people are losing their individualism," then added, "I feel I am a little too." In class he said, "Marcuse is brainwashing us." Questioning the dominant ideology is never a comfortable thing, and, as Robert Brooke has pointed out, it is not something students expect to do in classes. Robin's resistance to Marcuse's argument, his feeling that his "natural" beliefs in such things as individual freedom were being replaced by an alien ideology, is not so remarkable as his ability to allow himself to try out such an uncomfortable position.

It seemed clear to me as the quarter progressed that students were developing the kind of supportive relationships that might characterize an ideal discourse community, the kind of relationships that are necessary for trying out new perspectives. John and Rich, who were in the same group, developed a particularly close intellectual relationship. Neither were attracted to Marcuse's theories at first. In a journal entry early in the class, John wrote, "What does it matter whether my needs are true or false as long as I'm happy?" But by the second week, writing on the Marcuse Disk, John was beginning to understand the difference between what the class had been discussing as peer pressure and what Marcuse calls the "happy consciousness":

> I think that we are all getting caught up in our old viewpoints and not letting Marcuse's sink in. He doesn't tell us that society controls it's individuals but instead society is controlled by the system. As Dr. Cooper has said, there is nobody at the top, no controlling body, but instead a technological system. It is this system that sets the norms and the standards. Whatever it wants to be the "in"

thing is. It doesn't matter what your neighbor or the guy down the street thinks because they are controlled just as we are. Our ideas of "gross" and "unacceptable" will be the same because they are implanted in the same manner. It's a hard concept to grasp but I think if we put ourselves into Marcuse's shoes and feel his thoughts and give them a chance we might understand better what he is meaning to say. Maybe to get the true meaning of his writing we have to fight back the ideals and concepts that have been implanted throughout the years by the system? Who knows?

Following this entry, Rich wrote in a similar vein:

What [John] is trying to say is right, in my opinion. It is hard to try and see everything as Marcuse did. It may seem a little scary to try and think like him after seeing what he writes like. Anyway, back to the main point; Marcuse is warning all of us to be aware of what technology is doing to us, not just the working class, but even the people at the top of the social ladder. To me it seems as if technology was some kind of living thing taking control of every-thing we do—but it is something we cannot see or touch directly, it is just there. Maybe we are all conditioned to think a certain way so that we cannot think like Marcuse. Maybe this is how the "one dimensionality" fits in—we are conditioned to think that we have all the freedom we need. Technology does not give us the choice of whether or not we should get a VCR, but what kind.

The ideas that John and Rich are struggling with here are difficult ones: the idea that our ideas may not be entirely our own—that in order to understand something we may have to fight against ideals and values that have been implanted in us, that we have been conditioned to think we are free—and the idea that this repression is structural, that it is not a matter of intentional domination by an upper class. They are tentative in the way they express the ideas, asking questions, using qualifiers like 'maybe.' Rich jokes about Marcuse's impenetrable writing style. Most importantly, however, they address each other and their class members in their entries. They are certainly aware of my opinions and my control over the situation, but within this context they have made the problem of understanding Marcuse's arguments their own.

Eventually, I realized that my biggest contribution to making the course work was just this: not explaining ideas to them, answering ques-tions with questions, and in general doing something I'm pretty good at in other situations—listening more than talking. As Carl complained in class one day when I answered his question with another, "You want us to think!" By effacing my presence as much as possible, I allowed them to entertain ideas without having to commit themselves to them in any final way. I encouraged them to look to each other for support and for validation. And I helped them realize that they all had ideas and resources they could draw on.

Trying to understand Freud's notion of sublimation and Marcuse's notion of desublimation proved especially frustrating for some students. Margot asked me in class to explain sublimation but I refused, saying, "I think you can work it out." Later she wrote on the Marcuse Disk:

> Now I think I've got it—maybe! Does sublimation mean an act of transposing something bad into something good such as an instinct or an urge? . . . Maybe I don't have enough understanding of this concept yet, but I'll tell you it's pretty ridiculous to have to call a friend long distance to ask for help. Why do you keep us guessing?

The friend she called was a psychology major at another university. Other students writing on the Marcuse Disk tried other strategies to figure out what sublimation was. Peter wrote: "In normal text, doesn't sublimation mean to purify or make pure? If this is the case, I then understand that term in our text as making the bad seem good. . . . And I suppose that desublimation would be making that that is good for us seem bad." Robert wrote: "Even though I have read the Freud entry, I still am not exactly sure what sublimation is. From the comments added by the other students, I feel that I might understand a little of it." Eventually I wrote a short paragraph on sublimation and desublimation into the file, but I also explained to them that my refusal to define the concept for them had enabled them to discover useful research strategies: consulting an expert, examining language, talking with others.

In writing on the Marcuse Disk and in critiquing each other's drafts, students rarely addressed me directly and often seemed to ignore me in favor of each other as primary audience. Stan and Warren were particularly prone to joke with one another in their comments on each other's drafts. On one of Warren's one-page first drafts Stan wrote: "Well my friend, it seems as though you have an extremely good start, considering when you started it." Warren wrote on Stan's draft:

> Well, we meet again. I was going to senselessly rip your paper apart but decided not to stoop to your low level of intelligence and mantality. I agree that you have presented many good ideas and facts here. I think that if they were tied together with some choice quotes of Marcuse's you may just have a paper that is worthy of a C-, O.K. C, but that's as high as I go. More quotes. I give it a thumbs up and so does Siskel and Ebert.
>
> Staggaringly yours,
> Wang Chunk

(Like many students, Warren used a nickname to sign his comments and his entries on the Marcuse Disk.) Some of the language and type of comments Stan and Warren make here are based on the comments I made on their drafts—"this is a good start," "more quotes." But their approval of each other's work is strongly laced with a kind of sarcasm they appreciate, and Warren adds in language drawn from popular televised movie reviewers. This kind of fun is explicitly encouraged by the environment of the CCLI, where food and drinks are allowed; the walls are decorated with brightly colored weavings, paintings, and cartoons; and the PC's all have names of famous writers and are adorned with small stuffed animals and plastic "action" figures. But it also illustrates how these students created their own discourse and their own ways of interacting within the structure of the class research project.

The supportive relationships they developed also seemed to help them take chances in their formal papers. Stan and Warren's group chose shampoo as the product they would research in order to test Marcuse's claim that the technological society controls us through the illusion of freedom of choice. Linda wrote a fairly well-developed, if unfocused, first draft, and she received approving and helpful comments from the others:

> You have a really good start here. Where did you learn so much about hair? Damn! Maybe your discription is just a little too technical for us laypeople. I like it anyway, though. I think a little more on advertising and you may use a bit more detail in why you disagree with him. You're almost done. You're lucky.
>
> "Wang Chunk"

> The effort with the ingredients but I think some more discussion on the different ingredients are in different shampoos. Also some information on price of different shampoos might be helpful in proving your point.
>
> "Wang Chunk"

> I don't mean to be picky just because I researched the preference aspect of shampoo, but I think it deserves to be explained. I also think that maybe you should expand on the formaldehyde part. The fact that we are getting ingrediants that we may not want and definately don't know [about] may be important.
>
> "Me" [Stan]

> Thanks for the description on the hair. Now I don't have to [go] looking for it. You did good there. You need more on price though,

and also maybe what people liked. Other than that, good work. I'm proud of you.

Tater . . . [Peter]

Despite (or perhaps because of) comments like "You're almost done," and "I'm proud of you," Linda used the suggestions she received to do substantial revisions. In her final draft, she used only the first paragraph and a small section on the effect of shampoo on hair from her three-page first draft. She ignored their comments that she should discuss all the aspects of the research the group had done and instead picked up on Warren's request for more discussion of the different ingredients in shampoos and on Stan's suggestion that she talk more about formaldehyde, an ingredient she discussed in her introductory paragraph. The result was a five-page paper that focused on what she knew most about —the effects of various ingredients—and that made the point that although there are many brands of shampoo, all have basically the same ingredients and "none fulfill the consumers true needs," as they often contain unwanted and undesireable ingredients like formaldehyde.

Not all students were able to form such supportive relationships, however. Margaret was a working mother, whose car trouble, work schedule, and day-care problems distracted her and often kept her from writing on the Marcuse Disk, finishing drafts in enough time to get critiques from her group members, or attending classes. Furthermore, she was in a group with three young men, with whom she shared few interests (there were no other older students in the class and only three other women). Thus, the emphasis on collaborative thinking and discussion in the course was more of a handicap to her than a help. She had a particularly hard time understanding anything of what Marcuse was saying, even when she related some of his ideas to situations familiar to her. At the end of the course she commented, "I wish Marcuse were easier to understand. It has kept me from being able to write as I wanted because I always questioned my interpretation of his ideas and justly so, I was usually wrong in what I thought he was trying to say."

Margaret's inability to participate fully in the informal modes of writing kept her from achieving a confident understanding of Marcuse, for in the comments on drafts and entries in their journals and on the Marcuse Disk, students not only formed supportive relationships, but also used writing and reading conversationally, to collaboratively make sense of difficult ideas. Their writing on computer (comments on drafts and on the Marcuse Disk) exhibited the spontaneity of face-to-face conversation (cf. Spitzer 1986, 19)—their ideas were not completely worked out, their sentences changed direction in midstream, and there were many surface mistakes. To some extent, their handwritten journal entries, which engaged them in conversation with themselves and with me, exhibited some of the same features (suggesting, perhaps, that it is not the technology of writing that determines whether language use is more oral or literate).

Robin, who was learning disabled, was one student who benefited particularly from the freedom of expression the informal writing allowed. His entries on the Marcuse Disk were distinguished by wildly aberrant spellings and unexplained connections between thoughts, but these sur-face errors did not prevent him from contributing insightfully to the discussion. His classmates never commented on the errors (neither did I), but his logic sometimes confused them, even when they understood the gist of his comments. In discussing the topic of advertising, Robin wrote,

> Not only do advertisements appeal to us with the beatiful face and bodies, but they also insalt are intelligence. People will remember some one who tries to make them look stupid rather than another pretty face. But we don't think about that while we say later on did you see that stupid advertisement. And then in the stores we remember it again and we are not quite shore wear so we buy it to try it. The other advertisements that really stick in the back of our heads our the ones that make you feel left out. And there is nothing people can do because these are the things people remember and the agencies know it.

In the next entry, Stan wrote,

> What does this have to do with anything? I'm not quite sure what George [Robin's nickname] is trying to say but I agree with him on one thing. Advertisements are used as a kind of subliminal message. We see them and only vaguely remember them later, but the damage is done.

Still, despite his complaint (which was only partly serious), Stan did get Robin's main point. And however confused his ideas sometimes sounded, Robin was capable of working out some rather difficult concepts. In a journal entry he wrote:

> I almost finished chapter 6 last night and am a little confude about this objective/subjective thing. Could you tell me if I am on the right track. Everything that happens, happens wether or not we can explain it. In a tech. society people try to find wayse to look at things so that they can plug in the numbers and see if $A > B$ or $B > A$. And while in the objective world you can say $3 > 2$ and $2 > 1$ in the subjective world all the numbers lose there

meaning. Bill is not $>$ Paul because he makes more money. But in a tech. society those kinds of values hold true. The person with the most of the "good" stuf is better or greater than the rest. And we try to get on the open side of the $>$ sign. But most of all it makes us feel good to say we understand things that we can put into formulas when really there are millions of ways to get thouse same results in the subjective world.

In a later journal entry he expanded this idea:

> I could guess that he [is] saying we are becoming to much involved in our equations [so] that our lives are starting to resemble them, add good gpa with a little experience = stable job. Add high school diploma and summer jobs = no where land.

Writing in situations that allowed me—and his classmates—to ignore his difficulties with spelling and sentence structure, Robin was able to focus on explaining Marcuse's ideas in his own terms; he was able to use writing as a means to understanding something he wanted to know about.

Positive and fruitful interactions in writing gave Robin greater confidence as a writer, and his formal essays were sophisticated both in structure and in content. His essay on the illusion of freedom of choice concluded:

> Truth comes in two forms in Marcuses technological society, the real truth and the subconscious truth. People in the technological society know that the real truths, the one that tells us all light beers are the same and that we all are limited by one thing or another to what we can do in life, is right. While no matter how simple it seems people always choose the subconscious truths, that tell us the expensive light beers are different from the inexpensive ones and that success happened over night. Technology has conditioned people since their birth to think in a non-negative frame of mind. It would not be so bad except that it keeps people from thinking at all.

Robin's argument in this essay was complex, drawing on Marcuse's discussions of advertisements, modern literature, and language; his own observations of traditional values; and the research collected by his group. And, although I tried to avoid measuring a student's success by how well he or she understood Marcuse, Robin's grasp of—and agreement with —Marcuse's central thesis inevitably pleased me as much as his skillful elaboration of his argument.

Unavoidably, we teach our own values in writing courses as we teach the strategies of academic discourse. Some values are personal and we must try to make this clear to students; but other values—such as the value of taking different perspectives on a question—are central to certain types of academic discourse. In requiring these students to try to look at technology from a new perspective, I asked them to question beliefs some held very strongly. A student who had particular difficulty with this aspect of the course was Bartleby; his entries on the Marcuse Disk and his essays made it clear that there was no way he would entertain Marcuse's perspective on anything. Here are excerpts from two entries he wrote in response to Marcuse's comment that the press self-censors material that goes against the interests of the technological society:

> What is the true responsibilities of the press? Are these responsibilities to the people they serve or the government? The actions of the government are in some instances best left unstirred. The whole thing with the Iran arms sales every one is hearing so much about would probably have been best left untouched. . . . The whole idea of fredom of the press is supposed to provide for self-censorship but over the course of U.S. history they have grown to care more about sales then what is in the best interest of the majority of people. . . . Who does the covering up and the "self" censoring of the media? The large majority of the censoring is not DONE BY the press but rather the government. The majority of the censoring is in the best interest of the people. Imagine if the press would have released the impending attack on Libya earlyer this year. . . . The only issue of the media is money and anything to make money. Is a state run media all negative.

Bartleby's stance was familiar to me, as was the tenacity with which he held to it. I had encountered similar views in the first-quarter writing classes I taught. Bartleby's heavy use of absolutes—"the whole thing," "the whole idea," "the only issue"—would undoubtedly lead William Perry to call him a dualist, but I attributed his stance to a strongly conservative background he could not give up. Neither explanation, however, gave me any idea of how to deal with Bartleby, who virtually absented himself from the class project. He wrote on the Marcuse Disk rarely and was often not in class.

He did turn in all three formal essays. For his final essay he chose to discuss the problem of world hunger, using material drawn from a book I put on reserve in the library, Susan George's *How the Other Half Dies*. Again he disagreed with the perspective, denouncing it as "very socialistic": "The whole nature in which the book is written is that [those who] have something extra should freely and willingly give it to those who do not have enough." The problem with his paper, in terms of academic discourse, is that he thought of this characterization as a persuasive argument, as undoubtedly it would be in a dinner table discussion in his home.[9] My colleague who was grading the essays gave Bartleby an F for this paper on the basis that he did not even mention George's discussions of the points he raised. In Bartholomae's terms, Bartleby was unable to set out an academic project in his writing.

At the end of the course I asked students on the Marcuse Disk what they thought they had learned. Several students talked about the experience of dealing with a point of view that was quite different from their own. Sean wrote:

> I think that reading One-Dimensional Man has given me a chance to look at society from a different perspective. Marcuse brings up a lot of ideas that I think people may not want to talk about, but it is probably good for us to do so. As for something that I learned from him, I think I have learned to try and evaluate someone elses opinion positively even when I am not sure I agree with them.

Several students also noted the relevance of Marcuse's views to their career interests; Frank, a senior, was especially aware of this:

> I have not really learned much from Marcuse, what he has done is open my eyes to problems and things around me in society that I should try to change or that I should disagree with. Marcuse has caused me to look at things from a non-technological perspective. I grew up living and I am about to graduate into a technological society with a technical degree, but Marcuse has giving me the thought to be able to look at some things from his type of perspective. This will give me a more open view to the things I am trying to do and if I should disagree with what they or it is doing. The reading of Marcuse has expanded my vocabulary a little, having to always read the book with the dictionary right there. Was a tough class a lot of work but it was alright.

The experience of analyzing ideas from a new perspective was all I was hoping for them. It was not, after all, a course in social theory, but a research writing course. And indeed about half the class, even after trying sincerely to understand Marcuse, remained fairly impervious to his perspective. Robert wrote, "I have learned to try and figure out what someone elses opinion means. . . . As for false needs or wants as I brought up in my first paper, I think I will keep taking them if I can get them."

But for me the most significant evaluations of the course were those that indicated that the students had understood how reading and writing contribute to learning. Typically, they talked more about what they learned from reading than what they learned from writing, but it was the writing they did that enabled them to read in this new way. Tom wrote, "I think that reading this type of writing has helped me become a more observent reader because when you read Marcuse you have to understand every sentence you read." Margaret wrote, "I believe the thing that I learned most from reading 'One Dimensional Man' by Marcuse is to analyze things more—to think more about what is being said and to look more objectively at things and not just take them for face value." Best of all was this comment from Ronnie: "I think the most important thing I've learned from Marcuse is how to read and read and read until I understand. He has taught me how to learn and figure things out for myself."

I think this is a nice story. It makes me feel good about teaching writing. But I recount it here for another reason—not because we need to know that sometimes things do go right in writing classes (which of course we all do, on occasion, need to know), but because it illustrates how necessary it is to think about the social structure of writing in the classroom, to think about such things as our relationship to our students and the relationship of their purposes and experiences to the projects we propose for them. Composition research on the social aspect of writing has focused on two overlapping concepts: collaborative learning and, more recently, discourse communities. The two concepts are closely interrelated and articles dealing with either often treat the same issues —teacher/student roles and identities, student interaction and socialization, purposes for writing, the relation of educational institutions to the larger society. To begin with, then, I turn to this literature to help me make sense of my classroom experience.

Collaborative learning/writing—significantly, learning and writing are nearly synonymous in this context—is a label that applies to a rather broadly conceived phenomenon. In general it signals an interest in writing as a social activity, but beyond that it may also reflect an interest in the way in which ideas are developed collaboratively through the act of writing, an interest in group work in the classroom, or an interest in bringing writing in the classroom more in line with what we know about the social structure of writing practices in other contexts. Andrea Lunsford and Lisa Ede, in reporting preliminary results of their survey of writing practices in the workplace, conclude, "writing allows us to know, understand, and act on our world in unique ways; . . . through writing, in fact, we most often create these worlds" and "such creation is least often an isolated, solitary act created *ex nihilo*, and most often a communal, consensual act, one that is essentially and naturally collaborative" (1986, 76). Both the purpose and mode of writing is here seen to be social: we write to define our place in the social world; we write together.

Kenneth Bruffee also approves a shift away from the assumption that writing is individual and primarily competitive:

> How would it look if we no longer assumed that people write to persuade or to distinguish themselves and their points of view and to enhance their own individuality by gaining the acquiescence of other individuals? How would it look if we assumed instead that people write for the very opposite reason: that people write in order to be accepted, to join, to be regarded as another member of the culture or community that constitutes the writer's audience? (1984, 651)

Bruffee's remark illustrates how the idea that we write to define our place in the world leads to the concept of the discourse community. He also notes in this article how interest in collaboration in the classroom grows out of what we already know about other situations: "all that is new in collaborative learning, it seems, is the systematic application of collaborative principles to that last bastion of hierarchy and individualism, the American college classroom" (1984, 647).

Indeed, Bruffee has been arguing for collaborative learning for fifteen years, pointing out how traditional teaching conventions isolate students:

> they all assume a one-to-one relationship between student and teacher. . . . A student talks to the teacher, writes to the teacher, and determines his fate in relation to the teacher, individually. . . . Students are officially anonymous to one another, and isolated. Classroom learning is conceived of as an almost entirely individual process. (1972, 459)

Bruffee's solution to this crisis of "authority" in the classroom is to relegate faculty to "the edge of the action, once they have set the scene," to conceive of the teacher as "a *metteur en scène* whose responsibility and privilege is to arrange optimum conditions for other people to learn" (1972, 464, 470). His metaphor aptly describes what I was attempting to do in taking my students into the CCLI and in refusing to be the "donor" of knowledge (but see also Freire 1972).

In the same year that this article of Bruffee's appeared, Edwin Mason's book on collaborative learning was published in the United States. His diagnosis of the situation in the classroom is much the same as Bruffee's but more politically oriented; he assumes that the values of the educational system reflect those of the larger society:

> The present system is damaging to most of the people who are caught up in it, adult and young alike. . . . Most frightening of all

to me . . . is how this information environment reinforces the alienation of people. . . . How can we eliminate this energy-sapping rivalry and produce a system of schooling which encourages collaboration for everybody's sake? That is the question I mean to explore in this book. Since it runs so directly against the tide of working values, if not of face values of our society, where private enterprise is seen as bargaining for privileges and in no sense the giving of gifts, I do not expect a ready initial agreement that the question is even important. (1972, 12–17)[10]

Mason's analysis, by focusing on the source of the traditional values that permeate the educational system, explains the resistance I encountered both in the classroom and from other teachers to the way I conceived my role as a teacher in the research writing course. Students revealed their assumptions about what teachers should do in indirect but clearly understandable complaints: "Why do you keep us guessing?" "You want us to think." Other teachers sometimes accused me of being "cold-blooded" in making students tackle such a difficult text "on their own." In discussing how collaborative learning changes the role of the teacher, John Trimbur highlights Mason's insight and my experience: "Developing new teaching practices, Mason argues, is more difficult than developing new teaching materials because teachers are tied into a self-perpetuating system and set of expectations that are resistant to innovation" (1985, 104). Trimbur also cites Bruffee in this context, but Bruffee more clearly blames teachers rather than the system for the "latent authoritarianism" in higher education: "the first change we make is not in our students but in ourselves" (1972, 470).

The reason we wish to change the relation between teachers and students is deeply rooted in the concept of collaboration. It is not just that it enables students to "regain confidence in their innate ability . . . to learn without being taught" (Bruffee, 1972, 465). It is not just that it shifts the responsibility for learning—and the control over what is learned, when it is learned, and how fast it is learned—from teachers to students. Learning is not something one does to another person, except in a punitive context: "I'll learn you!" Paulo Freire points out that learning is not something one can do alone: "In the dialogical theory of action, Subjects meet in cooperation in order to transform the world" (1972, 167). As Greg Myers says:

Collaboration . . . makes for learning that is participatory. No longer is the teacher the exclusive source of information; rather, students, too, create knowledge, forging their own individually meaningful network of meanings. (1986, 48)

My students and I brought different resources and perspectives to bear on the task of making sense of Marcuse's theories in today's world. I brought in Freud and Marx and a reflection in popular culture of some of Marcuse's ideas—the movie *The Terminator*. They brought a more immediate knowledge of certain scientific and technological information than I had, and certainly more familiarity with not only *The Terminator* (some of them recited the lines along with the on-screen characters when we viewed the movie in class) but also other movies that exemplified Marcuse's critique of technology. I came to understand better the limitations of Marcuse's ideas in critiquing the present relation between technology and society (*One-Dimensional Man*, after all, was published in 1964); they came to understand better that some of Marcuse's ideas could help them explain their own experiences in the technological society (some of them had worked on automotive assembly lines) and in their classes in science and technology. Collaboration assumes an exchange, what Mason calls the giving of gifts. It assumes that differences among people are a resource, not something to be eliminated in the name of education, remediation, socialization. Mason notes, "Our haste to apply special remedies to people unlike us with no aim other than to make them *like* us (the ambiguity is intended) is not the least worrying manifestation of . . . human arrogance" (1972, 19).

Still, the goal of collaborative learning is not to make the teacher one of the guys, but to make the guys, as a group, more important. Just as the language children acquire reflects the forms of their peer group more than the forms their parents use, so too will peer groups in school incorporate ideas into their own structures for their own purposes. Each generation recreates the social world for themselves. And students in classes affect each other's learning whether we encourage it or not. Anne Haas Dyson reports an interesting study of second-grade writing behavior in which the peer networks within the class and the students' different "social interpretations of school writing tasks (whom writing tasks were completed for and why)" (1985, 210) were the dominant influences. When writing stories to be shared orally with the class, one student with few friends viewed her story as an opportunity to present herself positively while another more social student strove to entertain the class with her story.[11]

In my class I could contrast the experience of Margaret with that of Robin. As the only older student, Margaret had no particular friends in the class. When writing in the computer file, she rarely picked up topics from other students and never entered into direct debates. Often her drafts were not ready to share on computer with the members of her group and thus she did not receive the benefit of their comments. It seemed clear to me that her relative isolation from class discussion contributed to the difficulty she had in interpreting *One-Dimensional Man*.

Robin, on the other hand, was the same age as the rest of the class and had several good friends both inside and outside his group. He knew he had serious mechanical problems in writing, but because he felt secure socially he was able to write on the computer file and to share his drafts with no hesitation. And this engagement with class discussion helped him master the difficult and foreign ideas he encountered in the reading.

The emotional support students receive from collaborative learning practices is often noted (see Bruffee 1972; Gebhardt 1980). Peter Elbow memorably describes how essential it is to writers in particular:

> For improving your writing, you need at least some readers to be allies, persons who wholly *cooperate* in the communicative trans-action. When you pass them the potatoes they don't just sit there and look at you holding the bowl with a look that says, "If I had wanted the potatoes I would have *asked* you for them." They take the bowl and thank you for it. (1981, 24)

It is often difficult for teachers to sincerely thank student writers for what they receive. The collaborative writing group attempts to draw on the strength of the peer bond among students as a resource for building positive attitudes toward writing; students are encouraged to work to-gether to figure out what kind of writing they are supposed to be doing and why they should and how they can cope with these demands.

In their comments on each other's drafts, my students were able to acknowledge such things as the value of research ("Where did you learn so much about hair?"), the value of sharing ("Now I don't have to [go] looking for it"), and their common tendency to procrastinate ("an ex-tremely good start, considering when you started it"). They internalized the need for detail, expansion of ideas, and quotes. They encouraged each other in their own terms: "Wang Chunk" told Linda: "You're almost done," the ultimate goal of student writers. Writing on the Marcuse Disk, students tried out learning strategies: Rich and John reinforced each other's impulse toward adopting Marcuse's perspective by assuring each other that they would not therefore be committing themselves to believing in a particular ideology.

Ideally, collaborative learning techniques allow writing teachers to reform their relationship to their students and the relationships among students so that teachers become expert consultants to peer groups who understand assignments in their own way and develop and adapt ideas, purposes, and forms by working together and supporting one another. But when collaboration is placed in the context of the school or college classroom, its egalitarian basis is substantially altered by the institutional purpose of education. No matter how much we feel we learn from our students, no matter how accepting we are of their generational, class, ethnic, and other differences that lead them to display differences in learning strategies, values, and goals, we still, for better or for worse, are in the business of changing them. John Trimbur explains that one reason for the success of collaborative learning is that it deals with the problem of students who "often are not fully socialized to the discipline of the classroom and the rules and values of the academic game." He goes on:

> Learning in groups, Kurt Lewin and Paul Grabbe point out, is often more effective than learning individually because learning involves more than simply acquiring new information. It also involves the acceptance of new habits, values, beliefs, and ways of talking about things. To learn is to change: learning implies a shift in social standing—a transition from one status and identity to another and a reorientation of social allegiances. (1985, 90)

Alan C. Purves and William C. Purves, arguing that "most writing is done within the framework of a community," which they call a "culture," similarly point out that "when an individual is transplanted from one culture to another culture, the individual has a great deal both to unlearn and to learn if he or she is to be accepted as a writer in that culture" (1986, 193, 194).

For most students in our educational system, learning involves being transplanted into a different culture or cultures, joining a variety of different discourse communities. They can often deal better with the demands made on them by these changes when they work collaboratively, acknowledging to one another their difficulties and resistance as did many of the students in my classes. Bruffee, drawing on the work of Richard Rorty, explains the continuity between the notions of collaborative learning and discourse communities: "Collaborative learning provides the kind of social context, the kind of community, in which normal discourse occurs: a community of knowledgeable peers" (1984, 644). But in a college classroom, the type of community that forms is not primarily oriented to student needs nor is it determined by students: it is instead a distinctly academic discourse community, "a social context in which students can experience and practice the kinds of conversation valued by college teachers" (Bruffee 1984, 642).

I largely determined the nature of the discourse community that could form in my classes by choosing for them a particularly academic project, a project they certainly would not have chosen for themselves. Research on collaborative learning has helped me explain how the students, to a certain extent at least, made this academic project their own. The question that still must be answered is why this was an appropriate project for a first-year writing class.[12] I certainly don't believe that *One-*

Dimensional Man was the only text I could have chosen to base the course on, although it was particularly appropriate at my university and had an added advantage I will discuss later in this essay. But to define better why this general kind of project worked I turn now to the research on discourse communities. In particular, I want to look at the nature of the discourse community that students are asked to join in the writing class and why they should want to join it.

We often say that our goal in writing classes is to introduce students to the general academic discourse community, to ways of thinking and writing that will serve them in all their college courses. As James Reither says, "The business of knowledge communities is inquiry—coming to know" (1985, 625), and so we say that the discourse practices students master in first-year writing classes will enable them to learn. Group discussions of reading, informal writing in journals, and formal writing in essays enable them to synthesize new ideas and integrate them with their previous ideas and experiences. This is a familiar and to some extent a useful way of thinking about the purpose of writing classes. But though I would agree that writing should be the foundation of a college education, I see some real problems in the idea that what we are doing in writing classes is preparing students to join the academic discourse community.

The first problem is that instead of actually introducing students into the academic discourse community, we often assume that they must first master the appropriate discourse practices before they can take on the purposes of the community. But practices stripped of their purposes become sterile exercises. When, for example, we assign a research paper in a situation in which there is no ongoing inquiry, students not surprisingly see the assignment as pointless. As Reither points out:

> We need to help students learn how to do the kinds of learning that will allow them, in their writing, to use what they *can* know, through effective inquiry, rather than suffer the limits of what they already know. We need to bring curiosity, the ability to conduct productive inquiry, and an obligation for substantive knowing into our model of the process of writing. To do that, we need to find ways to immerse writing students in academic knowledge/discourse communities so they can write from within those communities. (1985, 624)

Instead of conceiving the writing class as a particular academic discourse community with particular discourse practices that serve particular purposes, we all too often conceive it as a skills acquisition course that will supposedly prepare students to enter the discourse communities they encounter in their other classes. This, of course, is the other problem with the idea that writing classes prepare students to enter the academic discourse community: there seems to be no reason to assume that there is a general academic discourse community, no strategies of inquiry or discourse practices that all the disciplines seem to hold in common. The discourse practices students are set to master in first-year writing classes are most often the specific practices of whatever discourse community the teachers belong to, practices that seem universal because they are the ones the teachers themselves use. Thus, the view widely held by students about their first-year writing classes is often true: the writing they do there takes the form of exercises, not real academic projects, and it usually has little relation to the writing they are required to do in their other classes.

The repressiveness of setting exercises as the focus of writing classes is particularly salient in the case of basic writers, writers who most of all need to know that writing is a way of acting on the world, not a mechanical skill to be acquired as an admission ticket to white-collar employment. Recently, in an upper-level class on literacy, I asked students to discuss a paragraph of description written by a student in a remedial writing class at a nearby institution:

> My teacher is wearing a cream sweater, stripe pants, and black shoes. Her hair is curly with a light brown color. She wears glasses, rings, and watches. Her height is about "5" feet even, but her weight should weigh about 120 pounds. The class like when she walks, because she don't walk, she stumps; However when she enters the class she always wear this red coat and have this blue book bag in her and.

Insistently they asked what might have been the student's purpose in writing this paragraph, as, apart from the fifth sentence, nothing that is said here would be news to the teacher,[13] nor is the topic one that the student shows much interest in. The obvious answer is not very satisfying: the student's purpose is to practice using detail in description. Using detail, of course, is a convention of a particular kind of academic writing, but what is essential to know about this convention—that it is a means of understanding what is being described by linking the particular with the general—cannot be grasped in a writing situation that obviates the over-all purpose of this academic community: to use writing as a means of coming to know. Marilyn Sternglass, studying the experience of basic writers, concludes:

> I found that the degree to which the student writers transformed the generalized tasks into ones that were personally meaningful to

them affected strongly their critical and creative thinking processes and their ability to utilize complex cognitive strategies in responding to the problems they had posed for themselves. (1986, 77)

Writing classes at all levels have to be places where meaningful inquiry is going on if students are to acquire the values and practices of knowledge communities.

In a case study of writing across the curriculum, Lucille Parkinson McCarthy also concluded that the student's success in his courses was strongly linked to his ability to see purposes for his writing other than demonstrating competence. Her claim that the various writing he did in the three classes she studied was similar in many ways suggests that it might be reasonable to think that first-year writing classes can train students in general academic writing practices. But her analyses show that in fact the writing in the three classes varied considerably in strategies, structures, and demands, being similar only in that it all could be characterized as "informational writing for the teacher-as-examiner" (1987, 243). And, most significantly, the student himself perceived the writing in the classes as being entirely different.

One of the similarities McCarthy claims for the writing in the three classes is the teachers' purpose for having students write: they wanted to enable "students to become competent in using the thinking and language of their disciplines" (1987, 244). The biology teacher says, "Students need to get a feeling for the journals, the questions people are asking, the answers they're getting, and the procedures they're using. It will give them a feeling for the excitement, the dynamic part of this field." The poetry teacher says, "The three critical essays you will write will make you say something quite specific about the meaning of a poem (your thesis) and demonstrate how far you've progressed in recognizing and dealing with the devices a poet uses to express his insights" (McCarthy 1987, 244). Both emphasize the link between thinking and writing: students writing in these classes are involved not only with the discourse practices of the disciplines but also with the particular concerns and modes of inquiry. And the concerns, modes of inquiry, and discourse practices are specific to the particular discipline. The purpose the composition teacher sees for her course is quite different:

> Ideas aren't going to do people much good if they can't find the means with which to communicate them. . . . When these students are more advanced, and the ability to produce coherent prose is internalized, then they can concentrate on ideas. That's why I'm teaching the analytic paper with a certain way of developing the thesis that's generalizable to their future writing. (244)

She makes no claim to be teaching students how people think in her discipline, and she offers to train them in no particular discourse practices but rather in general strategies. Unfortunately, like many other students, this student didn't see the way of developing the thesis taught by his composition teacher as generalizable to the writing he had to do in his other classes: "In Biology he was indeed concerned about his organization, but here it was the five-part scientific format he had been given, very different, it seemed to him, than the thesis/subpoint organization he had had to create for his freshman essays" (249). And, when we look at the four purposes that he articulated for writing in his composition class, we find that two have to do with inquiry: writing to explore topics of his choice and writing to participate with other students in the classroom.

The ideas that writing occurs most naturally within a discourse community and that within academic discourse communities a primary function of writing is to enable learning lie behind the move to embed writing instruction within courses in other departments. We often explain to our colleagues across the college or university that "the value of writing in any course should lie in its power to enable the discovery of knowledge" (Knoblauch and Brannon 1983, 466), and it is not difficult to design writing assignments that aid students in mastering not only the concepts presented in history, chemistry, or business courses, for example, but also the purposes and conventions for writing in these communities. Were it not for the fact that enrollments in writing courses are a primary means of supporting upper-level and graduate work in our own departments, we might argue more strongly for writing instruction to be carried on entirely within such communities. But our resistance to giving up writing courses also stems, I think, from our belief in the value of the purposes and conventions for writing of a particular discourse community that we call our own. In fact, it is the high value we place on these discourse practices that leads us to see them as characterizing academic discourse as a whole. When we recognize that the assignments we design for writing classes enable the discovery of knowledge in a particular field, that we are involving our students in a particular mode of inquiry just as much as their biology or poetry teachers do, we will be able to stop seeing the function of first-year writing classes as that of simply preparing students to do the "real" work of their other courses.

I argue that the discourse community we are inviting students into, in their first-year writing class, is the community of professional nonfiction writers, people who analyze ideas in writing as an occupation or as part of their occupation.[14] This is clearly not one of the discourse communities that is aligned with a single academic discipline; it is more like the discourse community of bird watchers, which might be seen to be particularly associated with the discipline of ornithology but which draws its membership from a much wider range of people and has different purposes and interests than its related discipline. Similarly, the community of nonfiction writers is associated with the discipline of literary studies, but it includes academic writers in such disciplines as history, psychology, astronomy, and archaeology; writers of trade nonfiction; and writers of newspaper and magazine columns and opinion pieces. This community values discourse practices that lead to a certain kind of knowing, a kind of knowing usually referred to as critical thinking. Critical thinking implies the ability and inclination to examine things from different points of view, to develop, test, and apply theories in order to come to understand experiences. Critical thinking is clearly not a value solely of this community, but for nonfiction writers it is a kind of knowing that is the result of writing and reading, a kind of knowledge that develops intertextually. (As always, purpose and practices interact to define the community.) When writing teachers define writing, it is often in these terms. Brooke argues that writing teachers "would have students see themselves as writers, as people who use the processes writing offers to explore, question, and change elements of their social lives" (1987, 151). To explore, question, and change society is not the purpose of all writers or of all writing, except in a very abstract sense. But it is the purpose of the writing that we find valuable and that we often teach in first-year writing classes.

This purpose is clearest in the first quarter or semester of writing, when we ask students to write from personal experience. Students' personal narratives are based on a genre—the personal essay—that is central to this discourse community and that suggests appropriate roles for students and teachers. Students explore insights based on personal experiences, and teachers respond as readers who are interested in insights derived from human experience and who can help students express their insights in a form acceptable in this community. But when we move on to "more advanced" assignments and ask students to write from sources, we sometimes ask them to write in genres that force them and us into uncomfortable and artificial roles and that serve purposes other than inquiry. Letters to the editor, for example, are primarily persuasive in purpose and rarely offer the scope in which to develop and analyze new insights. Further, when faced with an assignment to write a letter to the editor, students frequently find that the arguments and information they have to offer are old news to their readers—the general public and their teachers—and are thus not persuasive. Research reports, either on a national issue like AIDS or on some local issue such as how the city of Houghton suddenly found itself with no place to dispose of its garbage, have as their primary purpose the transmission of information. When the information they contain is neither new nor interesting to the reader, writing them will be a pointless exercise.

If we wish to focus research writing courses on inquiry and the discovery of knowledge, a better genre to assign would be the well-known, if not well-defined, genre of general analytic nonfiction. Its purpose is the critical examination of social phenomena from the point of view of current theories; the mode of writing is analysis, synthesis, hypothesis, and comment, not primarily persuasive or informational. The genre includes both academic writing of the less esoteric type (*One-Dimensional Man*, for example, or Mary Belenky et al.'s *Women's Ways of Knowing*, or George Steiner's *After Babel*, or Oliver Sacks's *The Man Who Mistook His Wife for a Hat*, or Stephen Jay Gould's *The Flamingo's Smile*), and some trade nonfiction (such as Andrea Dworkin's *Intercourse*, or William Greider's *Secrets of the Temple*, or Barry Lopez' *Arctic Dreams*). It is a genre that college-educated people are supposed to be comfortable with, and it is a genre that allows students in writing classes to move the base of their inquiry beyond the bounds of their personal experience. And, again, the genre projects workable roles for students and teachers: students write about social phenomena of interest to them using theories to explain them in ways that are interesting to educated people such as their teachers, who also are willing and able to help them perfect their mastery of this discourse genre.

Thomas Tryzna has similarly argued that "developing critical thinking skills is a primary objective for research writing," and that "we can begin by redefining research writing as an exercise in hypothesis development, as opposed to a task of reporting and reviewing" (1983, 204). If we want our students to think critically, to develop hypotheses, we must confront them with ideas that raise questions in their minds. By confronting my students with a theory that contradicted many of their assumptions, I encouraged them to question those assumptions and to search for ways to back them up or for new hypotheses to take their place. As prospective engineers, they were led to ask, for instance, whether formulas explained everything that is important about the world. To understand Marcuse's critique and to find answers to their questions, they had to read other texts, both theoretical and informational, and they had to examine their experiences and their observations in terms of his critique; research became a means to an end, not an end in itself. John, for example, reexamined information he had gathered for a high school report on the America's Cup race and concluded that interest in the race had shifted from a focus on national pride and individual skill and effort to a focus on the money that could be made in testing sail stress, developing new hull designs, and marketing the race to tourists. And they worked out their defenses of their beliefs, their new hypotheses, and their conclusions in informal and formal writing that I could respond to with interest because it relied on discourse practices that are used in our discourse community to expand the kind of knowledge we find valuable.

A benefit, then, of thinking of writing classes as part of the discourse community of nonfiction writers is that it highlights their purpose as the development of critical thinking through writing, a purpose that secures for writing instruction a central place in education. The development of critical thinking is a slippery idea, however, one that all too easily translates into the idea that educated people think in some objectively better way than uneducated people. Myers sums up a common view of how the collaborative learning that takes place in discourse communities stimulates "mature" thinking: "Students who may initially perceive the world in simplistic terms may be encouraged, through exposure to the diversity of their peer's outlooks, to grow into more accurately complex understandings that characterize mature intellectual processes" (1986, 49). By now, after Labov's and Scribner and Cole's refutations of claims that particular dialects or particular types of literacy lead to cognitive development, we should know enough to be wary of such claims as this. It is, of course, William Perry's study of the thought processes of Harvard undergraduates that provides the underpinning for this particular claim. But, as Patricia Bizzell has perceptively argued, what happens to students' thinking processes in the course of their education is not best characterized as cognitive development: "Perry's analysis describes the changes in student thinking that result from their socialization into the academic community" (1984, 452).[15] And she worries about what socialization does to some students, pointing out that "the student's very self . . . is altered by participation in any new discourse. These will not be changes the student can erase at will" (1986, 43).

When I think of the experiences of my students in this class, the changes—and resistance to change—in their ways of thinking seem to me to be best elucidated in these terms. They showed awareness of—and some discomfort at—the changes that were required of them. Bartleby, in particular, found these changes too threatening; he was perhaps more unwilling than unable to set out an academic project. In his final comment on the Marcuse Disk he explicitly repudiated hypothetical ways of thinking about the world: "The whole approach of any philosopher i have ever seem [seen] is idealistic bull." If we think of Bartleby's resistance as an unwillingness to change rather than as an inability to develop cognitive maturity, we are led to examine what is going on in our classes more closely. It is not that we want our students to be "better thinkers," but rather that we want them to join us, to be a part of one of our communities. I argue that it is only by participating in this community that students will come to understand it, and thus we must invite them in, by asking them questions whose answers will be significant within the community, by asking them to take up topics that are of interest to us as well as to them.

But what of students like Bartleby who refuse to accept the invitation? Bizzell suggests that we have perhaps been less than straightforward in our dealings with our students in this regard:

> it seems hypocritical to pretend that academic activity is value-neutral, that we are merely teaching "thinking," not thinking in a certain way. And it seems more respectful to our students to see what we are doing when we teach as attempting to persuade them to accept our values, not simply inculcating our values. (1984, 454)

Before students like Bartleby can bring themselves to try on other perspectives, especially perspectives that are opposed to the ones they are most comfortable with, they must see some reason for behaving in this way. They must see some value for themselves in accepting membership, even if only temporarily, in a new community.[16] Other students are more easily persuaded; for them the value of critical thinking is already established or closely enough related to other values they hold as to be readily acceptable. Like Ronnie, they see their socialization into the community as liberating: the course "has taught me how to learn and figure things out for myself."

We believe in the value of critical thinking, cognitive dissonance, and adopting different perspectives—all of which are based on the central value of coming to know through reading and writing. But that these things are the norms of our discourse community, that they are *our* values, is not in itself a sufficient reason for us to offer them to students so persuasively. *Why* are these things valuable to us and to our students? This is the question that is not addressed in the discussions of collaborative learning and discourse communities; it is the question we must answer if we are to persuade students to adopt our community as their own.

And it is here that Marcuse's theory is especially useful in the writing classroom, for built into his argument about the repressiveness of the technological society is an argument for the value of a particular kind of critical thinking.[17] Robin referred to it in the conclusion to his third paper: "Technology has conditioned people since their birth to think in a non-negative frame of mind. It would not be so bad except that it keeps people from thinking at all." The one-dimensionality of Marcuse's title refers to the loss of the negative power of the dialectic, the loss of alternative ways of thinking in the advanced industrial society. The technological society arranges the world in such a way that all other social values seem to be allied with productivity—what's good for GM is good for the nation. All alternatives to the established system thus appear to be irrational; all contradictions that might drive the dialectic force for change are systematically obscured. Marcuse argues that:

> this society is irrational as a whole. Its productivity is destructive of the free development of human needs and faculties, its peace maintained by the constant threat of war, its growth dependent on the repression of the real possibilities for pacifying the struggle for existence—individual, national, and international. . . . The fact that the vast majority of the population accepts, and is made to accept, this society does not render it less irrational and less reprehensible. The distinction between true and false consciousness, real and immediate interest still is meaningful. But this distinction itself must be validated. Men must come to see it and to find their way from false to true consciousness, from their immediate to their real interest. They can do so only if they live in need of changing their way of life, of denying the positive, of refusing. It is precisely this need which the established society manages to repress. . . . (1964, ix–x, xii–xiv)

The power of positive thinking overwhelms the negation that in the life of the mind leads us from the realm of sense-certainty to the realm of absolute knowing, that in the material world leads us out of slavery to the needs of the technological society to the freedom to fulfill our true needs, needs that are indeed our own.

In Hegel's terms, the power of negation comes from its power to define. To see what something is, one must see what it is not, and vice versa. The conflict between the two, the way they depend upon one another and interact, must be held in the mind, not allowed to resolve in favor of one or the other, if one is to understand, to be able to think critically about what one confronts. In daily experience in the technological society, Marcuse argues, such conflicts are instead harmonized:

> I take a walk in the country. Everything is as it should be: Nature at its best. Birds, sun, soft grass, a view through the trees of the mountains, nobody around, no radio, no smell of gasoline. Then the path turns and ends on the highway. I am back among the billboards, service stations, motels, and roadhouses. I was in a National Park, and I now know that this was not reality. It was a "reservation," something that is being preserved like a species dying out. If it were not for the government, the billboards, hot dog stands, and motels would long since have invaded that piece of Nature. I am grateful to the government; we have it much better than before . . . (1964, 226)

The crucial move in this train of thought is the point at which the awareness of the way the surrounding area contradicts the "naturalness" of the park is suppressed by the ideology of the National Park system. The negative value of the experience of returning to reality, which may lead to questions about why elaborate systems are necessary to protect nature from technology, is contained by the harmonizing "realization" that it is only because of the prosperity of the government, well-supported by the profits of technology, that these reservations can exist at all. (Yosemite Valley might be seen as a microcosmic image of the irrationality of this train of thought.) My students often demonstrated the pervasiveness of such "positive thinking," responding to the unease created by considering Marcuse's theories with harmonizing realizations like "What does it matter if my needs are true or false as long as I'm happy?" Comforted by such realizations, we cease to see the contradiction as a contradiction; we cease to think about it as a problem with alternative solutions; we cease to think about it at all.

Our ability to find our way to true consciousness, to see our real interests, depends on our ability to think about these contradictions, to see in them not only the established reality but also the alternative possibilities they contain. This is the function of the kind of critical thinking Marcuse calls for: "Critical thought strives to define the irrational character of the established rationality (which becomes increasingly obvious) and to define the tendencies which cause this rationality to define its own transformation" (1964, 227). The power of critical thought to enable us to see irrational aspects of our society as irrational and to find ways to transform them is the basis for the value we place in the writing classroom on critical thinking, on cognitive dissonance (the appearance of negation), on the ability to adopt different perspectives. Adopting different perspectives means, in Sean's words, "to try and evaluate someone elses opinion positively even when I am not sure I agree with them"—or, as Marcuse would say, *especially* when, given the omnipresence of technological rationality, we are not sure we agree. This is the kind of thinking we mean when we say that writing is thinking.

It is true that, as Bruffee says, one purpose of writing is to join a community. But it makes some difference which discourse community you wish to join through writing. In the writing classroom our goal is not to create just any discourse community, not just to use collaborative learning techniques to help students forge "their own individually meaningful network of meanings" (Myers 1986, 48), but rather to persuade students to join a particular discourse community. And we do so because we believe the practices of this discourse community are of some social value.

Our primary goal in first-year writing classes often seems to be to make our students happy. Particularly at universities where first-year students are generally in large classes, the small writing class is seen as the one where students get the kind of intellectual and emotional support that will "improve student retention." We are supposed to teach students skills that will make them more successful in their other classes; we give them a break from structured knowledge acquisition lessons—the "banking" concept of education (Freire 1972)—and we help them express their feelings and opinions and develop new ideas. We take care that the readings are interesting, the assignments engaging. Our role seems to be to make college life palatable, or at least bearable. To an extent, it may be a good role; certainly it is a good thing to support students who are overwhelmed at first by college life. But just as certainly, within the context of our particular educational institutions, this role also causes students to see writing classes as different, marginal, subordinate to the "real" classes that form the substance of their education.[18]

If they are to see their writing classes as we do, as central to their education, we must be prepared to persuade them of the value of what we are asking them to do. We are asking them not only to question values assumed by their home communities but also to question certain practices of institutions of higher learning, practices that subvert critical thinking. Brooke points out that the type of rebellion we wish them to engage in, an attempt "to undermine the nature of the institution and posit a different one in its place" (1987, 151), is a type of behavior that discomforts them. And, he argues, "it is in this desire to shift roles, from student to writer, from teacher-pleaser to original thinker, that writing instruction comes into greatest conflict with the existing educational system, and also has the most to offer to it" (152). What we offer is immersion in the kind of critical thinking in writing that indeed can be useful in all academic disciplines but that also enables one to act on and in one's social environments. In order to make good on that offer we must remember that our central role is not to make our students happy, that the goal of writing is not the comfort that comes with conformity but rather the unhappiness that leads to understanding. We must remember that our role is to try to give to our students the ability to criticize and change the world and thereby to claim it as their own:

> it is as if the world had for [the Unhappy Consciousness] only now come into being; previously it did not understand the world; it desired it and worked on it, withdrew from it into itself and abolished it as an existence on its own account . . . it discovers the world as *its* new real world, which in its permanence holds an interest for it which previously lay only in its transiency: for the *existence* of the world becomes for self-consciousness its own *truth* and *presence*; it is certain of experiencing only itself therein. (Hegel 1977, 139–40)

Marilyn M. Cooper

Notes

1. Thomas N. Tryzna has also argued that the problem with "research papers" is the assumption that research essentially involves searches in libraries: "So-called 'research papers' are often mere assemblies of barely related facts. This situation is hardly surprising because the basic premise of much library research training—that information is available on students' topics—is misleading. It is *not* possible to find information about many interesting topics because no one else is writing about precisely those topics"—which is, of course, why such topics are interesting (1986, 217).

2. The course was actually designed and implemented in collaboration with my colleague Joseph Roberts; we each taught two sections of the course. However, since I do not wish to try to distinguish who had which ideas and insights about the course and do not wish to burden him with responsibility for views with which he may not agree, I will use the first person throughout this article. The examples of writing cited are from students in my sections only.

3. Cf. Bruffee, who notes that students in one experimental course "regain the ability to learn as children often learn at play" (1972, 465).

4. Cf. Reither, quoting from his colleague Russell Hunt's course description: "the course should be 'organized as a collaborative investigation of a scholarly field rather than the delivery of a body of knowledge' " (1985, 624–25).

5. I got this idea from Dixie Goswami, who described her use of "class notebooks" at a symposium on writing across the curriculum held at Michigan Tech in September 1986; as she described them then, however, her notebooks were handwritten.

6. Michael Spitzer points out that computer conferences reward those who write well and think clearly (1986, 20); thus, the Marcuse Disk was not just another class discussion, but a supplementary mode of class discussion that allowed some of those students who did not speak much in face-to-face discussions to add their voices and insights to the ongoing process of research.

7. See Janice Lauer's discussion of " 'cognitive dissonance,' which springs from the perception of a gap between a current set of beliefs or values and some new experience or idea that seems to violate or confound those beliefs. This clash engenders puzzlement, curiosity, a sense of enigma, sometimes of wonder, a pressure to restore equilibrium" (1982, 90).

8. Apart from inserting obviously omitted words such as the "when" in this sentence, I have not edited students' writing.

9. Cf. Bartholomae's discussion of the authority roles most often taken on by basic writers: "the voice of a teacher giving a lesson or the voice of a parent lecturing at the dinner table" (1985, 136).

10. Both Mason's book and Bruffee's article are steeped in nostalgia for people like me who were undergraduates during the student revolutions of the 1960s. Bruffee's article is "a critical survey of innovations in college teaching with special reference to" a 1971 special issue of *College English* on "authority in the classroom"; Mason ends his introduction with an allusion to the Beatles: "We can all get by with (maybe more than a little) help from our friends" (1972, 27). But the impulse toward collaborative learning now is

possibly not unrelated to the student movement of the 1960s, for as that generation takes control of the working world, we find that the collaborative methods of student political organizations are finding new expression in corporate and governmental working relationships (see Lunsford and Ede 1986; Odell, Goswami, and Quick 1983).

11. Carol Berkenkotter similarly notes that "a number of subtle emotional and intellectual factors" (1984, 318) influence the kinds of comments students make on each other's papers and how they respond to peer comments.

12. When I submitted a proposal on this course to a panel on the teaching of first-year writing, the organizer checked with me to make sure the course was a writing course and not a sociology course before accepting the proposal.

13. All the other sentences fail to fulfill Grice's second quantity maxim and Searle's second preparatory condition on assertions; their application here, I would argue, is blocked by the conventions of the institution of education. Searle similarly separates exam questions from real questions on the basis of the sincerity condition: "In real questions S wants to know (find out) the answer; in exam questions, S wants to know if H knows" (1969, 67).

14. It is sometimes argued that students in first-year writing classes should be invited into the discourse community of writing researchers; this is, I believe, rather too narrow and esoteric a community to be of value to most students.

15. Similarly, although not writing in reference to Perry, Mina Shaughnessy repudiates the notion that basic writers must first be taught to think before they can learn to write, saying that such a pedagogy "minimizes both the intellectual sophistication of the students and the extent to which 'thought' is narrowly equated with those styles of thinking and ordering that dominate academic discourse" (1977, 237).

16. For further discussion of Bartleby's experience and my reaction see "Why Are We Talking About Discourse Communities?" pp. 218–19.

17. *One-Dimensional Man* was, after all, a central text for the student revolution of the 1960s out of which grew, among other things, the concept of collaborative learning; see above, note 10.

18. This is perhaps most clear at institutions like mine, where most of the students are not majoring in humanistic disciplines.

Many of my colleagues helped me with this essay. I want to thank in particular Diana George, whose insights on teaching writing far surpass mine.

4

Evaluation in Adult Literacy Programs

It is useful to think about types of evaluation in terms of implicit social ideals rather than in terms of techniques, which usually receive the most attention. The unquestioning assumption of middle-class values of one well-known system in the United States—the Adult Performance Level (APL) scale—is almost too easy a target for satire, but there are similar issues in the seemingly opposite English tradition, which accepts "affective measures" as sufficient.

The question of the evaluation of the "progress" of adult learners is intimately connected to issues of funding and control in many adult basic education programs. In budget and planning discussions concerning adult basic education programs, "accountability," which is often said to justify inappropriate forms of testing, is a way in which programmatic, curricular control can be exercised under the guise of seemingly neutral management procedures. Challenging the validity of the testing criteria is then perceived by the administrators of the programs in question as a challenge to their power and political interests.

I suppose they are right.

□　　□　　□

Issues of adult literacy are usually associated with the literacy campaigns of revolutionary governments (Russia, China, Cuba, Nicaragua) or with initiatives sponsored by international agencies, such as UNESCO, intent on achieving "development" among the lesser developed nations of the Third World (Chad, Ethiopia, Iran, Mali, Tanzania). Concern about the large numbers of adult illiterates in countries otherwise highly developed appears to be peculiar to Britain and the United States, where adult illiteracy is primarily a *result* of schooling, rather than an artifact of a lack of educational facilities.[1] While the long-term solution to the problem of adult literacy in the United States and Britain is probably to be found in school reform, a consideration of issues involved with adult literacy—and adult education generally—is itself of interest for educators and policy makers in both countries. A convenient focus for such a consideration is the question of evaluation: How are literacy education efforts to be gauged?

The issue of how literacy is to be defined is itself somewhat difficult. We have learned from the research of Vygotsky, Luria, Graff, and Scribner and Cole, among others, that the question of literacy is not without a context; that it is entwined with those of schooling and culture; also, that the mind of an illiterate is not at all innocent of knowledge about and contacts with the world of literacy. Even if we retreat from these ethnographic complexities and simply take illiteracy as the inability to read or write *anything* (which is not a very fruitful definition), we are still faced with the problem of how to define literacy before we can approach the evaluation of efforts to achieve it. Literacy is clearly not the ability to read or write *anything*. Just as we find that there is not in fact some absolute wordless primitive of illiteracy, so there are degrees of literacy. A conservative definition of literacy would perhaps refer to the continuing practice of reading and writing *some* things. What those things are, and when they are referenced, is almost certainly highly contingent. In other words, the search for a definition of literacy and a framework for evaluating its achievement must first go through these questions: literacy for whom? literacy for what? If we take this approach we will soon grow accustomed to considering literacies, rather than some timeless paradigmatic and singular literacy.

I think it might be best to continue by occupying ourselves with description rather than definition. In some contexts literacies can be described by means of an ethnography of their cultures when viewed through the optic that their literacy practices provide.[2] Something like a series of "thick descriptions" in the tradition of Clifford Geertz would then be necessary to begin to come to grips with this. We are fortunate to have an American instance of such a description in Shirley Brice Heath's *Ways With Words*. If other such studies are generated in sufficient quantity, we may someday have a degree of understanding of the points at issue. We can already judge that an ethnography of literacy for the United States or Britain as a whole would be highly stratified. In some areas and social situations early nineteenth-century "signature" literacy (the ability to sign one's name, which is taken to indicate the ability to read) might still suffice; in some, the "literacy test" ability to read previously unknown passages from books or manuals might do; in others the ability to perform literacy tasks of the highest order of technical complexity based on broad or highly specialized sources of written knowledge would be necessary.[3]

It is evident from these and other considerations that the design of literacy instruction must be closely tied to the needs and desires of those receiving that instruction as well as to perceived national priorities or expert decisions. These definitional and descriptive issues of literacy are also basic to those of evaluation—the evaluation of both individual and programmatic literacy achievement. As such, they are intimately tied to literacy education policy and its goals. In the United States and in Britain much effort has gone into adult literacy programs, often without a preliminary fundamental agreement on the goals envisioned. However, in the British instance we do possess a valuable partially retrospective analysis of the goals of the first British adult literacy "campaign," which occurred between 1974 and 1978 under the auspices of the Adult Literacy Resource Agency.[4] Many of the issues central to a consideration of adult literacy policies in a developed country are dealt with in that study, which will serve as a point of departure for the observations in the following pages.

The Concept of Success in Adult Literacy, by A. H. Charnley and H. A. Jones, examines what might be called an administrative preoccupation with degrees of literacy as demonstrated by individuals taken as insufficiently educated. In both Britain and the United States the question is usually posed not in the ethnographic phrase "What literacy activities involve this individual?" but as the pedagogical-legalistic question: "How literate is this person?" The form of the answer provided to this latter question often then determines the form of education provided. Matters are further made complex by the circumstance that historically the question has been asked by governmental agencies not specifically charged with educational concerns, agencies that usually frame it with a reference to years of schooling. In the U.S., a level as high as the completion of twelve years of schooling is now frequently used in such bureaucratic definitions of the threshold for literacy. Entire job categories are restricted to those with high school diplomas or the equivalent, without regard, on the one hand, to the actual literacy requirements of the work, or, on the other hand, to the nature of the accomplishments indicated by a diploma from a given school system.

A seemingly useful step beyond this census-form definition of literacy is to evaluate actual performance on a test keyed to years of schooling or grade level equivalencies. However, Charnley and Jones (among others) are also critical of this most common set of evaluative standards for literacy. They point out that

> reading ages depend on two parallel progressions of which one, chronological age, is immutable: nothing can stop a child of eight

from becoming nine in a year's time. That immutability is an essential part of the measurement, for it offers a prediction of future
progress: a normal child's reading age will also rise by one year for
each year of chronological age. . . . Among adults no such prediction can be made. Not only is there an ethical and humane
objection to describing a man of 29 as having a reading age of nine,
there is also the practical objection that the measurement points
nowhere: can he be expected to have attained a reading age of 16
by his thirty-sixth birthday? Or should it be a reading age of 18 by
his fifty-eighth? (1979, 9)

Experience with adult literacy programs in the United States supports
Charnley and Jones's position. In particular, the commonly reported
phenomenon of extremely rapid breakthrough improvements in reading
levels—a grade level per month is not unusual under certain
circumstances—indicates a lack of commonality between that measured
for children and that measured for adults by reading level calibrated tests
rather than proof of the efficacy of whatever technique is being evaluated.

What is nonetheless the commonplace and unreflecting acceptance
of the validity of reading-level or grade-level reference points for literacy
programs is perhaps rooted in an unspoken assumption that adult literacy
students are in some sense unschooled, and, that like children who fail
a year of school because of illness or inattention, they must be set back
to "do it over." Unfortunately, the usual case is nearly the opposite:
native born adults in need of literacy tuition in the United States and
Britain usually have been *schooled* into illiteracy. Having much experience of that offered by conventional methods of reading and writing
instruction, they are not in need of more of the same. As their
illiteracy—relative or complete—is not like that of the unschooled child,
it is not at all clear that their learning patterns will have anything to do
with those of children.[5] Arguing along these lines, Charnley and Jones
claim that "the type of progress implied in standardised tests for children
is largely inappropriate to adults."

> Tests of readability, for example, which measure difficulty in re-
> lation to reading age, depend heavily on the counting of polysyll-
> ables, since children start to read with monosyllables and progress
> to two- and three-syllable words. Experience with adults shows a
> quite different order of difficulty. Often they readily grasp polysyl-
> labic nouns, especially social sight words like *telephone* or *tickets* or
> *post office*, but then have great difficulty with monosyllables whose
> function is syntactic rather than denotative—prepositions, con-
> junctions, auxiliary verbs. (1979, 10)

Thomas Sticht has similar objections to grade level equivalencies as applied in adult education contexts:

> The elementary school point of view . . . tries to prepare adults for future needs, but it does so by analyzing what happens to children in the kindergarten through twelfth (K-12) grade school system, and then applies the objectives, methods, and contents of the school system to adults. . . . (1986, 169)

Sticht goes on to point out that this theoretical misconception has quite specific programmatic repercussions:

> Because children first go to school to learn the basic skills, and then they go to work, the basic skills, or literacy, are viewed as something we first must get that can then be applied. Hence, adult literacy programs are usually cast in the childhood, school days mold. That is, literacy programs are offered prior to job skills training to 'remediate deficiencies' and raise levels to those needed for training. (169–71)

The argument against the use of grade-level equivalencies in the evaluation of adults for certification purposes or, say, for admission to an employment skills program, is twofold: as we have seen, grade levels provide an inappropriate scale, misleading in its implications; in addition, the tests used to place performance on the scale are also inappropriate. Testing vocabulary recognition, identification of parts of speech, spelling, and other decontextualized matters is not, of course, testing literacy (unless we perversely define it in this way); it is testing vocabulary recognition, identification of parts of speech, etc. and, crucially, the willingness and ability to take decontextualized tests. Although few would include such "achievements" in a list of varieties of literacy (such as that given above), operationally this form of socialization becomes the essential definition of literacy in many education contexts.[6]

Having rejected grade-level equivalencies, Charnley and Jones consider two alternative bases for evaluation: performative and functional literacy. The performative theorists are typified by the developers of the University of Texas Adult Performance Level (APL) scale. In this regard Charnley and Jones comment that "here the focus is not upon the competent display of skills but upon their result."

> Three indices of personal success in life are employed: income level, educational level and occupational status. These are associated with three states of functional competence: APL-1 (adults who function

with difficulty), with income at or below poverty level, education up to eight years' schooling or less and unemployment or low job status; APL-2 (functional adults), with income more than poverty level but no discretionary income, education of nine to 11 years of schooling and middle-range job status; and APL-3 (proficient adults), with high levels of income, education through high school or beyond and high levels of job status. (1979, 12)

The educational policy and pedagogical importance of this matrix of income, education, and job status is that it is linked with various "competences," which are then taken as predictive.

The competences associated with these levels of success consist of four sets of basic skills—communication (speaking, listening, reading, writing), number, problem-solving and interpersonal skills. These are assessed in five areas of general knowledge or activity: consumer economics, job-related knowledge, use of community resources, health, and knowledge of government and law. According to an individual's performance in the exercise of these skills, a prediction of his success is made and this is compared with his actual success. (12)

The list of basic skills is fairly routine, although "interpersonal skills" does appear an anomalous term in the series. But the list of "areas of general knowledge or activity" gives the impression of nearly arbitrary selection. Why consumer economics and not, say, automotive repair? How is the "job-related knowledge" of the unemployed or leisured measured? Why is there no aesthetic category? No religious category?

It is probably with these or similar questions in mind that after giving their summary of the APL standards Charnley and Jones comment—rather kindly as it happens—that

severe criticisms have been advanced of the indices used in the APL study, especially the concentration on material success in income and occupation. But the purpose being to measure performance in a particular culture, the results do demonstrate the relationship between the demands of a given society and command of certain basic skills. (1979, 13)

Perhaps, though, they are going too far in giving the performance theorists the benefit of the doubt. It is not certain that the conscious purpose of these social scientists was limited to that of measuring performance "in a particular culture," nor what "given society" is in question here. Indeed, the United States is neither a "particular culture" nor a "given society." Like all complex societies, it is many cultures, many societies, and the values inherent in the APL levels apply only to certain of its cultures, certain aspects of its social matrix. The claim to be inclusive and objective while implicitly holding certain unstated values is the very nature of the ideological, the antithesis of a Weberian "value-free" social science. An example might help here. When one considers, say, adults with advanced degrees in the humanities or artists or ministers vis a vis the entrepreneurs whose production is apparently envisioned as the proper end of the educational system by the APL system, the ideological nature of this system of classification should become apparent (at least to humanists, artists, and ministers, one presumes). Given its ideological bias, the APL system is, as Charnley and Jones point out, rather more useful as an ethnocentric schematic then as a framework for educational improvement.

Even if it is granted that the APL system tells us much about certain aspects of American culture, it is doubtful whether this "type of study yields evidence upon which an educational strategy can be built . . . certainly it gives little help towards the qualitative assessment of the progress of individual students towards the acquisition of literacy in a different cultural milieu" (Charnley and Jones 1979, 13). It tells us— or purports to tell us—only what certain influential groups in the United States value. As such it might have a certain limited use. For instance, this sort of study would be helpful in the design of a literacy program for those who believe that literacy programs should be designed with the social and ethical values of the dominant groups in a given country in view, rather than with reference to some more general conception of educational value or to the particular values of the adult learners in question.

The third basis Charnley and Jones review for evaluating the success of literacy education is functional literacy. The term "functional literacy" itself came into currency with the Experimental World Literacy Program (EWLP) begun by UNESCO in 1967, which sought to achieve literacy as a part of technical or vocational training in about 20 countries in five years. The standard work on the subject is *The Experimental World Literacy Programme: A Critical Assessment*, a highly critical appraisal of the programs, which concludes that most were failures. These failures were often due to a lack of cooperation between national governments and international agencies or, more interestingly, due to a lack of appreciation by the program designers of the realities of life in the Third World, where literacy for its own sake apparently is valued as little as in the United States. The primary lesson of these programs would seem to be that literacy must be of use to the individual and reinforced by the society if it is to be acquired and maintained.

In England these lessons have been applied by the Adult Literacy

Resource Agency and its successor organizations. The ALRA booklet *An Approach to Functional Literacy* includes three primary features for a successful literacy program: "first, the identification of functional tasks as a teaching medium; second, the placing on the student the onus of selecting tasks that relate to his perceptions and intentions; and third, the self-assessment built into each task" (Charnley and Jones 1979, 13 –14). This is not nearly as straightforward a procedure as it might appear. The entire question of the "functional task" is itself highly questionable. What is a functional task? Does this method involve the reduction of literacy to a technical decipherment/inscription skill? Many workers in the field of adult education would have it so, partially, perhaps, because of the ease with which this concept can be linked to an objective driven curriculum and procedure, which, in its turn, can be neatly packaged and readily evaluated. But Charnley and Jones tell us that even "in technical courses there has been ground for doubt."

> Chatfield (1973) examined a technicians' course in Workshop Technology . . . to assess each item of the syllabus according to the uses made of it by technicians in a group of engineering factories serving the motor industry. For over half the items the actual use in industry was relatively rare and the potential for use was little greater. There was thus a strong argument for slimming down the syllabus. Yet the technicians interviewed asserted almost unani- mously that all items of the syllabus should be retained because together they constituted an important and coherent body of knowl- edge. In their severely practical view, specific behavioural objectives could define only a part of a total desirable training. (17)

The point here is that a knowledge-world is a unified realm not amenable to analysis in terms of scientific management. Charnley and Jones appear to be arguing for drawing a line between knowledge for immediate use and knowledge for broader purposes. The force of the argument is con- siderable and its implications profound.

The EWLP and its *Critical Assessment* demonstrated the difficulty of adding an arbitrary and self-contained unit to a culture. Literacy— like capital itself—could not simply flow into the social problematic; it had to be set within the local culture, tied to it and integrated if it were not to either suffer rejection akin to that of a mismatched tissue transplant or cause serious disruptions in the society in question.

A corollary is that even individuals in a highly literate culture are not well-taught if they are given discrete "bite-size" units of literacy strictly tied to some expert-derived set of learning objectives. One prob- lem is that identified by the technicians quoted above: knowledge— useful knowledge—is not always linearly quantifiable, and that which is linearly quantifiable is frequently only that which we *can* measure, not that which we might wish to measure. It is a mistake when results of the former effort are then taken uncritically as equivalent to the latter goal. "Improvement" as measured by, say, quantifiable test scores is often enough only that and not necessarily an indication of progress in education.

If one problem with competency-based evaluation is this methodological issue—the question of exactly what is being measured—another equally serious problem is that of the appropriateness of objectives. Charnley and Jones begin their discussion of this point by noting that

> in relation to literacy, there have been a number of studies of what adults actually read and frequency-lists have been prepared. . . . Newspapers, popular fiction and nonfiction books and magazines and personal correspondence are usually at the head of these frequency lists. But . . . an index of items of reading regarded as essential has little in common with the frequency lists: dosage instructions, danger/warning signs, emergency procedures, traffic signs and the like then take precedence. . . . (1979, 17)

They then cite a typical interpretation of this distinction: "The filling in of an application form for a driving license may be a once in a lifetime occurrence, but must be regarded as more critically important than the daily occurrence of reading a newspaper" and ask

> regarded . . . by whom? Who shall set the objectives of a basic process like literacy and on what grounds? Might it be that the daily occurrence of reading the newspaper could be more important to the would-be literate than an occasional matter like an application form, for which he would be accustomed to asking for help anyway? (17)

It is from such considerations as these that the second of the ALRA maxims derives, that the "onus" for the selection of tasks relating to the student's perceptions and intentions be on the student. This is certainly a step forward, apart from the choice of terms, but one has reservations. Charnley and Jones have eloquently stated their position in relationship to the problematic:

> For the teacher, adult literacy tuition will usually appear to be predictive: the student will eventually "be able to read." There is then the temptation for the teacher to import instrumental objectives, as in the stages of a formal reading scheme. If we ask what it is that the adult will learn to read, for what purpose, with what

depth of understanding, with what result, we see that there is no linear progress here, such as could be assessed by an advancing series of objective tests. Each piece of reading or writing is a domain of its own, defined by the student's purpose and these purposes derive from his status as an autonomous adult, exercising will and judgement within the context of his own life and aspirations. (1979, 18)

And then crucially: "Only a child can learn to read; an adult learns to read something and to some end" (18).[7]

But the individual student is no more a Cartesian subject than anyone else. As Paul Willis taught us long ago, the perceptions and intentions of an individual member of, for instance, the English working class are fundamentally social. They are based, on the one hand, on pressures from the dominant forces in a given society, and, on the other, on countervailing pressures from the working class itself.

Simply asking an adult education student what he or she wants to learn is disingenuous. Given years of a certain kind of schooling and more years of the formation of consciousness by the various media and class pressures, how are they to know what there is to be learned and what is important for their purposes for them to learn? (How are any of us to know?)[8] They will know what teachers normally expect to hear, in general; they will know what their teachers normally have expected to hear from them, in particular. Under these circumstances a question about goals would not be expected, in good practice, to lead inevitably to an "answer" that can be translated directly into an individualized curriculum.

Charnley and Jones, and to some extent much of the English adult education effort, take this argument to imply a shift from thinking about the "needs" of adult learners to discovering their "intentions." The emphasis changes from one of social utility to an interest in the expressive desires of individuals. Although Charnley and Jones call upon the experience of the Experimental World Literacy Program and its *Critical Assessment* for support in this, it is important to maintain the distinction that the criticisms of the latter were directed at the process by which international experts ascertained the needs of nations, while the English situation is that of middle class educators assessing—or refusing to assess—the needs of individual members of the working class. A refusal to presume may be as much a class stance as an assumption of the right to judge.

The questioning process here (What is it the student wishes to learn?) should be as much political as pedagogical in order to avoid the danger of a certain irresponsibility that might inadvertently be built into this otherwise very attractive approach to education. This is another aspect of the problematic which more often pivots on the relationship between someone who "has something to give"—who has placed his or herself in a position to give something—and someone who "is in need." The former, in this English tradition, then tries to respond positively to the requests of the latter, tries "not to impose their values." The model is paternalistic, as surely as that which it was developed to replace, the model of the wise teacher who "knows best." It is difficult to see a way out of their binary opposition: What is a democratic model for education?

Where the *Critical Assessment* tends toward a model in which decisions about adult education are made on a wide social basis of political and cultural values and aims, Charnley and Jones wish to highlight the individual emotions of learners, highlight them to such an extent that they begin with the notion that "progress in literacy is bound up with the growth of the student's confidence" (1979, 18) and conclude with the ranking of "affective personal achievement" as the most important outcome of literacy programs. The others are "cognitive achievements," that which was learned; "enactive achievements," that which was done with what was learned; "socio-economic achievements;" and "affective social achievements."

The category of affective personal achievement as a basis for evaluation is Charnley and Jones's most original contribution to the discussion. Their other categories are traditional, and assessment within them takes traditional forms, granted the context of an emphasis on the students' judgments of what is valuable.[9] We can compare this measure with the grade level and age equivalencies of conventional assessment, the achievement criteria of APL, the functional utility of the military programs examined (and created) by Sticht. Is it too much to say that in each case the criteria reflect the social views of those who developed them? that affective personal achievement is a satisfactory criterion in a society seemingly reconciled to a permanently unemployed 10–15 percent of its population, what had once been the classical working class of the mills and mines? that, on the other hand, grade level equivalencies are actually—and quite brutally—meaningful in a society in which one of the primary instruments of control over access to employment is the schools?

When adults are told (and they *are* so told, repeatedly) that they read and write only as well as children in the third or fifth grade, surely something other than objective evaluation is being accomplished. One of the achievements of grade- and age-level standards of literacy evaluation is to exclude people from the system of literacy and to persuade them that they deserve little more. Assessment, which appears to be a bureaucratic necessity or a function of scientific pedagogy, is all too often used as a means to—once more—limit access to opportunity for those whose access is already pitifully limited. Whether it is the clumsy and slightly sinister scale of APL achievement, or the benevolent restrictions of "affective personal achievement," most of the standards used to measure adult literacy are extensions of the same system in the United States and Britain that produce the phenomenon of adult illiteracy itself. After generations of universal education in both countries, it is an inescapable logical conclusion (as well as the result of empirical observation) that most native born adult illiterates are products of the schools. In the United States, the types of assessment used with such success in the schools are then reapplied to those who as adults seek the education that eluded them as children. We need not be surprised that these means of assessment interfere with education under those circumstances, also.

Adult education is of interest to those interested in education in general, because in this neglected and underfunded area the relevant issues appear clearly against a background of great individual misery. Assessment—of individual achievement, of teaching, of programs—is central to educational policy at all levels of the system. It can be used by learners as an aid to their education (it can be performed by learners as part of learning). It can be used by teachers as an aid to their teaching (its methods can be devised by teachers, individually and collaboratively). It can be used by administrators to improve their programs. A humane assessment procedure in adult literacy programs, and, by extension, in most education, adult or otherwise, would be used in these ways. If this were done, there would probably be little reference to criteria such as grade or APL levels, test scores, and the like. Assessment would be a matter of reference—How's it going?—measures of practice against goals arrived at by a dialogue between personal aims and social realities. This dialogue would itself be fundamentally educational.

We can lay down as a general rule that direct methods of assessment are superior to indirect ones, that tests generally fail to reach this standard. How often, after all, do we wish merely to know how well a person does on a test? Tests are meant to be indicators, indirect means to ascertain how a person might do with one task by reference to another. A valid assessment procedure, then, should be direct. It should also be programmatically valid; it should refer to the goals of the educational situation. This criterion receives little attention, as the emphasis on skills and knowledge acquisition in the schools is taken as the model of all education. In the schools, the valid direct measure is, perhaps, criteria-referenced holistic scoring of actual school writing assignments. But the programs described by Charnley and Jones have other goals, including those of personal satisfaction. Their survey instruments are more appropriate means of assessment than the analysis of writing samples. In other adult education venues, such as that of the Literacy Volunteers of New York, the programmatic goal is that social activity become mediated by literacy activities. In this case an ethnographic record of these actions, appropriately coded, might be a suitable direct measure.

These are three examples of assessment that would serve the needs of teachers and learners. All too often, however, assessment is used only by administrators, and then only as a method of policing the system. The conceptual distance between such policing and the true educational goal of promoting learning is a measure of the distance from that which all too often is to that which might be.

Michael Holzman

Notes

1. It is generally the case in Britain, and most often the case in the United States, that illiterate adults have been to school. As literacy is a fairly easily acquired skill, particularly in a literate society, it is apparent that schooled illiterate adults are illiterate at least in part as a consequence of the type of schooling they have encountered. Here I am putting aside, for the moment, issues of English as a second language and new immigrant populations.
2. We must be careful to avoid believing that simply because a literacy-centered ethnography is possible it is therefore the "proper" point of view for the analysis of culture, any more than religion, say, or economics. See Geertz (1980).
3. For a sketch of the concept of historical literacies, see Resnick and Resnick (1977, 370–85).
4. The effort to achieve universal adult literacy continues in Britain and is now the responsibility of a successor organization, the Adult Literacy and Basic Skills Unit (ALBSU).
5. However, it is possible that the patterns will be similar to those of adult second-language learning. There is an emerging fruitful collaboration between the fields at certain centers in the United States and in Britain.
6. We might note in passing at this point that the programs used to prepare people for these tests at best prepare people to take these tests; they do not necessarily improve their literacy in any other sense. But this is not to say that the willingness to acquire the ability to do well on these tests is unconnected with the possibility of more general educational achievement. Just as the inculcation of unquestioning obedience of trivial or nonsensical orders in basic training is apparently a prerequisite to discipline on the battlefield, so there appears to be something in common between the willingness to work through a GED degree program, say, and success in other forms of training and work.
7. Peter Johnston has pointed out the faulty assumption here that children learn to read without context, an assumption that contributes to the school operation by means of which children learn how not to read.
8. "If people in general do not write effectively, that is as much to do with their not being able to envisage what writing could do for them as with lack of skills, since these would be developed if the perceived gains were large enough." (Medway 1986, 25).
9. For example, the subcategories within that of cognitive achievement are: 1)

increase in word recognition skills; 2) increase in sentence recognition skills; 3) increase in comprehension skills; 4) increase in the ability to read informational texts; 5) increase in the ability to read texts beyond the purely informational levels; 6) increase in the ability to read newspapers (Charnley and Jones 1979, 103).

5

Talking About Protocols

Composition theory is a new academic discipline. As such it draws on theories and methodologies from other disciplines—rhetoric, linguistics, literary theory, cognitive psychology, linguistic anthropology, sociology, political theory—which it translates, modifies, and creatively combines. Our concern in this essay is with this process. In particular, we argue here that our discipline's perspective on writing is discrete and that theories and methodologies drawn from other disciplines must be carefully scrutinized and adapted for use in our study of writing. Much of the writing research extant stems from the teacher-researcher projects of the Bread Loaf School of English and various sites of the National Writing Project. Almost all of this is in the form of case studies performed with ethnographic methodologies. The "protocol" research at Carnegie-Mellon University is a major exception in both tradition and method. In the context of this collection of essays, an obvious issue is the privileging of the individual as isolated writer that underlies, if not the protocol method per se, at least the use to which it has been put at CMU.

We have pointed out that some of the theory on which this research relies is underdeveloped and that the usefulness of the protocol methodology is more limited than what is often claimed for it. The most serious of our criticisms, perhaps, was the recurrent slippage we noted in discussions of the relation between theory and practice: rather than assuming a dialectical relationship in which theory informs practice and vice versa, Flower and Hayes sometimes seem to assume that theory describes practice. This conflation of discourse and reality also affects their use of protocol data, which are then seen as descriptions of writers' cognitive processes. But we were also concerned about the validity of the protocol method as applied to writing, and it is this part of our critique that has received the most attention.

□   □   □

The "cognitive process theory of writing," expounded by Linda Flower and John R. Hayes in the December, 1981 issue of *College Composition and Communication* and elsewhere, is attractive; as they argue, it improves on previous theories of composing by emphasizing the processes followed by the writer instead of describing "stages" in the completion of the product and by better accounting for the recursive nature of those processes through the use of a hierarchical rather than a linear description. But their casual reliance on unarticulated theories and an unsound methodology, while it does nothing to detract from our intuitive satisfaction with their conclusions, deprives them of any real support. Our acceptance of such work, if we accord it, will lead us away from, rather than toward, valid understanding of how writers write.

Two facets of their work are particularly questionable: their theory of cognitive processes and their methodology for producing and analyzing protocols. Neither of these facets is new with Flower and Hayes. The cognitive processes they descry in writing are in large part those processes involved in purposive behavior. In discussing writing as a goal-directed activity, they rely on the concepts of goals, plans, and scripts developed by cognitive psychologists (Miller, Galanter and Pribram 1960; Schank and Abelson 1977). But their discussion obfuscates much that is clear in their sources and thus seriously weakens their claims for the validity of their theory. Their methodology for psychological research dates from Plato and was made scientifically respectable in the nineteenth century by Wilhelm Wundt, who named it introspection. But early and late critics of introspection have emphasized the limitations of the methodology, precisely as it is applied to the investigation of cognitive processes—limitations that Flower and Hayes ignore. In what follows we will discuss first the troublesome problems with their theory, and then pass on to the more serious problems with their methodology.

In elaborating their model of the composing process, Flower and Hayes, especially in their most recent work, seem to ignore its status as a model and consequently to ignore the question of whether it is valid. Rules for social scientific model building were first clearly formulated by Max Weber. He pointed out, in connection with his theory of ideal types, that such models are not literal descriptions of reality, but, rather, are abstract descriptions of certain aspects of social life by which such aspects can be held constant so that they can be investigated more thoroughly than might otherwise be possible. Similarly, and more recently, models of language production—the grammars developed by Chomsky and others—do not describe the real cognitive processes used by people to produce and interpret sentences but rather postulate abstract rules that allow even nonspeakers of the language to produce correct sentences, sentences that native speakers would produce and would judge to be correct.

As Chomsky explains,

> We observe what people say and do, how they react and respond, often in situations contrived so that this behavior will provide some evidence (we hope) concerning the operative mechanisms. We then try, as best we can, to devise a theory of some depth and significance with regard to these mechanisms, testing our theory by its success in providing explanations for selected phenomena. (1980, 191)

The reason for such caution in making claims for models is a serious concern for their validity. Direct evidence of cognitive processes is un-available: Chomsky uses the analogy of the impossibility of collecting direct evidence about the nature of the thermonuclear reactions that take place in the interior of stars. Thus, models of cognitive processes cannot, in principle, be valid as literal descriptions.

Rather alarmingly, in their most recent discussions, Flower and Hayes often suggest that their theory is an actual description of mental processes: what is wanted, they claim, is "a theoretical system that would reflect the process of a real writer" (1981a, 368). Again: "The model of the writing process . . . attempts to account for the major thinking processes and constraints we saw at work in these protocols" (369). Perhaps the word "reflect" in the first quotation and the word "account" in the second are metaphorical; still, Flower and Hayes seem confident that they "saw" processes at work in the protocols. While actions resulting from cognitive processes can be observed (although such observation is itself not free of problems), the processes themselves simply cannot be. But here's what Flower and Hayes have to say about one protocol:

> At the end of episode 2c, the writer reaches tentative closure with the statement, "By God, I can change that notion for them." There are significantly long pauses on both sides of this statement, which appears to consolidate much of the writer's previous exploration. (1981a, 383)[1]

On what basis do they conclude he has reached closure? Or that up to this point he has been exploring? What he has been doing, according to his own account, is "doodling" some thoughts under "audience." His description of his actions and his pauses before and after the statement "By God, I can change that notion for them" are all that is observable. Protocols, far from being "extraordinarily rich in data" (Flower and Hayes 1981a, 368) are exceedingly impoverished sources of information on what writers are thinking about. Flower and Hayes concede this problem in an earlier article, where their caution in their claims for the model is more apparent that it has been recently:

> Typically, though, protocols are incomplete. Many processes occur during the performance of a task that the subject can't or doesn't report. The psychologist's task in analyzing a protocol is to take the incomplete record that the protocol provides together with his knowledge of the nature of the task and of human capabilities and to infer from these a model of the underlying psychological processes by which the subject performs the task.
>
> Analyzing a protocol is like following the tracks of a porpoise, which occasionally reveals itself by breaking the surface of the sea. (Hayes and Flower 1980, 9)

Claiming that a model literally describes real processes not only misstates the value of the model, it also encourages others to apply the model directly, to teach students to behave as the model says people behave. For example, teachers who thought that transformational rules were meant to be real descriptions of how people talk might teach the rules to their students as processes for them to follow to ensure syntactic fluency. As we all know, translating a theory into pedagogical practice is difficult, often precisely because models are not realistic descriptions. Flower and Hayes know this and sometimes mention it (in dependent clauses): "since a model is primarily a tool for thinking with, . . ." (1981a, 368). But, increasingly, they have ignored the abstractness of models and the problems in application that this abstractness entails.

A typical cognitive process model is that of scripts, plans, and goals, developed by Roger Schank and Robert Abelson in their eponymous book on the subject. This model is located firmly in the tradition of cognitive psychology and represents a well-developed form of the current standard theory. Schank and Abelson define goals as consciously-desired ends of behavior. Plans are projected series of actions, and scripts are the highly detailed arrangements of building blocks used to achieve those plans. (Thus, knowledge of how to walk, putting one foot in front of another, is a possible *script* for reaching a location, while a statement like "I will walk to the corner" is part of a *plan* for achieving a *goal* such as buying a newspaper.) The center of interest for theorists are the scripts, nearly unconscious sequences of behavior. The test for validity in building formal models of human behavior is that enunciated by Turing fifty years ago: the possibility that communications from a computer following a model script (say, an artificial intelligence computer program) will be taken as communications from a human being. The important thing to notice about this test is that it is the action resulting from following a script that is under investigation, not the script itself—in other words, the product and not the process.

The cognitive process model of human behavior allows us to build scripts that result in actions similar to those of persons in situations similar to that described in the script. It does not claim that the scripts produced by the model are the same as those used by people. As a matter of fact, formal scripts are "native" only to machines. Most people follow partial scripts which they can, and do, abandon or change from moment to moment. These inconsistencies do not bother the theorist. One does not hope to eliminate them—an impossible task. It is exactly at the "fuzzy" edges that a model is interesting. The point of model building in the social sciences is to create a model that produces effects close enough to human behavior so that departures from those actions predicted by the model can be detected and carefully investigated, thus enabling us to refine our knowledge of how people function in the world.

Turing's test for validity points to a second, and more serious, problem with the Flower and Hayes's model as a model: it is too underspecified to be testable. Testability is the basis on which theorists claim validity for models, and to be testable a model must be described in enough detail that we can tell what evidence might support and what evidence might falsify it. Testing Flower and Hayes's central hypothesis, that writing is a goal-directed process, requires a definition of goals and a discussion of the distinctions and relationships between at least goals and plans if not also between goals and scripts. Without such definitions, anything can be called a goal and no possible evidence could falsify the hypothesis that writing is goal-directed. Though Flower and Hayes talk about types of goals and what role goals play in writing, they never define goals, nor do they distinguish goals from plans. Notice how *goal* and *plan* are used interchangeably in the following passage:

> In this rather complex instance of planning the writer is exploring possibilities and setting up tentative, even alternate *goals*. In considering possible ways to focus her discussion she is stimulating her readers' response and using their interest to both guide and evaluate her *plans*. And although some of these *goals* deal with content, they do not take the form of proposed or even proto text. The range of what the writer could say, given either *plan*, is enormous. (1981b, 232–33; italics added)

Indeed, they apparently see no need for a distinction between plans and goals:

> A note on our terminology: in order to focus on the overall structure of goals and sub-goals in a writer's thinking, we have treated the

writer's plans and strategies all as sub-goals or operational definitions of the larger goal. (1981a, 385)

In Schank and Abelson's terms, the desired outcome of the activity would be the goal, while the detailed actions designed to lead to the outcome would be the plan or scripts. Although they do not discuss goals, Miller, Galanter, and Pribram's definition of plans accords with that of Schank and Abelson: "*A plan is any hierarchical process in the organism that can control the order in which a sequence of operations is to be performed*" (1960, 5–6). For serious researchers, these distinctions between plans, goals, and scripts are what is important about the cognitive process model of thought and action; they make claims about goal-directed behavior that can be supported or falsified by evidence from plans observed in operation. Flower and Hayes do not test details of their model with their research, but instead merely use their model as a source of labels for data in the protocols, labels that thus have no explanatory power. Experiments properly using the cognitive model of goals, plans, and scripts would focus on just those matters ignored by Flower and Hayes: the difference between goals and plans, say, or the various lengths and the detailing of scripts used in pre-writing, writing, and revision.

Neither, in this unarticulated form, is the theory particularly useful in the classroom. In Flower's composition textbook, students are urged to create goals for their writing and to make their goals "operational" by developing sub-goals (1981, 63–64). At a very low level, equating sub-goals and plans is reasonable.[2] But do we want to say, as Flower and Hayes's thoroughgoing equation of plans and goals implies, that all of a writer's goals automatically call up associated plans? Isn't it instead the case that achieving a goal involves not simply the setting of sub-goals (instrumental goals) but more importantly involves knowing what actions might be useful in achieving the goal, knowing how to choose which actions to take, and knowing how these actions can be arranged into a coherent series? For example, in one expert protocol Flower and Hayes discern this process goal: "write an introduction" (1981a, 378). That which helps a writer achieve this goal is not merely his setting sub-goals, but rather developing a plan—a series of actions (state, explain, recount) that will achieve the goal. And in orchestrating these actions, a writer may also call upon any of a variety of scripts he has internalized for writing introductions (narrate an incident, start with a quotation, etc.). In other words, in addition to being an action, writing is a matter of knowledge, knowledge about writing.

With Flower and Hayes, the question of how writers are to develop plans to accomplish their goals remains unanswered, and the scripts that skilled writers unconsciously use are not described. Indeed, uncovering these scripts is what is difficult, both for composition teachers and for writers talking about their writing processes, because often they are so well learned as to be almost invisible. Still, models of some of these scripts have been attempted—the classical parts of an oration, for example. Donald Murray's "signals which say 'write' " (1978, 377–80) work because they have well-learned scripts associated with them. Every skilled writer instinctively knows, for instance, how to build a piece around an image: set up an image early on, refer to it, allude to it, expand it here and there, and end with a (preferably oblique) reference to it, perhaps in a slightly altered form. A well-developed cognitive process theory of composition would aim at constructing models of such scripts and thus bring us new knowledge about these important, and too-long neglected, aspects of what writers know. What scripts *are* used by skilled writers? Are rhetorical figures scripts? Are certain organizational patterns scripts? Similarly with plans—these are things that we want to know; they are not, as Flower and Hayes apparently assume, things that we know already.

We offer these criticisms of Flower and Hayes's recent discussion of their model in the hope of strengthening their promising work. But as we take up the problems in their methodology of producing and analyzing protocols, we are less hopeful. Their accounts of the "protocol method" reveal that it is what is more commonly known, both in everyday speech and in the history of cognitive psychology, as *introspection*.[3] Wilhelm Wundt, generally regarded as the first modern psychologist, differentiated psychology from philosophy in part by drawing a crucial distinction between meditation and introspection, his term for the scientific investigation of the geography of the conscious mind. As is common with the founding gestures of a new discipline, Wundt defined psychology as that discipline—that area of research—that could be studied through the application of a particular technique, introspection.

> Wundt recognized that conscious contents are fleeting and in continual flux; he therefore laid down explicit rules for proper use of the introspective method: 1) the observer, if at all possible, must be in a position to determine when the process is to be introduced; 2) he must be in a state of "strained attention"; 3) the observation must be capable of being repeated several times; 4) the conditions of the experiment must be such that they are capable of variation through introduction or elimination of certain stimuli and through variation of the strength and quality of the stimuli. (Watson 1963, 277)

Wundt found that these investigations were best conducted through the use of highly trained "introspectors," research assistants who were able to verbalize their mental states. Critics of the new science pointed out that the technique was limited to static and relatively simple mental states, and that the consideration of *process* had to be put to one side, because mental processes are not simply additive—each new complexity changes the entire process or state of mind. Since Wundt, the technique has come under attack from two other quarters: the discovery of the unconscious has cast doubt on the "transparency" of mental processes, in principle; and in practice there are many doubts as to the general applicability of results obtained in so special a way, from what is necessarily a small number of people who have been trained to have mental processes different from the general population. (We might note here that the Flower/Hayes articles are apparently based on just four protocol transcriptions [see 1981b, 233], and that their introspectors are also trained, or instructed, and do their work under quite special conditions.)

It is, after all, rather an odd thing to talk about what you are thinking about while you are doing something. Only those particularly trained to perform this trick, or those with special talents in this direction, can be sources for the data. When they succeed, the results are usually not the clear and reasonable accounts found in the work of Flower and Hayes, but something much stranger. For instance, in one of her essays, Virginia Woolf describes the supposed vagueness of her knowledge of American literature:

> Somewhere upon the horizon of the mind, not recognizable yet in existence, "Typee" and "Omoo" together with the name of Herman Melville, float in company. But since Herman Melville is apt to become Whyte Melville or Herman Merivale and "Omoo" for some less obvious reason connects itself with the adventures of an imaginary bushranger who is liable to turn jockey and then play a part in the drama of "Uncle Tom's Cabin," it is evident that a mist, due to ignorance or the lapse of time, must have descended upon those far distant regions. . . . Waves are breaking; there is a rough white frill of surf; and how to describe it one does not know, but there is, simultaneously, a sense of palm trees, yellow limbs, and coral beneath clear water. (1977, 80)

Although we all appreciate these passages of literary introspection, we might as well say at once that the charm of this is how far the sensibilities of Virginia Woolf differ from our own. Her description of the way her mind wanders while writing seems possible, but only in a highly stylized way, only to a particularly sensitive mind. We recognize digressive moments in our own writing process (noting belly rumbles while typing this, or seeing the reflection of the office lights on the word processor's screen), but realize that the baroque explication of them is an artistic production, a creation. Nonetheless, Woolf's meditation reminds us that the thoughts that run through our heads while we are writing (or, in fact, while engaged in almost any activity) are diffuse, highly branched, visual as well as verbal. Turning from Woolf's "protocol" to those presented by Flower and Hayes, we note how focused the latter are. Their introspectors notice virtually nothing other than that which is to the point. Do these people never fantasize about, say, lunch? Or were they instructed never to mention such things? Or were the transcriptions of the protocols edited? Do protocols "capture a detailed record" (1981a, 368), or invent one, one as literary in its own way as those of Woolf and other writers?

Flower and Hayes apparently claim that protocols provide direct access to writers' cognitive processes. We have argued that this claim cannot be granted on both theoretical and methodological grounds. But, more fundamentally, the way in which protocols are elicited raises serious questions about their validity—questions not limited to the protocol method, but applicable to all research concerning human thought and behavior. Michael Cole and his associates offer a powerful critique of formal investigations of behavior in a treatise that should be studied by all psychological investigators: *Ecological Niche Picking: Ecological Invalidity as an Axiom of Experimental Cognitive Psychology*. They remark:

> it appears that since its inception as a science, psychology has used task environments which assume a framework of analysis in which stimulus causes precede response effects, coupled with a strong claim that preassigned, initial stimuli are *the* stimuli to which some later indicator of individual behavior is assigned the status of *the* response. (87)

What stimulus are the writers of the Flower/Hayes protocols responding to? Is it only that of the writing process, or is there something special about the conditions of the writing task set them in this instance? How are we to know that even the same writers would produce similar protocols in a different environment? For, as Cole points out, "In so far as we are unable to specify formal equivalence of tasks across settings, we cannot generalize about the behavior of individuals from one setting to another" (89). Other researchers have asked similar questions, questions that we might also address to Flower and Hayes:

> Does the test elicit the same behavior as would the *same* tasks embedded in a *real*, noncontrived situation? . . . even to speak of the *same* task across contexts requires a model of the structure of the task. In the absence of such a model, one does not know where the equivalence lies. (Schwartz and Taylor, 1978, 54)

This is a serious problem. How are we to investigate cognitive processes in general, or the writing process in particular, so that we know that our results are generally applicable? There is some doubt that this can be done under controlled conditions as a matter of principle:

> where experimental procedures systematically preclude determining features of non-laboratory tasks, they limit the possibility of obtaining the required formal equivalence. Therefore, as currently conceived, laboratory experiments are *ecologically invalid*; they cannot serve as a vehicle for making statements about the cognitive processing of individuals across settings. (Cole, Hood, and McDermott, 89)

Can protocol analysis tell us anything about the writing processes of people outside the laboratory? Lester Faigley and Stephen Witte remark in their discussion of revision, "What we learn from protocol analysis . . . is uncertain. . . . the writing situation is artificial" (1981, 412). In their own study, they measured their results against "the actual revisions of practicing writers of various sorts" and "again . . . found considerable variation" in the way expert writers revise, a variation not observable in the experimental situation (1981, 410).

As Faigley and Witte's work suggests, ecological validity is a problem not limited to Flower and Hayes's methodology; in fact, a great deal of recent empirical work in composition theory is open to the same charge. A recent issue of *Research in the Teaching of English* discusses ethnographic studies of writing, which avoid the artificiality of experimental methodologies by instead creating "thick description of contextual phenomena, based principally upon data collected by participant observation" (Kantor, Kirby, and Goetz 1981, 298). This is precisely what Cole is calling for: "cognitive skills have to be specified in terms of the activities (environments) in which they occur" (Cole, Hood, and McDermott 109). In his ground-breaking work in sociolinguistics, William Labov argued persuasively for the value of this approach in the study of language behavior:

> Through the direct study of language in its social context, the amount of available data expands enormously, and offers us ways and means for deciding which of the many possible analyses is right. (1972b, 202)

Another possible way to achieve greater validity is a methodology that produces data without appearing to be an experiment at all. An example of such a technique may be found in the current research of Mark Olson at the University of Southern California. His subjects, randomly selected composition students, write their regular class compositions with the aid of a computerized text processor. From the point of view of these students all that has happened is that they have been given a fancy typewriter; they are not aware of being "in an experiment" (although the usual permissions are secured at the beginning of the course). And the text processor makes it easy for them to revise and to produce perfect typed essays. Meanwhile, Olson has programmed the computer to record every editing function that they invoke: substitution, deletion, transposition; it also notes whenever they re-read their text, and counts such things as word and sentence length. This is a less ambitious methodology than that of protocol analysis, but it represents an approach that may well be "capturing" the writing process in a more valid fashion.

Yes, certainly writing is a recursive, complex process. And cognitive psychology's model of scripts, plans, and goals may help us understand this process. But if it is to do so, it must be tested by an ecologically valid, replicable research methodology. We believe that Flower and Hayes have taken pioneering steps in this direction, identifying the proper goal, but their plans seem vague and their scripts not those we wish to encourage.

Marilyn Cooper and Michael Holzman

Notes

1. We like Ann E. Berthoff and Warner B. Berthoff's definition of closure: "In a protocol, after the *Hmmm* and before the *Uhhh*," (1980, 84). The division of protocols into episodes, discussed in another Flower and Hayes article (1981b) is highly suspect. Episode boundaries are not marked by pauses, though they supposedly correspond to silent pauses noted in other research. They are arrived at through intuitive judgments of readers well-acquainted with the protocols who "were merely instructed to look for units of concentration in the writer's process and to mark a boundary when they saw the writer shifting focus, changing a train of thought, or setting up a new plan" (237). That the resulting "episodes seem to be organized around *goals*" (238) is hardly surprising, given these instructions.

2. In discussing how goals and plans interact, Schank and Abelson reveal why the two can be equated. They first distinguish operating or main goals from instrumental goals (instrumental goals are "necessary partial accomplishments along the path to the main goal," 1977, 74). They then distinguish specific from general instrumental goals and name these general instrumental goals, which involve the idea of change, D-goals. These low level D-goals

   are defined by the set of possible actions (henceforth called planboxes) that they call up to achieve their goal. The D-goals are thus no more than a set of planboxes. This is analogous to the primitive acts which are no more than the set of inferences they give rise to when invoked. (75)

An example of a D-goal is "changing proximity," which simply involves moving from one place to another. Here we lose nothing by equating the goal with the plan for achieving it, since the connection between the two is deeply ingrained in our everyday behavior. The connection between goals and scripts is equally strong, as evidenced by the example from Miller, Galanter, and Pribram, above.

3. Flower and Hayes sometimes confuse *introspection* and *retrospection*. At one point they contrast their method of protocol analysis to introspective analysis (1981a, 368), but as a later comment reveals, the contrast they actually have in mind is between protocols and *retrospection*: "thinking aloud protocols tell us things retrospection doesn't" (377). They make the same point elsewhere: "protocols avoid the unreliability of retrospective generalization" (1981b, 233).

6

More Talk About Protocols

Linda Flower and John R. Hayes responded to our critique of their work, and the following essay is a reply to that response. We were surprised by several aspects of their reply. They implied that critiques of research are an inappropriate mode of scholarship in this discipline: they wrote, "we . . . would find reasoned, alternative hypotheses from data a more productive approach than arguments to cease doing research" (Flower and Hayes 1985, 94). In the conclusion to their remarks they explicitly rejected metadiscourse: "The best way to test a method and to argue about research is to develop alternative hypotheses supported by substantive arguments about the process of writing itself" (97). They did not respond to our discussion of the relation between theory and practice, nor to our request for a more specific—and testable—definition of goals in their model. Instead, they concluded that what we wanted was that their "results should fit more neatly into the categories (script, plan, and goal) which Schank and Abelson use to model story comprehension," and they argued that "when the data as we observe them are more complex than our expectations or other theories suggest, it seems best to make the theory reflect the data" (94). Certainly when one is confronted with data that falsifies a theory, the need for a new theory may be suggested, but the development of a new theory, a new model, demands more of researchers than simply making the theory "reflect" the data.

The central purpose of their reply was to argue for the distinction between introspection and protocol methodology and for the validity of the protocol method. They pointed out that Wundt's method of introspection required subjects to attend in a special way to what they observed and necessitated a lengthy training process for subjects. And they referred us to the work of Ericsson and Simon on the validity of the protocol method. After summarizing Ericsson and Simon's analysis of how various reporting situations affect the mental processes being reported, Flower and Hayes explained, "reporting methods which direct subjects in how they should attend or what they should attend to are likely to modify the processes being observed. Reporting methods which do not do so may slow processes but not change their course or structure" (1985, 96). Since writing protocol methods, unlike Wundt's method of introspection, do not direct subjects to attend to particular things in a particular way, Flower and Hayes conclude that doing protocols does not distort the writing processes reported.

Though we had had commonsense worries about the way in which doing protocols might affect the writing process of subjects, we did not address this particular problem in our original critique where we were more concerned with the ecological validity of methods that depended on a laboratory setting. But after studying Ericsson and Simon's "Verbal Reports as Data" we noted that, unfortunately, Flower and Hayes had oversimplified the theory they were depending on and that, in fact, there were some very good reasons to question the validity of protocol methods.

Our critique of the protocol method, along with that of others, was the subject of a pair of articles published in *College English* in 1986. In an Afterword appended to this essay we comment on the continuation of this debate.

□   □   □

We were "trying to tell you that the search for explicative laws in natural facts proceeds in a tortuous fashion" (Eco 1980, 305). We were not arguing for an end to empirical research in rhetoric, but we were arguing that such research should be carefully designed. Flower and Hayes proposed an object of study, a theory about that object, and a methodology for the testing of the theory. We contended that the *object of research*, writing, which they implicitly defined as a cognitive process, could not be distinguished from certain other cognitive processes: for instance, from the purely mental preparation of an oration and its delivery without notes or transcription—a process that shades off into inner speech and conversation—or from surrealist automatic writing, which shades off into the purely physical act of inscription. We believe that in order to design research to investigate this object, Flower and Hayes needed to explain not only what, if anything, is distinctive about writing as a cognitive process, but also how that distinctive character should be defined and why it should be defined in that particular way. This initial difficulty is crucial, for if writing cannot be clearly defined as a cognitive process, it will be impossible to construct a testable theory about it. And if it can be strictly defined, Flower and Hayes still faced the task of justifying this definition as the most useful or most appropriate one if their research was to have any applications.

We have shown that even if they were investigating a well-defined object of study, their *theory* was not well-defined. We suggested the adoption of a more fully elaborated version of the model Flower and Hayes originally cited; if they found that even this model is not complex enough to enable them to analyze all of their data, we would have expected them to produce a more adequate theory. As a theory is useful to science only when applied to a well-defined object of research, so a methodology is useful only to the extent that it can be used to test a carefully articulated theory. Flower and Hayes have repeatedly empha-sized (see Swarts, Flower, and Hayes, 1984) the importance of theory in analyzing protocols; what they did not seem to realize is that the theory must be defined exactly enough that some possible data might falsify it. Their refusal to see the importance of defining processes for study and of strictly elaborating a theory that would clearly model the processes being studied rendered their hypotheses untestable in principle.

Our doubts about their protocol *methodology* have become more serious. We raised the specter of Wilhelm Wundt to suggest that the verbal reporting of cognitive processes must be an artificial situation. Wundt, in response to criticism, developed a highly controlled meth-odology, which he acknowledged could not be applied to cognitive pro-cesses, only to cognitive states. Hayes and Flower deny the artificiality of the writing situation they study. They fail to recognize that the writers from whom they have taken protocols (as they identify them in 1980, 23) do not constitute a random sample of the writing population, but are, like Wundt's introspectors, a carefully selected (if not explicitly trained) group. Thus, their responses to their situations—restricted to a particular place, restricted in time, and responding to assignments to write particular kinds of essays—are not necessarily generalizable to other situations, other populations; and these limitations drastically affect the way the subjects manage their apparent writing process. The students strive to do what their instructors have suggested, rather than concen-trating on developing their ideas in words (37). The NEH fellows who worked with Flower and Hayes, prevented from such activities as talking to colleagues, reading, and skulking around the library or department halls, immediately recognize the situation as artificial and proceed, like the teachers they are, to a demonstration of what they take to be the writing process (Flower and Hayes 1981a, 383). This research method-ology is neither ecologically valid nor carefully controlled. It produces interesting narratives, data for a theory about what certain writers will say about the writing process, but not data about *the* writing process, nor even, given its limitations, particularly useful data about the cognitive processes of writers in this particular situation.

Flower and Hayes cite the methodological authority of Ericsson and

Simon. But the latter team's discussion of verbal reports as data reveals the limitations of the methodology used by Flower and Hayes. In order to make this crucial point clear, we will have to summarize some of Ericsson and Simon's findings. Ericsson and Simon define in their own work a model in which *"only information in focal attention"* (defined as the contents of short-term memory) will be verbalized (1980, 235). Thus, any processes that do not make use of short-term memory and any situation that overloads short-term memory will result in a distorted verbalization of the processes. Highly skilled writers tend to automate processes, which do not then make use of short-term memory; and, as Ericsson and Simon predict, "verbal explanation of automated activities would be cumbersome and would change the course of the processing from a largely perceptual (recognition) to a more cognitive one" (234), one in which they would expect "more frequent interjection of metastatements (explicit statements about the process itself) replacing statements about inputs and outputs" (227). Even a cursory glance at the few excerpts from protocols by experts that Flower and Hayes have published bears out these crucial predictions (Flower and Hayes 1981b, 235; Hayes and Flower 1980, 24). Such systematic differences in the protocols that experts and novices produce limit seriously the conclusions one can draw from them about differences between experts' and novices' writing processes.

But even when processes are represented in short-term memory, they might not be reported in the verbalization. One situation Ericsson and Simon note suggests a reason for Flower and Hayes's inability to distinguish plans and goals in the protocols they have collected: "Under thinking-aloud conditions, it has been observed that information that leads to the direct recognition of the appropriate action often tends not to be verbalized" (1980, 238). Another situation that blocks verbalization of information in short-term memory is being under "high cognitive load" (237); thus, "reasonable protocols" (whatever they might be) are more likely to be produced in situations where the writing process, either because the task is easy or because it is well practiced, is proceeding smoothly. On the one hand, Ericsson and Simon show, as Wundt had acknowledged, that laboratory protocol methodologies cannot deal with complicated cognitive processes; on the other hand, common experience shows that cognitive processes in nonlaboratory conditions are also unreachable in this fashion. We thought, at one point, that we might enliven this response by including a protocol of our writing process in producing it. But we were stymied by our inability to talk aloud in the situations in which much of the process took place—while listening to jazz at the Vine Street Bar and Grill, while swimming laps at the Sports Connection.

One level of our complaint against Flower and Hayes's method is epitomized in this problem: any research methodology that simply ignores the context in which writing takes place cannot produce valid data. But our complaint about the protocol method is, in a sense, beside the point. Flower and Hayes could not hope to produce valid results with *any* methodology until they solved their basic problems of definition and theory.

And, indeed, now they have begun to do this. In their recently published article in the inaugural issue of *Written Communication* (Flower and Hayes 1984), Flower and Hayes define their research question more clearly ("How do writers actually use different forms of knowing to create prose?"), define what they mean by planning ("the purposeful act of representing current meaning to oneself"), and, again, are cautious in their claims about protocol data ("The data we garner is only a sample of the phenomena we would study"). These are steps in the right direction. With a more precisely defined theory we can move to a consideration of substantive matters rather than those of research design.

Though our critique has been limited to Flower and Hayes, these problems are clearly not found only in their work. Quite simply, we call for all those who would do empirical research on writing to do it right: to define and defend their choice of an object of study, to articulate a testable theory (one that could be falsified by some results), to develop a methodology appropriate to testing the theory, and to take into account the effect of the methodology on the data. But, on another level, our goal in this critique was not simply negative. It was to reassert that because scholarship in rhetoric does not consist only of empirical research, we must have a lively exchange of theoretical work and critique, as well as careful empirical studies, if the field is to continue to be an area of scholarly and scientific interest. This means that we must be and train theorists as well as experimentalists; scientists as well as scholars.

Afterword

In November 1986, a pair of articles appeared in *College English* debating again the status and validity of the protocol method of collecting data on writing processes. Though our original critique was much cited by both Erwin R. Steinberg and David N. Dobrin, neither Flower and Hayes's reply to our critique nor our response to their reply was cited. Steinberg, a senior colleague of Flower and Hayes, offered a detailed refutation of criticism of the protocol method; Dobrin offered an elegant argument questioning the validity of the model of writing that protocol analysis assumes.

Dobrin argues that the model of writing as a problem-solving process mischaracterizes the process, that the evidence provided by protocols is contaminated, and that protocols do not provide "an illuminating trace" of the process. But, most tellingly, he also suggests that writing is not a problem-solving process, at least not the kind of closed process that protocol analysis was designed to investigate: "Unlike mathematics problems, writing problems are not generally well-formulated, and again unlike mathematics problems, they have no single solution. They don't even have a class of solutions we would agree are satisfactory" (1986, 722). He then invites his reader to engage in a commonsense, do-it-yourself proof of this claim, based on the explanation of the CMU model in his article.

Interestingly, Steinberg also relies on commonsense proofs at crucial moments in his article. Since Marilyn did a protocol for a colleague recently, we were particularly interested in Steinberg's claim that "a protocol adequately represents focused mental activity during problem solving" (1986, 699). Steinberg offers his own and Donald Murray's experiences with protocols as proof. Steinberg says, "My attention . . . remained firmly focused on the task at hand. . . . And what I said aloud that was captured by the tape recorder adequately represented that focused attention and the cognitive processes involved in my writing or revision" (698). Murray agreed: "I do not assume, and neither did my researcher, that what I said reflected all that was taking place. It did reflect what I was conscious of doing, and a bit more. My articulation was an accurate reflection of the kind of talking I do to myself while planning to write, while writing, and while revising" (1978, 698).

I did not have the same experience. My attention never remains firmly focused on the task at hand when I am writing, although, for the sake of this argument, I am willing to agree with Murray that what I said should not necessarily reflect *everything* that was taking place. (But where does one draw the line?) The problem is, what I said was far short of reflecting what I was conscious of doing, even of reflecting what I was conscious of doing that I would normally characterize as writing activities—even, dare I say it, of reflecting what I was conscious of in the line of cognitive writing activities. My researcher noted that my protocol was strikingly different from others she had gathered in that it consisted almost entirely of rehearsals of wording. It also contained rather long silences. My researcher was not present to urge me to speak as continuously as possible, but I was trying to do so and I was not drawing blanks (at least not most of the time). I did try to verbalize everything that was verbal or propositional in my thinking as I wrote. But I did not verbalize my conscious writing intentions that were spatial—I feel such things as ideas and argument structures as arcs and circles and shapes of indeterminate kinds—and had I tried to do so it would certainly have interfered with my writing (as Ericsson and Simon predict).

So here is another do-it-yourself proof. If you feel as Steinberg or

Murray do when you write, then you will believe that protocols can accurately reflect the cognitive part of the writing process. If you feel as I do, you won't.

We certainly would agree with Dobrin that if they are interpreted in the way that all verbal accounts must be interpreted, protocols can be useful sources of information about what certain people do when they write in certain circumstances. His critique of the model of mind that must hold if protocol analysis is to have any special claim as a methodology is a useful complement to our own critique. But our primary concern, here as elsewhere in this collection, is with the social world, how well theories and methodologies work in that world, how the practice of writing instruction might make sense in that real world of uncontrolled phenomena.

Marilyn Cooper and Michael Holzman

7

Cohesion, Coherence, and Incoherence

Our central concern in this essay is very much the same as what concerns us about the methodology of protocol analysis. M. A. K. Halliday and Ruqaiya Hasan's catalogue of means of achieving cohesion in texts has been adopted by many composition researchers as the Ur-text on how to make essays hang together. But as a work of theoretical linguistics, it is not particularly well-adapted to this use. This fact was brought to our attention most strikingly when we attended a lecture by Hasan at UCLA. She was puzzled by—and not particularly interested in—our questions. This is not surprising. Why should we expect linguists to be able to tell us about the rhetorical features of texts?

In what follows, we draw on the work of composition theorists, discourse analysts, reading researchers, and artificial intelligence researchers to make the case that coherence is not a textual feature but rather a judgment made by readers. Our particular contribution to this conversation is to point out that this judgment depends on more than a knowledge of the conventions and strategies that lead readers to see texts as coherent. The extent to which a text must demontrate cohesion and coherence explicitly, we argue, is a function of the social situation in which the text is embedded, and as writing teachers, our goal should be to alert student writers to the possibility of such situations and to the limited ways in which uses of conventions of coherence may help them avoid having their texts being judged incoherent.

□　□　□

Both cohesion and coherence received a great deal of attention in the years following the publication of *Cohesion in English* (Halliday and

Hasan 1976). The two terms were defined and redefined and their relationship speculated on, and innumerable texts were scrutinized to find out why they were judged to be coherent. Many attempts have also been made to distinguish cohesion from coherence, as Witte and Faigley have pointed out. Referring to Grimes, van Dijk, Enkvist, and de Beaugrande, Witte and Faigley say:

> They limit cohesion to explicit mechanisms in the text, both the types of cohesive ties that Halliday and Hasan describe and other elements that bind texts such as parallelism, consistency of verb tense, and what literary scholars have called "point of view." Coherence conditions, on the other hand, allow a text to be understood in a real-world setting. (1981, 199)

Smith reaffirmed the distinction:

> Recently . . . theorists have formulated a new, reader-centered definition of coherence which distinguishes the quality of connected sentences, now termed *cohesion*, from the larger, global quality of text structure, or *coherence*. . . . Thus through a text-centered approach we can account for cohesion, but in order to analyze coherence we must consider the context, or, in particular, the reader. (1984, 9)

Still, the terms were—and still are—frequently used interchangeably, as two articles demonstrate: Markels extends cohesion to refer to readers' expectations that texts will make sense (1983, 450); Fahnestock, in an opposite move, distinguishes levels of coherence and notes that her article "will deal only with the first level, sentence-by-sentence coherence" (1983, 401).

We believe that the distinction can be most clearly delineated not on the basis of level (cohesion as connections between sentences, coherence as a more global concern) but on the basis of function: *cohesion* is a linguistic feature of texts; *coherence* is a judgment made by readers about what they read. On the basis of this distinction, we argue that although coherence is an important concern of composition theorists and writing teachers, cohesion is not. Markers of cohesion are formal features of texts that contribute to the coherence of a text only insofar as they are recognized as signaling recognizable connections between ideas. Thus, compendia of such markers are of little interest to us or to our students, however interesting they may be to other scholars. What is of interest are the social conventions and strategies that writers and readers use to make their texts coherent. These should be the focus of research on coherence by composition theorists.

Making such a claim requires that we first look rather closely at what use writers and readers make of the markers of cohesion. Halliday and Hasan define cohesion as a textual function, but when we look at how readers process markers of cohesion we discover that the amount of extra-linguistic knowledge a reader must bring to this task seriously qualifies this notion. Many researchers interested in teaching reading and writing have taken issue with Halliday and Hasan's definition of cohesion as the "relations of meaning that exist within the text, and that define it as a text" (1976, 4). In a survey of some of this criticism, Carrell pinpoints the objectionable assumption; she says, "Cohesion refers to the semantic relations in a text which Halliday and Hasan claim make the text cohere" (1982, 481). Halliday and Hasan's critics argue that they have it backwards, that instead, as Morgan and Sellner say, "cohesion, insofar as any sense can be made of Halliday and Hasan's description of it, is an epiphenomenon of content coherence" (1980, 179). Morgan and Sellner go on to point out the range of factors that impel a reader to judge a discourse as coherent. Referring to Halliday and Hasan's much cited example—"Wash and core six cooking apples. Put them into a fireproof dish."—they say,

> It is not knowledge of language that supplies [the] conclusion [that *them* refers to cooking apples]. It is our knowledge of cooking and of the author's purpose, our ability to reason, and the assumption that the recipe is coherent. Without this latter assumption, there would be no way of knowing what *them* is intended to refer to; the recipe might have been written by a madman or produced by a computer. (1980, 180)

This is exactly our point, that cohesion by itself does not create coherence. As a criticism of Halliday and Hasan, however, it is not so apt, for they also point out that readers

> insist on interpreting any passage as text if there is the remotest possibility of doing so. . . . If one can imagine a situation in which someone is faced with a string of words picked at random from a dictionary, but which has been made to look or sound as if it was structured, then it is safe to predict that he will go to great lengths to interpret it as text, and as related to some accessible features of the situation. (1976, 23–24)

Nor is it the case that Halliday and Hasan believe that cohesive ties are links between words on the page, as many of their critics contend. Halliday and Hasan argue that "A text is best regarded as a semantic unit: a unit not of form but of meaning. . . . A text does not CONSIST OF sentences; it is REALIZED BY, or encoded in, sentences" (2). With reference to their cooking apples example, they say,

> The cohesive agency in this instance, that which provides the texture, is the coreferentiality of *them* and *six cooking apples*. The signal, or the expression, of this coreferentiality is the presence of the potentially anaphoric item *them* in the second sentence together with a potential target item *six cooking apples* in the first. (3)

Nor do Halliday and Hasan insist that cohesive ties be explicitly realized in the text. Pointing to the example, "They fought a battle. Afterwards, it snowed," they say,

> although . . . the cohesion is achieved through the conjunctive expression *afterwards*, it is the underlying semantic relation of succession in time that actually has the cohesive power. This explains how it is that we are often prepared to recognize the presence of a relation of this kind even when it is not expressed overtly at all. We are prepared to supply it for ourselves, and thus to assume that there is cohesion, even though it has not been explicitly demonstrated. (229)

In these examples coreference and succession in time are signalled syntactically but realized in the semantic structure of the text, which is considered to be a linguistic structure to the extent that any native reader of the language would process the syntactic signals in the same way. The problem Morgan and Sellner—and anyone who is primarily interested in language use—have with this explanation is that it accounts for such a minimal part of the process of understanding texts. It does not—nor does it intend to—account for how readers know to interpret the first example as a recipe, the second as a narrative, for example. Nor does it take any account of the social situation of texts and their readers and writers, which may cause them to process structures differently.

Still, one may question the extent to which linguistic structure is independent of readers' extra-linguistic knowledge. Two aspects of Halliday and Hasan's model are particularly vulnerable to this line of argument: their restriction of cohesion to endophoric coreference (that is, coreference within the text) and their inclusion of lexical collocations as cohesive ties. Brown and Yule argue that if one looks at how readers process coreference, the distinction between endophoric and exophoric falls apart. Considering remote anaphoric coreferences, as in characters' names in novels, they argue that it seems more likely that the [reader] establishes a referent in his mental representation of the discourse and relates subsequent references to that referent back to his mental representation, rather than to the original verbal expression in the text. . . . [Thus] in both [endophoric and exophoric coreference], we must suppose, the [reader] has a mental representation. In the one case he has a mental representation of what is in the world, in the other he has a mental representation of a world created in the discourse. In each case he must look into his mental representation to determine reference. (1983, 201)

Reading researchers have similarly argued that readers do not remember the linguistic forms of a text. Thus, it becomes difficult to see coreference as merely a function of a text rather than as a cognitive process in the reader responding to a text.

Lexical collocations present a different case, one in which coherence depends on writers' and readers' knowledge of real-world schemas. Halliday and Hasan do note that this is "the most problematical part of lexical cohesion, cohesion that is achieved through the association of lexical items that regularly co-occur" (1976, 284). The problem is, as they point out, that there are numerous ways in which the co-occurring items can be related. Some of these relations might be considered semantic: the best case can be made for synonymity, as with *disease/illness/ sickness*, and for the relation between general and particular nouns, as with *children/girls*. But with other relations, such as complementarity (*boys/girls*), antonymity (*love/hate* or *wet/dry*), ordered series (*Tuesday/ Thursday* or *dollar/cent*), unordered sets (*basement/roof*), and particularly with collocations based on unspecified relations—some examples Halliday and Hasan offer include *laugh/joke, blade/sharp*, and *mountaineering/ Yosemite/summit peaks/climb*—coherence is due not to any formal textual links but rather to schemas associated with such things as measures of time, houses, and mountaineering. Significantly, it is just these markers that have been singled out by researchers as correlating with readers' judgments that texts are coherent (see McCulley, 1985).

As Brown and Yule observe, however, much of this contextual criticism is beside the point, for Halliday and Hasan "are not concerned to produce a description which accounts for how texts are understood. They are, rather, concerned to examine the linguistic resources available to the speaker [and] writer to mark cohesive relationships" (1983, 204). Thus, Brown and Yule explain, the problem is not in Halliday and Hasan's model but rather in the use of this model by discourse analysts, who, Brown and Yule warn, "should not assume that the account of textual relations produced as a *post hoc* analysis of the structure of a completed text should necessarily be revealing" about how a reader experiences that text (203).

Cohesive markers are, of course, of great interest for, and are particularly suited to, linguistic study. Theoretical linguistics, as a pure science, is not concerned with the real-world application of the patterns it discerns but rather finds its motivation in a nearly aesthetic interest in the perfection of theory that is the central motivation of the tradition descending from Pythagoras to Feynman, or, in this case, Chomsky. When Hasan, for instance, is investigating pronominal cohesion in English, she is doing so in order to produce an elegant set of rules that apply to the general case. We can then test her rules against particular texts:

> As on a festal day in early spring
> The tidelands maneuver and the air is quick with imitations:
> Ships, hats appear. And those,
> The mind-readers, who are never far off. But
> To get to know them we must avoid them.
>
> And so, into our darkness life seeps,
> Keeping its part of the bargain. But what of
> Houses, standing ruined, desolate just now:
> Is this not also beautiful and wonderful?
> For where a mirage has once been, life must be.
>
> The pageant, growing ever more curious, reaches
> An ultimate turning point. Now everything is going to be
> Not dark, but on the contrary, charged with so much light
> It looks dark, because things are now packed so closely together.
> We see it with our teeth . . .
>   (John Ashbery, "Voyage in the Blue," 1976, 25)

"We see it with our teeth." The "it" here is an obvious cohesive marker; it must refer to something earlier in the text, but what? Perhaps "thing"? This is not going to work. And yet the poem is coherent. One can, then, have a coherent text in which the cohesive function of pronouns is simply flouted. As a matter of fact, the distinctive nature of Ashbery's poetry, that which allows us to recognize his poems, is this flouting of pronominal cohesion. One might say that this demonstrates nothing, that poetry is such a special case that it must be ignored. Hasan has said exactly that, and, speaking as a linguist, she is entirely correct. But as rhetoricians, we are interested in precisely such special cases, cases in which writers exploit to the maximum the expressive possibilities of the rules of language. For the rhetorician, language is not a set of rules to be modeled, it is an integral part of our cultural world and the display of its possibilities, as language, is one of its uses, as rhetoric.

The great promise of research such as that of Halliday and Hasan is that it allows linguistic theory to proceed on beyond the sentence to larger units of discourse. This would be a great contribution to linguistics. But it would have little to do with composition, for if it is truly a discovery in the field of linguistics, it would not be something that could necessarily be taught—it would be "natural" rather than "cultural." We do not *teach* our beginning students how to put together phrases and sentences. A basic working knowledge of the function of cohesion in doing this comes with the language.

An analysis of cohesive markers in texts does not necessarily tell us anything about the process by which that text was produced nor about the process by which a reader judges it to be coherent. Though Markels' discussion of cohesion paradigms in paragraphs is a significant improvement on Halliday and Hasan's description of cohesion, it does not, as she attempts to argue, lead to a practical pedagogy for writing teachers. Cohesion is a result—not a cause—of good writing skills. Witte and Faigley's study (1981) suggested that students with greater skill in invention produced more coherent texts; Stotsky's analysis of types of lexical cohesion (1983) suggested that what writers need in order to create cohesive texts is a "huge repertoire of words" for expressing relationships; Tierney and Mosenthal conclude that

> comprehensibility in text might best be approached from an argumentation perspective. It is essential, though, that the argument not be misinterpreted as structure. In other words, the text need not be architecturally bound from beginning to end, but the status of the argument must be comprehensible at any point in the text. (1983, 227)

Direct instruction in the use of cohesive markers, like direct instruction in grammar, is not likely to produce good writing. In each case it is conceivable that direct instruction could result in the learning of the skill in question—a writer could consult a memorized list of cohesive markers, say, before writing each sentence—it is just that such methodologies are inefficient and almost willfully perverse.

In contrast, coherence, as a judgment made by readers, is clearly an object for composition research. We, as composition teachers and researchers, are especially interested in such matters as readings performed by *certain types* of readers. We are concerned with readers of student writing, on the one hand, and with students as readers, on the other. In other words, we are concerned with what readers of writers taken to be inexpert notice; with what readers, taken to be inexpert, do not notice and need to be taught to notice in their own work and that of their fellows. One thing the first class of readers notice is coherence, whether a text is understandable to them.

Writers and readers draw on a variety of conventions and strategies to make their texts coherent. As these conventions and strategies are social in origin, they can be acquired through experience with texts, and they can also be explicitly taught. Learning how to use these conventions and strategies may help some readers and writers who are taken to be inexpert. But often writers who are labeled inexpert are simply the victims of readers who refuse to apply these conventions and strategies to a student's text, insisting instead that everything in the text must be absolutely explicit if the text is to be understandable to them. A brief sketch of some of these conventions and strategies will demonstrate that the lack of explicit markers of cohesion is not what these readers are reacting to.

Coherence can derive from the structural conditions on genres of discourse. For instance, the five paragraph essay.

> In this essay I will say three things.
> First this.
> Then this.
> Then this.
> In conclusion I will conclude.

A smaller unit of discourse is the adjacency pair, such as proposition/acceptance:

> HE: I've just bought a pretty Baskerville Catullus.
> SHE: I'd like to see it.

Smith demonstrates persuasively that adjacency pairs are not restricted to spoken dialogue. Like markers of cohesion, these structures do not create coherence. But from their use in particular social situations, these conventional structures have acquired a force that compels readers to see texts employing them as coherent. Teachers have a difficult time explaining low grades for the perfectly executed but vapid five-paragraph essay; and everyone has a hard time saying anything in reply to a proposal that cannot be interpreted as an acceptance or rejection.

Several other conventions of coherence derive from the ways people in a particular society characteristically think about topics. These ways include the use of schemas, logic, and real-world relationships. For instance, here's a version of a text reading comprehension researchers often use:

> They dropped their clothes on the floor. Separate piles. Then they went down to the basement. She got out the liquids. He prepared the machine. They liked to do things like this together.

You may find this incoherent until you infer the schema of someone washing clothes, whereupon the text is immediately coherent, because you can neatly fit all the information into the slots the schema provides. (That you may have at first found it coherent using a different schema further illustrates the reader's contribution to coherence.)

Logical relations can also provide coherence, as in the following narrative:

> He went to a bookstore the other day. The quarto Baskerville Catullus was too beautiful to leave. So he took it, even though it was more expensive than the octavo Baskerville on La Cienega.

How do you know, in this narrative, that what he took was the Baskerville Catullus and not the many other things that *it* could refer to? Halliday and Hasan would say it is because you know that *it* and *Baskerville Catullus* are coreferential. But how do you know that? Partly because you know that leaving and taking are mutually exclusive actions, and thus you logically infer that the thing stated to be too beautiful to leave will indeed be taken.

And finally there is topical coherence that results from real-world relationships, such as that someone who likes eighteenth-century printing will most likely want to see a Baskerville Catullus, or that there are rare bookstores on La Cienega, or that unsupported items fall to the ground, often breaking and making a noise, which is the source of coherence in the following anecdote:

> Startled by the scene in the bedroom, the maid loosed her grip on the Ming vase she was dusting. They found the crash distracting.

As perceptions of real-world relationships vary widely from individual to individual this type of topical coherence is more liable to fail, as might these examples for readers who know little of rare books, Los Angeles, or Ming vases, as does a piece of student writing discussed by Dillon in which knowing something about high school lunch rooms is necessary for a reader to find a text coherent (1981, 33–34).

Readers and their judgments are the ultimate location of coherence, and we would argue that these judgments are, in the final analysis, social.

Note that even with generic coherence and topical coherence it is people's *perception* of genres and of schemas, logic, and relationships that leads them to see a text as coherent. And other sources of coherence are more purely attributable to writers and readers.

One of the primary sources of coherence in discourse is the reader's grasp of a writer's purpose; Widdowson (1978) sees it as the sole source. The desire to be perceived as acting in a particular way—suggesting, disputing, acknowledging—motivates what will be said and renders the result a coherent action. For example, here is a paragraph from a business letter:

> Our present shipment of Teak Benches has been delayed in England under circumstances beyond our control. We feel very badly about this, so I am taking this opportunity to write to you and apologize. This is not a computer letter cranking out mechanical copy. All of us here strive to deliver the best customer service humanly possible, and we feel frustrated when we cannot deliver it.

The writer of the letter made his purpose explicit—to apologize—and other sentences in the paragraph thus can be seen as coherent in that they are related to this purpose. The first sentence explains the reason an apology is called for; the slightly surprising third sentence is an indirect assertion of the sincerity of the apology, which depends on the reader knowing that businesses do on occasion crank out "apologies" without the requisite accompanying feelings. The final sentence asserts the sincerity of the apology more directly. The importance of a writer's purpose in confering coherence on a text is revealed in readers' reactions when they cannot infer a purpose: "Why are you telling me all these things?"

Texts can also be rendered coherent by the writer's individual associations and memories, though the coherence may not be acknowledged until the reader can ascertain (via further reading or inquiry) what the associations are. For example, Vardaman in *As I Lay Dying*:

> And so if Cash nails the box up, she is not a rabbit. And so if she is not a rabbit I couldn't breathe in the crib and Cash is going to nail it up. And so if she lets him it is not her. I know. I was there. I saw when it did not be her. I saw. They think it is and Cash is going to nail it up. (Faulkner 1964, 63)

In Vardaman's mind, rabbits are associated with death, and putting his dead mother in the coffin is associated with the time he got trapped in a corn crib. Readers know these associations and thus the passage is coherent.

But readers are not necessarily—or even usually—more interested in a writer's intentions and associations than in their own. Single-minded readers can almost always find a text coherent in line with their own purposes and associations. For example, the plumber who, when the research lab wrote him saying that the use of hydrochloric acid to clean pipes was incompatible with metallic permanence and likely to produce toxic residues, wrote back thanking them for their approval of his procedure. Instead, it is the reader's willingness to confer coherence, as Halliday and Hasan pointed out, that is the most important thing. All texts are incredibly gappy, all must be filled in with bridging assumptions. It is by means of these contextual bridging assumptions that the reader confers meaning on cohesive ties. All scholars interested in discourse insist on this, from linguists like Halliday and Hasan to composition theorists like Markels to discourse analysts like Brown and Yule to anthropologists like Gumperz, who says,

> Cohesion or coherence does not inhere in the text as such. It is the listener's search for a relationship, along with their failure to find anything to contradict the assumption that a connection must exist, that motivates the interpretation. (1982, 33)

If a reader withholds that commitment of energy and intelligence —as so often we do as writing teachers who are concerned to help our students "perfect" their texts—there is nothing a writer can do to make a text coherent for that reader. We can see this when Fahnestock downplays the reader's role:

> Of course readers are often patient with minor confusions and will sometimes actively endow a piece with meaning (as any composition teacher knows who has heard students explaining one another's writing); nevertheless, bridging the gap or "synapse" between adjacent clauses is still the writer's fundamental responsibility. (1983, 401)

Moskovit points out that this depends on who the writer is: "I tend to be diffident when faced with difficulties in writers of proven worth. If the reference of *this* appears to be unclear in John Stuart Mill or Samuel Johnson, I will think long and hard before finding fault" (1983, 466). But he also offers a rationalization for pedagogical practice that puts more responsibility on the student writer: "As teachers of beginning students, we often have to oversimplify and therefore imply more rigid criteria than we actually believe in" (467). One of the questions that arises out of this view of coherence is, why do writing teachers place so much emphasis on the use of cohesive markers?

Often, when readers of student writing comment about coherence, or its lack, they are actually commenting about their overall reaction to the quality of the writing at hand. If they like it, they say it's coherent. If they do not like it, they often say it's incoherent. Why this is so becomes clear in the work on modeling comprehension by artificial intelligence researchers. Some sources of coherence—genres, schemas, relationships—are stable enough for researchers to be able to program computers to "read" texts that are not too surprising. If they are too surprising, everything falls apart. Imagine a computer program that "reads" student essays. Using its student essay genre rules, its schemas for the various student essay topics—summer vacations, people who have influenced the author, descriptions of places—and a list of cohesive markers, it would look for lexical collocations, decide on the basis of the collocations found which kind of student essay it was dealing with, then grade or classify the essay—possibly holistically—on the basis of how well it matched the assumed genre and schema. Such a program would mimic the behavior of the usual readers of student essays. (One dimension along which this would be an accurate imitation of the behavior of the usual readers of student essays would be that the computer would not engage in imitations of behavior appropriate outside the classroom: boredom, admiration, opposition, agreement.)

Now, some very good student writers are deviant. Essays that are structured analogically or that are written in a highly ironic mode, for instance, may not allow computer programs to properly classify them. Human readers, if more flexible than programs, might simply go on to find the implicit sources of coherence—but if they are not in sympathy with what the writer seems to be saying or the way in which she is saying it they may instead refuse to find it comprehensible. In short, if a text fits a genre, schema, or way of thinking we are familiar with, we are more likely to see it as coherent. If not, we will stigmatize it as incoherent, if we are reading as writing teachers; or we will simply refuse—or fail—to understand it, if the text itself carries some authority. Often readers are resistant to new ideas and new genres; this is a truism. Too often, writing teachers are resistant to the unfamiliar ideas and conventions of their students and find it easier to insist that students conform to familiar, more "explicit" patterns rather than to help students find ways to make their unfamiliar patterns more accessible to their readers.

There are structural and lexical stimuli that lead readers to respond with judgments of coherence, and thus approval. Some work has been done with this type of coherence (Bamberg 1984; Smith 1984). Much more—properly, composition research—could be done. It might also be useful to point out to students that readers will assume that essays about certain topics will employ certain conventions of coherence, that by overtly referring to those conventions, especially when one's readers are expected to be hostile, the essay will be less likely to be rejected as incoherent.

Still, it is also true that writers do frequently produce texts that even they themselves see as incoherent. If readers' willingness to find a text coherent is all-important, it seems that it would be virtually impossible to produce a text that is incoherent for every reader. Witte and Faigley's attempt,

> The quarterback threw the ball toward the tight end. Balls are used in many sports. Most balls are spheres, but footballs are ellipsoid. The tight end leaped to catch the ball. (1981, 201)

could be read as an ironic account of an incomplete pass. Enkvist's example of the inadequacy of cohesive ties,

> I bought a Ford. A car in which President Wilson rode down the Champs Elysees was black. Black English has been widely discussed. The discussions between the presidents ended last week. A week has seven days. Every day I feed my cat. Cats have four legs. The cat is on the mat. Mat has three letters. (1978, 110)

becomes coherent with the assumption that it was written by a disoriented linguist (hence the mention of Black English and the notorious sentence 'The cat is on the mat') with a passion for enumeration. Any ingenious—or naive—reader can find such short texts coherent. Indeed, to do so is a common academic exercise of which this is an example.

In longer texts a judgment of incoherence can stem from a number of sources, the least of which is failure to adequately signal the source of coherence. Other problems that may provoke a judgment of incoherence are failure to fulfill the conventions associated with the intended genre of discourse, failure to fill in slots in the intended topical schema, failure to follow logical reasoning patterns, failure to supply relevant background information, failure to fulfill conditions associated with achieving the intended purpose, failure to clarify idiosyncratic associations, and failure to resolve the competing claims of different sources of coherence, as when an argument requires the alteration of a widely accepted and powerful frame, or when a description is cast in terms of a riddle, or when irony distorts the logical relations in an essay. In short, teaching students to avoid incoherence is not a simple matter, not restricted to a few lessons on cohesive ties or devices for signaling coherence. It involves encouraging students to use the various conventions and strategies of coherence, some of which they already have tacit understanding of and use in other discourse, to the fullest in their writing.

Composition research concerning judgments of coherence has much to tell us about the judges, much to tell us about pedagogical goals. It may lead us into questions primarily of narrow professional interest, such as how we might go about factoring holistic evaluations of student compositions. Present analytical scales presume certain things about holistic judgments. Some work has been done toward clarifying these presuppositions (Hake and Williams 1981). It is generally best to allow the data based on readers' responses to speak—not in some crudely positivistic fashion, we hasten to add—within a theoretical framework. Research in coherence could advance this work. One potentially fruitful field for such research would be the effects of contrasting cultural backgrounds between readers and writers.

Other paths might take us into issues of wider interest, such as the question of the text itself. We no longer believe that the text lies there, passively inscribed on the page; we hardly remember ever having believed this. The text, we (now) know, is dynamic, flowing into the minds of writer and reader, flowing out onto Sixth Street and up Fairfax into the wider culture, say, of Melrose Avenue. Examining the conventions and strategies of coherence in more detail may allow us to arrive at a clearer understanding of these matters.

In studying coherence and its creation by the reader, we are led to remember that texts are very much a part of the social world and that we understand them in much the same way we understand other things. Thus, just as we would not cede the study of texts to literary critics, neither would we cede it to linguists. As Morgan and Sellner point out,

> Given the powerful common-sense abilities that are brought to bear in just making sense of the world and other people, it is thoroughly implausible to suppose that these abilities are suppressed when texts are encountered in favor of some arcane, strictly linguistic mechanism whose sole function is to process and understand discourse. (1980, 196)

Marilyn Cooper and Michael Holzman

8

Context as Vehicle: Implicatures in Writing

This is the oldest essay in this collection and, as such, represents our approach to writing in an embryonic form. My view of social context here is fairly narrow and is characterized in cognitive terms—what writers know—but in insisting that the differences between spoken and written communication lie in the conventions specific to each rather than in the acontextuality of writing, I lay the groundwork for an argument that writing is essentially an action, not an internalized process. However, the essay also demonstrates how a cognitive theory and a social theory of writing can be seen as continuous rather than contradictory. Writers do think as well as act; our position differs from cognitive theorists in that we emphasize the dialectical relationship between what writers think and do and their social context—the effects that society has on what writers know and the effects that writers have on society.

The essay also contains a reworking of the speech-act theory of Paul Grice that is, I believe, more radical than I thought it was at the time I wrote it. In my version of how implicatures work, convention, in the form of the interpretive beliefs and conventions that define when maxims have been violated, plays a larger role than intention—certainly not an outcome that Grice would be pleased with.[1] In this way I attempted to rid the theory of implicatures of its psychologistic slant in order to highlight its hypothesis of a sociolinguistic strategy central to communication.

□   □   □

Writing theory often concerns itself primarily with what writers know about themselves and their intentions and what they know about their readers' needs and wants. But writers also take into account what they know about the world they find themselves in and what they know about the activity of writing. What writers know about the world is more or less what everyone knows: facts, empirical laws, and various culture-bound conventions—laws, social codes, religious rites, and so forth. What writers know about writing is more specialized knowledge: written works themselves and linguistic and genre conventions. How do writers use this variety of information in forming their works, and how do they relate this larger context to the immediate problem of communicating with their readers? Using H. Paul Grice's theory of implicatures, I will explain the various ways in which writers draw on and exploit context to communicate their intentions.

First, I must make explicit something about the context of my writing. I assume that writing is a communicative act. To some, this is a truism, but it entails two beliefs less widely acceded to: that writers and readers operate on the basis of the same knowledge, and that the meaning of texts, as with all other communications, depends heavily on contexts. The only chance writers have of communicating their meanings is by assuming that potential readers have largely the same knowledge of those facts about the world relevant to their meanings as they themselves do, and that readers will, when faced with a text (an object that is always multiply ambiguous), use the same interpretive strategies that the writers would. Writing and interpreting are mirror-image processes, as Stanley Fish explains:

> what utterers do is give hearers and readers the opportunity to make meanings (and texts) by inviting them to put into execution a set of strategies. It is presumed that the invitation will be recognized, and that presumption rests on a projection on the part of a speaker or author of the moves *he* would make if confronted by the sounds or marks he is uttering or setting down. (1980, 173)

This depiction is intuitively satisfying, especially when we consider how writers, in revising, read over their texts to test the meanings produced by the interpretive strategies they assume their readers will use. There are, of course, breakdowns in communication, most of which arise from a mismatch between writers' and readers' knowledge. Nevertheless, writers always act from the belief that communication is possible.

Because in writing the means of communication—the text—is more concrete and long lasting than in speaking, writing is usually considered to be a much less situated communicative act than is speaking. Teachers often point out to beginning writers that many contextual determinants of meaning available in speaking situations are lacking in writing—intonation, gestures, facial expressions, and location in time and space. As Mina Shaughnessy has explained, basic writers know this lesson only too well:

> For the BW student, academic writing is a trap, not a way of saying something to someone. The spoken language, looping back and forth between speakers, offering chances for groping and backing up and even hiding, leaving room for the language of hands and faces, of pitch and pauses, is generous and inviting. Next to this rich orchestration, writing is but a line that moves haltingly across the page, exposing as it goes all that the writer doesn't know, then passing into the hands of a stranger who reads it with a lawyer's eyes, searching for flaws. (1977, 7)

But no one denies that student writing takes place in a context, and one thing these writers need to learn is how to deal with it. The power imbalance between students and teacher is aggravated by their not knowing how to code gestures and intonation in linguistic forms or how to successfully hedge, equivocate, and predict the response of their reader.

James Britton terms this type of writing transactional, writing that "is intended to fit into, to articulate with, the ongoing activities of participants" (1970, 174–75). Transactional writing is the focus of most composition courses and programs, but it is only one type. Britton terms the other type of public writing poetic writing, and it is with this type that acontextuality is most strongly insisted on. Britton says that poetic writing, rather than articulating with the activities of participants, interrupts them "by presenting an object to be contemplated in itself and for itself. . . . A reader is asked to respond to a particular verbal construct which remains quite distinct from any other verbal construct anybody else might offer. A response in kind is not therefore inherent in the situation" (174). Jay Schleusener concisely summarizes the position of many literary theorists:

> works of literature differ from ordinary speech because they are not tied to an immediate social context. . . . Authors and readers . . . can hardly be said to meet anywhere at all. Their only common ground is the text, and they share nothing but the words that pass between them. Meanings that might be clear enough in the social context of ordinary speech tend toward ambiguity in this circumstantial void where author and reader must do without a common world of reference and make the best of a language that cannot rely on the casual support of facts. (1980, 669–70)

Texts are admittedly easier to decontextualize than are utterances: writers' names are more easily separated from their texts than speakers' presences are from their utterances, and because texts are, in a sense, physical objects, they are more permanent and portable, and thus more likely to turn up in alien contexts. But this is as true of nonliterary as literary texts. Nor is this any argument that writers or readers ever treat texts as acontextual.

Few teachers of literature would agree that literary language does not "rely on the casual support of facts." To take just two examples, I. A. Richards laments his students' "surprising unfamiliarity with the elements of the Christian religion" (1929, 42). And Martha Banta, discussing the cause of her literature students' "will to ignorance," notes:

> Over and over, against the grain of all my experiences, out of my unending hope and innocence, I keep asking, if only because a novel or poem or essay is waiting for its built-in references to be cleared up before we can go any further: "What is meant by 'He has met his Waterloo?' " and "Who was Cupid's mother?" and "Why did Lazarus stink?" and "Who did Jacob wrestle with and why?" and "Why did Leda get mixed up with a swan?" and "Who was Thor and why was Thoreau interested in him?" and "Who *was* Dwight David Eisenhower?" I ask; I rarely receive. (1980, 111)

When Richards asked his students to respond to and comment on unidentified poems, the students continually attempted to make sense of the poems by providing the missing contexts. They guessed at the authorship: "a spinster devoted to good works, and sentimentally inclined, or perhaps Wordsworth" (Richards 1929, 23). They guessed at the literary period: "Reminded of the pitched-up movement or strong artificial accent of post-Elizabethans. But this is without their complexity of thought. . . . a deliberate loading of rhythm—influence of the didactic pretentions. Wordsworth? Spurious. Mid-Victorian poetic drama?" (23). They compared the poems with other poems they knew: " 'Tho' world of wanwood leafmeal lie'—gloriously melancholy (worthy of Keats' 'La Belle Dame sans Merci')" (81). They drew on what they knew of poetic method: "This is clearly an experiment in sound and in striving after effect the sense suffers considerably" (86). They guessed at the author's pragmatic intentions by projecting the purpose the poem fulfilled for them: "An atmosphere of peace, and deep reverence, which transports the reader into another world, more pure and white than this" (95). To interpret the actions of the people in the poems, they drew on their beliefs about how people should act: "The parent or whoever it is advising Margaret is a bitter, hard individual who seems to be trying to take away all the hope and happiness of the child. I don't think that any really kind person would feel so little sympathy for a child's trivial sorrow, and make her unhappy by telling her the worse is yet to come" (83). And they guessed at the intentions of the writers by projecting their own attitudes toward subjects of the poems: "if we are meant to take the situation in profound meditation closing in self-absorbing remorse, then the whole thing is clearly vicious and preposterous. The idea of an eternity spent in turning up the files of other people's sins or crouching to cry *peccavi* for our own is either amusing or disgusting or both" (169).

Meanings carried by the conventional rules of language are exceedingly impoverished. Clearly, reading and writing require the reader and writer to hypothesize a whole communicative situation, just as in conversing face-to-face we assume many things about the situation we are in. The encounter between writer and reader is in one sense less immediate than the encounter between speaker and hearer: Writers and readers are not (usually) physically in each other's presence and cannot respond directly to each other. But actual presence makes little difference in the communicative process. Readers typically have a strong sense of the writer's immediate presence, and skilled writers develop the same sense of their readers' presence. Interaction does occur. As readers, have you never asked of a writer, "What are you referring to here?" and searched back through the text or in your knowledge of context for a clue? As writers, have you never asked, "What must I tell my readers next?" as you thought about how they would understand what you were writing? Schleusener concludes:

> We come to know the author in much the same way that we come to know anyone else: not by historical research or by hypothetical deduction but on our own authority and through our own experience. To the extent that we succeed in developing a useful notion of his character, our assessment is legitimized by our understanding of the conventions he has used and by our familiarity with the relevant notions of agency and action. We could do little more to legitimize our acquaintance with persons we meet face to face. (1980, 679)

I have insisted on the similarities between communicating in writing and communicating in speaking because the widespread tendency to dwell on the differences between the two obscures the fact that the fundamental communicative process remains the same. Readers and hearers use both their knowledge of linguistic and other conventions and their knowledge of the relevant aspects of context to assign meanings to texts and to utterances, and writers and speakers count on their ability to do this. The differences between writing and speaking are differences in the conventions that are employed, not differences in the means of employing them.

Beginning writers, it is often observed, use the same situational devices in writing that they use in talking with their friends. One of my colleagues received an essay that began, "This is the place I work at that's suppose to be a gas station." The meaning of his utterance depends on a context in which he and the person he's addressing are standing in front of the gas station: the deictic *this* refers to an object present in the addressee's world; the definite article *the* marks the place as known to the addressee, as it would be if he or she were standing near the place referred to. The intended sarcastic tone depends on intonation—a stress on *suppose*. But the writer and his reader are not in the context his meaning depends on, which imperils the success of his communication. *This* and *the place* may refer perfectly successfully in conversation, but in writing reference depends on definite descriptions and proper names that create the objects referred to in the readers' minds. The emphasis on *suppose* will convey sarcasm in conversation, but in writing that emphasis must somehow be marked typographically (typically by italics or under-lining) or be specified lexically. I could suggest that the student rewrite his sentence as follows: *The gas station where I work is a sadly deficient token of its type.* (Of course, I wouldn't.) In suggesting these changes to him, am I simply telling him to reduce his dependence on context and increase his dependence on convention? No. But I am telling him the two contexts are different and different conventions are needed to com-municate his intentions. Note that the reference of *I* remains, strictly speaking, ambiguous; *I* will be identified with whichever name is written at the top of the page or whoever hands the text to the teacher. *This* and a stress on *suppose* are just as conventional as the definite description of the gas station and the lexical meaning of *sadly deficient*. Furthermore, note that the revised sentence, if spoken by a person standing in front of the gas station where he works, is just as vulnerable to misinterpretation as the spoken version is when it's handed to a teacher as an essay. Both versions use conventions adapted to the demands of the contexts in which they are to be received. In fact, given the actual context of the student's writing, he would not be best advised to write as explicitly as I have in my first revision of his text. The student knew that his reader knew that he had been assigned to write about a familiar place he had some attitude toward, and he knew that his reader knew that most of his students had part-time jobs. I would better advise him to write simply, *The place where I work is* **supposed** *to be a gas station*—which preserves his "voice" while removing the undesirable marks of illiteracy (*at*, and misspelling of *supposed*).

How much readers rely on context in interpreting texts can be demonstrated by one further example. The other day, I picked up my copy of the October 6 issue of *The New Yorker* and turned to "The Talk of the Town." On reading the first sentence—"In 1969, when 'The Selling of the President,' by Joe McGinniss, was published, showing that

Richard Nixon had used Madison Avenue advertising techniques to the full in his recent election campaign, the book was regarded as an exposé" (47)—I said to myself, with this year's campaigns you wouldn't need an exposé. As I read on, my meaning prediction was verified: the argument of the piece was that in current political campaigns "the techniques by which public opinion is manipulated are proudly displayed to the world" (47). How did I (and several other readers I asked about this article) so quickly grasp the writer's intended meaning? The answer is obvious: as a longtime reader of *The New Yorker* I am well acquainted with that eye-glassed gentleman who regularly discourses on current events in these pages. I know what subjects are likely to interest him and what attitude he is likely to take toward them. I know that the first piece in this section is often a serious political commentary. I know that, if the first sentence of such a piece refers to a long past event, that event most likely provides a context relevant to the subject the writer intends to discuss. I know this piece was written fairly recently and that it will relate to something that has just happened or is still happening. I know that we are once again (as I read) in the middle of a presidential campaign: I have seen the candidates' television advertisements and read their aides' explanations of how engaging in debates would affect their candidates' images. In short, what I know about the writer's interests and attitudes, about the conventions of *The New Yorker*, and about the political situation at the time and place of the publication of this text allows me to correctly infer a meaning from relatively few linguistic cues. I certainly did not read each word in the first sentence, either, and I probably needed only five words to cue the meaning: *advertising techniques, election campaign, exposé*. That the writer of this piece used more than these five words to convey his meaning does not mean that he does not rely on his readers' having this knowledge, for no matter how much he writes he knows that any change in readers' knowledge will affect their interpretation of his meaning.

Most texts come richly provided with contexts. The student's paper was produced at a particular time (1970s) at a particular place (Minneapolis) in a particular course (composition) at a particular school (University of Minnesota) in a particular society (which includes the concepts of "working" and "gas station") in response to a particular teacher's particular assignment with particular intentions on the student's part (to fulfill the teacher's assignment, to pass composition, and possibly to explore his own feelings about the place where he works)—all of which is known by both reader and writer. Similarly, *The New Yorker* arrived in my mailbox in Los Angeles on about October 6 (the date on its cover); its format (paper cover, staple binding, ads interspersed with articles) and weekly appearance marked it as a known type of cultural artifact (weekly magazine) designed to sell products by offering information and diversion; the subtitle of the section ("Notes and Comments") and the subjects addressed in the section marked that as a known journalistic genre (editorial column) in which writers express opinions on current happenings—and all this is known to both the writer and the readers of *The New Yorker*. Very rarely do we encounter texts stripped of all this information. Richards in his experiment noted that "the precise conditions of this test are not duplicated in our everyday commerce with literature" (1929, 5), and he not surprisingly discovered that under these conditions readers have exceeding difficulty in "*making out the plain sense of poetry*" (12).

Communicating meanings depends on knowledge: interpretations are inferences based on beliefs and conventions.[2] As Richard Young and his colleagues explain in their composition textbook, "there can be no interaction between writer and reader, and no change in their thinking, unless they hold certain things in common, such as shared experiences, shared knowledge, shared beliefs, values, and attitudes, shared language" (1970, 172). The mix of knowledge called up by any communication varies. In the gas station example, readers use linguistic conventions and nonconventional beliefs such as that discourse is normally oriented to the speaker and that gas stations are places of business. In the *New Yorker* example, readers use linguistic conventions and genre conventions and nonconventional beliefs about the writer's personality and the current political situation. But many communicative acts are even more dependent on context than are these two. In his lectures on "Logic and Conversation,"[3] Grice describes communicative acts in which what is meant departs radically from the conventional meaning of the words that were used. He elaborates a set of nonconventional beliefs about how conversants interact that help us to perform and to understand these "indirect" communicative acts that he calls implicatures.[4] Implicatures are common in everyday conversations, as Grice reveals. But they are also common in writing, and what he says about conversation applies equally well to all communication.

Grice argues that conversation is a cooperative endeavor, that what enables conversation to proceed is an underlying assumption that we as conversants have purposes for conversing and that we recognize that these purposes are more likely to be fulfilled if we cooperate.[5] These purposes can vary greatly, they can be mixed, and they might not be shared by all participants in the conversation. We nevertheless assume, unless there are indications to the contrary, that we have a shared purpose for conversing, and our actions reflect this assumption. Grice states the assumption as an imperative and calls it the Cooperative Principle (CP): "Make your conversational contribution such as is required, at the stage at which it occurs, by the accepted purpose or direction of the talk exchange in which you are engaged" (1975, 45). From the CP he derives a series of "maxims":

Quantity
1. Make your contribution as informative as is required (for the current purposes of the exchange).
2. Do not make your contribution more informative than is required.

Quality
1. Do not say what you believe to be false.
2. Do not say that for which you lack adequate evidence.

Relation
Be relevant.

Manner
1. Avoid obscurity of expression.
2. Avoid ambiguity.
3. Be brief (avoid unnecessary prolixity).
4. Be orderly.

Although these maxims are also stated as imperatives, they do not rule conversation in any sense. We rarely violate the maxims casually, for no reason, but we do violate them intentionally for a variety of reasons. The most interesting reason for violating a maxim is to thereby say something indirectly; Grice calls this strategy an implicature. Other reasons for violating maxims are: (a) to mislead, in which case the violation will be hidden from hearers; (b) to "opt out" of a conversation in which we do not want to participate; and (c) to avoid violating another maxim. And we may unintentionally, through ineptitude, negligence, or absent-mindedness, violate a maxim.

Speakers who wish to implicate something violate maxims in a characteristic way: they violate them in a way that draws their hearers' attention to the violation; they blatantly violate them; Grice says they "flout" the maxims. Hearers who assume that the speakers are being cooperative are forced to look for a reason for the violation in what they know of the speaker's knowledge or beliefs, and what they infer about this reason is what the speaker has implicated. Implicatures can also arise when no maxims are clearly violated,[6] as in Grice's initial example:

SITUATION: A and B are talking about a mutual friend C who is working in a bank. A asks how C is getting on in his job, and B replies:
SAID: Oh, quite well, I think; he likes his colleagues and he hasn't been to prison yet.

REASONING: B in saying "he hasn't been to prison yet" has apparently failed to fulfill the maxim of relation. There is no reason to assume B is not fulfilling the CP. B must think that:
IMPLICATED: C is potentially dishonest. (1975, 43, 50)

In this way speakers can convey meaning beyond that carried by the conventional meaning of what they say. Grice offers a formal definition of the notion of conversational implicature:

A man who, by (in, when) saying (or making as if to say) that p, has implicated that q, provided that (1) he is to be presumed to be observing the conversational maxims, or at least the cooperative principle; (2) the supposition that he is aware that, or thinks that, q is required in order to make his saying or making as if to say p (or doing so in *those* terms) consistent with this presumption; and (3) the speaker thinks (and would expect the hearer to think that the speaker thinks) that it is within the competence of the hearer to work out, or grasp intuitively, that the supposition mentioned in (2) *is* required. (1975, 49–50)

Grice emphasizes that implicatures must be intentional; speakers must know they are violating a conversational maxim and must intend their hearers to know that too and know that they are observing the CP, for the communication of meaning depends on this knowledge. What is implicated is thus determined by speakers' intentions, even though in some instances, when there are several possible suppositions that could be consistent with the presumption that speakers are being cooperative, what is implicated may be indeterminate from the hearers' point of view.

Grice formulated his maxims with representatives in mind, but clearly all types of speech acts can be used to implicate. In order to emphasize the generality of the maxims and to rid them of their misleading imperative form, I have proposed the following restatement of the CP and maxims. A "no" answer to a question marks a maxim violation.

CP: Is the conversational act such as is required at the stage at which it occurs by the accepted purpose or direction of the talk exchange in which we are engaged?

Quantity
1. Is the act sufficient?
2. Is the act not more than sufficient?

Quality
1. Does the act accord with the speaker's beliefs and feelings?
2. Is there an adequate reason for the act?

Relation
Is the act relevant?

Manner
1. Is the act perspicuous?
2. Is the act unambiguous?
3. Is the act brief?
4. Is the act organized?
5. Is the act consistent?

Quantity 1: Is the act sufficient? If the act is an assertion, speakers provide the required amount of information; if the act is a question, speakers make sure that the hearer knows what information has been requested; if the act is a promise, speakers say enough to make clear to hearers what they are undertaking an obligation to do; if the act is a congratulation, speakers make sure hearers know for what they are being congratulated. Grice's professor writing a recommendation in which he fails to comment on the applicant's skill at philosophy violates this maxim. So does Alice when she asks directions of the Cheshire Cat: "Would you tell me, please, which way I ought to go from here?" The cat reasonably responds that he cannot answer the question as phrased: "That depends a good deal on where you want to get to." [7]

Quantity 2: Is the act not more than sufficient? Speakers avoid asserting what need not be asserted, asking for information their hearers would have volunteered anyway, making promises to do things they would have done anyway, and so forth. Grice feels this maxim may be disputable, in that overinformativeness is "merely a waste of time" and that it overlaps the maxim of relation. But overinformativeness can be uncooperative if it deliberately impedes the exchange of information. In a paper on "Conversation as Paranoia," one reason for violating this maxim is explained as "The principle of maximizing talking, or the fillibuster principle": "Always try to talk as much as possible, in order to keep other people from saying what they want to say" (Aelgh 1978, 75). Furthermore, this maxim can be flouted to produce implicatures. For example, X and Y are rigging a sailboat, and X, an experienced sailor, has made a series of absent-minded errors, dropping cotter pins overboard, attaching the mainsail to the jib halyard, and cleating the main sheet before raising the sail. Finally they are ready to put out, and Y says to X, "If you want to turn the boat, shove on the tiller," flouting the second quantity maxim and implicating that X has not demonstrated much skill at this activity so far. An act that is too informative because the information is not needed violates this maxim; an act that is too informative because the information is not relevant violates the maxim of relation. Grice's example, "A wants to know whether *p*, and B volunteers not only the information that *p*, but information to the effect that it is certain that *p*, and that the evidence for its being the case that *p* is so-and-so and such-and-such" (1975, 52), is indeed an example of the violation of the second maxim of quantity; the excess information is relevant but was not in question to begin with.

Quality 1: Does the act accord with the speaker's beliefs and feelings? This maxim is equivalent to Searle's sincerity condition. Speakers believe their assertions, want answers to their questions, intend to do things they promise to do, are pleased about the events they congratulate others for, and so forth. Rhetorical questions violate this maxim, for the questioner does not want an answer, whether the answer is known to him or not. In the opening scene of Pinter's *The Collection*, Harry asks the voice on the phone, "Do you know it's four o'clock in the morning?"[8] Harry does not really know the answer to his question, but it is clear he does not want an answer either. By flouting this maxim he implicates his annoyance at the early morning phone call. Ironic utterances also characteristically flout this maxim.

Quality 2: Is there an adequate reason for the act? Speakers assert things they have reason to believe are true; they ask questions to which they do not know the answers and believe their hearers can answer; they promise to do things they can do and their hearers want them to do; they congratulate people for real accomplishments. Exam questions violate this maxim; examiners know the answers to the questions they ask (usually) but still want the questions answered.

Relation: Is the act relevant? When Grice proposed this maxim, he observed that "its formulation conceals a number of problems that exercise me a good deal: questions about what different kinds and focuses of relevance there may be, how these shift in the course of a talk exchange, how to allow for the fact that subjects of conversation are legitimately changed, and so on" (1975, 46). He repeated his concern in his fifth lecture: "Also needed: . . . . a more precise specification of when relevance is expected" (Grice 1967). Ruth Kempson notes that the maxim "is normally construed as the relation between utterance and event, or between utterance and utterance" (1975, 195), and she suggests an additional relation maxim: "Make the form of your utterance relevant to its content" (196). Grice had already suggested much the same thing in his third lecture, where he notes that in explaining the meaning of stress it might be useful to "introduce a slight extension to the maxim enjoining relevance, making it apply not only to what is said, but to features of the means used for saying what is said (1978, 122). Kent Bach and Robert Harnish suggest a sequencing submaxim of the relation maxim to the effect that the force of the utterance be appropriate to the stage of the talk exchange: "questions are to be answered, requests and commitments acknowledged, greetings reciprocated, constatives concurred with (or dissented from, or elaborated upon), and so on" (1979, 63).

Conversants' judgments about the relevance of a conversational act can be based either on the content or on the form of the act. Changing the subject of a conversation, I think, always violates the maxim of relation; conversants attempt to figure out the reason for the violation and may or may not allow the subject change. The violation may be the result of a clash with the first maxim of quantity—speakers may have nothing more to say on this subject. Or the violation may signal that speakers are opting out, not wanting to talk about the subject further. Grice's example of the faux pas at the tea party (1975, 54) is an example of a change of subject that results in an implicature.

And using an inappropriate illocutionary force-indicating device (a device that conventionally marks the illocutionary force of an utterance)[9] is a common way of violating this maxim to produce an implicature. For example, a child arrives home two hours after school has let out and greets his father, "Hi, Dad." His father sternly replies, "Where have you been?" His utterance does not violate the quantity and quality maxims for questions: His son knows what information is being requested; it is not obvious that the boy would, unprompted, provide the information; and the father doesn't know where the boy has been and wants to know. Nor is the content of the utterance irrelevant to the situation: The boy has been absent from home for quite a while, and people who are close usually have an interest in each other's activities. But the interrogative form of the utterance violates the sequencing submaxim; greetings should be reciprocated. By flouting the relation maxim, the father here implicates he is angry about not knowing where the boy has been for the last two hours, and his utterance, marked as a question, has the force of both a question and a reproof.

Manner: Manner maxims might seem to overlap some of the other maxims. Acts that are obscure, ambiguous, and/or disorganized might also be insufficient or irrelevant; acts that are inconsistent might also belie the speaker's beliefs and/or feelings. Grice takes some care to distinguish the manner maxims (1975, 54–56), and in all cases manner maxims apply after it has been determined that the other maxims are holding; they apply to the way in which the act has been realized. An act may be sufficient for the purposes of the conversation yet still be obscure, ambiguous, or disorganized; conversants then ask themselves why the act is embodied in this form. Prolix acts are judged to be such if they add more words but no more information. And inconsistent acts may accord with the speaker's beliefs and/or feelings at the time of the utterance, although they conflict with beliefs and/or feelings evidenced earlier in the conversation.

Although I argue that Grice's maxims are universal—that they are used by all conversing (and, indeed, all cooperating) persons—the standards for compliance with the maxims may vary from society to society. Elinor Keenan notes that in Malagasy society conversants are much more secretive than in Western societies, and, in our judgment, they might be seen to be continually violating the first quantity maxim (1977, 258). But the maxims provide axes for interpretation, not rigid standards against which conversational contributions are to be measured. Within societies, judgments about whether maxims have been violated will be relatively uniform.

More interesting is the way in which the maxims interact with other beliefs and conventions in the interpretive process. Communicators are always performing mediating acts in their minds, adjudicating between the demands of various beliefs and conventions. Beliefs about speakers' and writers' intentions, as I mentioned earlier (p. 116), cause maxim violations to be interpreted in different ways: Those who hide their violations (and are caught) are taken to be liars and disbelieved; those who violate maxims so as to obstruct communication are taken to have reasons for their uncooperativeness; those who do not know they have violated a maxim are taken to be psychologically or mentally deficient in some way; and maxim violations that come about as a result of desires not to violate other maxims or other conventional standards or nonconventional principles[10] are simply not regarded as significant. Only when speakers and writers intentionally, overtly, and cooperatively violate maxims do implicatures occur, and speakers and writers are taken to be communicating something indirectly.

When a maxim suggests that in a particular communicative situation a particular act is required, another belief or convention, more important in the situation, may cause a speaker or writer to violate the maxim. To the extent that the hearer or reader knows that the other belief or convention is the cause of the violation and believes that it is indeed more important, the maxim violation will not be marked. Speakers and writers are commonly faced with clashes between maxims and a wide variety of other beliefs and conventions. Beliefs about politeness (explored in detail in Brown and Levinson 1978) often clash with the quality maxims, causing "white lies." Such violations, explains Sissela Bok, "deceive no one, except possibly those unfamiliar with the language" (1979, 61). Conventions of courtship also supersede quality maxims; in Sonnet 130 Shakespeare satirizes lovers who obviously cannot believe what they say: "My mistress' eyes are nothing like the sun."

Conventions of written genres clash with maxims too. Newspaper reports, structured for readers who may read only the first paragraph or two, repeat information, thus violating the first quantity maxim. An article in the *Los Angeles Times* headlined "No deal has been made to free hostages, Muskie says" repeats this information in the first sentence—"Secretary of State Edmund S. Muskie on Saturday repeated Administration denials that a secret deal has been worked out to free the 52 Americans in Iran"—and again in the sixth paragraph—" 'There is no deal,' he said." In articles like *Time* magazine's regular "Essay," writers surveying a broad perspective are not held strictly accountable to quality maxims. How can Lance Morrow know what he seems to know in the opening paragraph of his essay on revenge? "Americans found themselves thinking about it a little more than usual last week as they watched Iranians displaying charred American bodies in front of the Tehran embassy" (Morrow 1980). This convention is a kind of synecdoche; the writer's reactions to an event are allowed to stand for the reactions of a whole group of people. In the next paragraph, the writer follows a more common linguistic convention and again violates the quality maxims: "Such scenes open a little trap door at the base of the brain. From that ancient root cellar they summon up dark, flapping fantasies of revenge" (Morrow 1980). [11]

Thus, maxim violations may be rendered insignificant when the maxims conflict with other beliefs and with conventions. The opposite is true in the case of implicatures. Maxim violations (and maxim invocations) exist only by virtue of other beliefs and conventions. What is required in any communicative situation can be ascertained by reviewing the other beliefs and conventions that the people involved in the situation hold. In Grice's example of the bank employee (see pp. 116–17), A knows that B has failed to fulfill the maxim of relation because he knows, among other things, that the information B volunteers about C's situation is meant to explain, or give cause for, B's judgment that C is doing "quite well" in his job. Thus A knows that the statement *he hasn't been to prison yet* is meant to be related to the statement that C is doing quite well (and in writing, the relation is marked by the use of the semicolon), though, on the face of it, the two statements do not seem to be related. B in his remark raises the question of how the two statements can be related, thus invoking the relation maxim and implicating that C is potentially dishonest. (See Table 8–1, #1.[12])

Other beliefs and conventions not only define maxim violations and evocations, they also serve as the basis on which we work out what's been implicated. Look again at Grice's bank employee example. We decide that B believes C is potentially dishonest on the basis of things we believe about the world, specifically things we believe about prisons and banks. A variety of scholars have recently proposed that our knowledge of the world can best be represented as frames, or structures of associated facts.[13] Teun van Dijk defines frames as "knowledge representations about the 'world' which enable us to perform such basic cognitive acts as perception, action, and language comprehension" (1977, 19). And, of course, language production. Grice's example depends on two

TABLE 8–1
Written Implicatures

Linguistic form	Facilitating beliefs and/or conventions	Maxim violated	Interpretive beliefs and/or conventions	Implicated
1. Oh, quite well, I think; he likes his colleagues and he hasn't been to prison yet.	"Judgment" frame Punctuation convention (;)	Relation	"Bank" frame "Prison" frame	C is potentially dishonest.
2. We think they qualify at least for something like the New Egalitarianism.	"Wage level" frame "Inheritance" frame	Quality 1	"U.S. principles" frame	These proposals are unfair and bad.
3. We will probably find shores that have been ravaged by man.	"Human powers" frame	Quality 2	"Environmental action" frame	Too many people value the acquisition of resources over the protection of the environment.
4. Will the Governor charge $60 an hour? (etc.)	"Governor" frame	Relation	"Psychiatrist" frame	Psychiatrists might make bad governors.
5. Mr. X's command of English is excellent, and his attendance at tutorials has been regular.	"Recommendation" frame "Philosophy" frame	Quantity 1	"Criticism" frame	Mr. X is no good at philosophy.

TABLE 8–1
Continued

Linguistic form	Facilitating beliefs and/or conventions	Maxim violated	Interpretive beliefs and/or conventions	Implicated
6. A woman was murdered . . . the real killer was never found.	Text coherence convention	Relation	"Murder" frame "Marriage" frame	Her husband was suspected of her murder; the butcher knife was the murder weapon.
7. That, too, is nature.	Text coherence convention	Quantity 1	"Predation" frame	This series presents an idealized view of nature.
8. My copy has margin notes: Pages 1, 11, 16, 37.	Text coherence convention	Quantity 1	"Reading for erotic stimulation" frame "Reviewing" frame	This book is best considered a piece of eroticism.
9. I'll protect you.	Narrative convention (abstract)	Relation	"Game" frame "Family" frame	Foster is still of some use.
10. Since [the erotic passages] are the reason thou mayst covet it . . .	Archaic forms	Quality 1	"Bible" frame	This book offers sinful delights.

11. Well, sir, it sure would pleasure a feller . . .	Dialect forms	Quality 1	"Backwoods" frame	This series is pleasant but misleading.
12. Be as *complete* and *specific* in your answers as possible: I am not a mind reader.	Punctuation convention (:)	Relation	"Communication" frame "Examination" frame	Implicit answers will not count.
13. This was a tool whose only purpose was to make holes in human beings. (etc.)	Past tense form	Quantity 2	"Time" frame	You are not my intended audience.
14. We at Boise Cascade haven't been able to . . . yet.	Negation	Quantity 2	"Corporate image" frame	Boise Cascade is a good corporation.
15. Nobody does it better.	Deixis (pronoun reference)	Manner 1	"Product" frame	No one produces better cigarettes than Winston.
			"Worker" frame	Winston smokers are good workers.
			"Sexual relations" frame	Winston smokers are good lovers.

frames to convey the implicature: the "bank" frame, which includes the notion that bank employees are faced with temptations to be dishonest, and the "prison" frame, which includes the notion that people are sent to prison for illegal acts, one of which is dishonesty. (See also Black, Wilkes-Gibbs, and Gibbs' [1982] discussion of scripts, plans, goals, and themes.)

In communicating their meanings, speakers and writers always depend on context much more than they do on the linguistic shape of their utterances or texts. Implicatures are simply the most radical cases, in which speakers and writers draw on and exploit mutual knowledge of beliefs and conventions in order to communicate meanings that are in no way encoded in linguistic forms or that contradict the conventional meanings of the linguistic forms used. To demonstrate the variety of knowledge of context writers can exploit in implicating meanings, I will, in the rest of this discussion, examine an array of examples of implicatures in writing.

The contextual knowledge writers draw on most heavily is the beliefs they share with their readers about the world they inhabit. In some implicatures, frame knowledge both defines the maxim violation and serves as the basis for interpreting what was meant. An editorial in the *Los Angeles Times* entitled "Laying Golden Eggs" (#2) commented on two economic proposals made by Ronald Reagan: one to abolish the minimum wage "without favoritism. . . . for adults and teenagers alike" and another to abolish the inheritance tax "without partiality. . . . no inheritance tax for either the rich or the poor." The writer remarked: "He did not seem to think that they warranted a grandiose label like the New Deal or the Reagan Doctrine, but we think he was too modest. We think they qualify at least for something like the New Egalitarianism" ("Laying Golden Eggs," 1980). Despite the approving tone of these remarks, readers know that the writer is not applauding Reagan's new policy direction. The writer is being ironic: by flouting the first maxim of quality that you believe what you say, he implicates that Reagan's proposals are unfair and thus are bad proposals.[14] Two frames reveal the insincerity of the egalitarian label: the "wage level" frame, which includes the fact that teenagers are paid less than adults, and the "inheritance" frame, which includes the fact that the poor inherit much less than the rich. The writer cannot believe that such unfair policies are laudable, and by referring to the "U.S. principles" frame, which stipulates, among other things, that government policies ensure equal opportunity for all, readers infer that the writer thinks the proposals are bad.

A letter to the editor of the *Times* in response to an article about sea otters (#3) similarly depends on a value frame to convey its meaning. The writer fails to fulfill the second quality maxim, for she has no way to know her prediction will come true. She says, "we would be delighted to find a sea otter population, the sign of a healthy marine environment, south of Point Conception in 15 years, but instead we will probably find shores that have been ravaged by man—stripped of their resources and smeared with oil" (Fulton 1980). We know that people's powers do not include seeing into the future (a fact in the "human powers" frame), but by referring to the "environmental action" frame the writer evokes we can infer a proposition that she does have reason to believe is true: too many people value the acquisition of resources over the protection of the environment.[15]

One tactic writers often use to implicate is the evocation of two apparently unrelated frames. Roger Rosenblatt in writing about the psychiatrist who was running for Governor of the state of Washington (#4) asks: "Will the Governor charge $60 an hour? Will his hours last 45 minutes? Will his staff know each other's last names? More urgent: Where will he be in August?" (1980). Rosenblatt invokes the maxim of relation: These questions have no apparent referents within the "governor" frame. But the "psychiatrist" frame contains the propositions questioned as part of the knowledge we have of psychiatrist's terms of employment. By thus juxtaposing the frames, Rosenblatt allows readers to conclude that the psychiatrist might be tempted to retain his old terms of employment in his new job, and that such a course of action might not be in the public's best interest. Grice's example of the professor who, in writing a letter of recommendation, violates the first quantity maxim by not commenting on the applicant's skill at philosophy (#5) is also facilitated by a frame that explains what information is necessary: letters of recommendation are characterized by their containing information bearing on the subject of the letter's qualifications for the position in question.

Invoking the relation maxim as a way of implicating meanings is facilitated by a fundamental convention of written discourse: the presumption that all propositions in a single text are somehow related. Coherence is largely an inference writers allow readers to make, as van Dijk explains: "Linear coherence . . . depends on interpolated propositions that remain implicit in the expressed discourse and are inferred from the other propositions of the discourse with the help of lexical meaning postulates and frame information" (1977, 18). Here's an example (#6) of a text that invokes the maxim of relation in that its individual propositions do not seem to cohere:

> A woman was murdered in this room last year. The police suspected her husband. The butcher knife turned up in the garden two months after her death. But the real killer was never found.

Propositions that remain implicit in this text are that the woman's husband was suspected of her murder and that the murder was done with a

butcher knife. Readers, because of the text coherence convention, assume the sentences are meant to be related and use the "murder" frame
evoked in the first sentence to assign roles to the husband and the butcher
knife and reasons for the action of the police.[16] (The "marriage" frame
also helps explain why the police suspected the husband.) The implicit
propositions are what the writer has implicated.

Written texts that do not state their central point often implicate
it. The convention of text coherence not only demands that all propositions in a text be related but also demands that there be some proposition to which all other propositions in the text can be related. If such
a proposition is not stated in the text, the writer fails to fulfill the first
maxim of quantity. Reviewers often implicate their judgment of the work
they are reviewing via this route. Robert MacKenzie began a review of
the television show "The Life and Times of Grizzly Adams" (#7) by
posing the question, "What's in Grizzly Adams' stew?" He noted that
"this may be one television series that could be accused of unnecessary
nonviolence" and reflected on how the meat for that stew must be
procured: "when we're not looking, Grizzly Adams konks one of his little
furry friends with an ax." He concluded: "That, too, is nature" (1977).
By failing to fulfill the quantity maxim and by evoking the "predation"
frame, MacKenzie implicates that this series presents an idealized view
of nature.

In reviewing Gay Talese's *Thy Neighbor's Wife*, Harvey Mindess
also fails to fulfill the first maxim of quantity and implicates his opinion
of the value of the book (#8): that it serves best as a piece of eroticism.
He quotes a particularly vivid description of an orgy scene and says, "my
copy has margin notes: Pages 1, 11, 17, 37" (1980, 10). He repeats this
ploy three more times in the review, each time listing page numbers.
Those remarks cannot be directly related to anything Mindess says in
the review about his opinion of the book, though he does comment that
the book, "like an overrated call girl . . . fails to live up to her hype"
(1), and that the writing is on the level of *Esquire* and *Playboy*: "topical,
clever, flashy, and crass (10). But the listing of pages evokes a frame
that might be called "reading for erotic stimulation," and Mindess ex-
ploits this piece of shared knowledge to implicate what the primary value
of the book is.

A narrative convention similarly helps story writers implicate the
point or "message" of their stories. William Labov remarks that in oral
narratives he has elicited, "it is not uncommon for narrators to begin
with one or two clauses summarizing the whole story" (1972a, 363). He
calls this part of the narrative the abstract, that part which encapsulates
the point of the narrative. In written narratives, the title often serves
the function of abstract, and the propositions in the story are supposed
to be related to such a title. Thus, writers often invoke the relation

maxim in order to implicate how the story embodies the title. John Updike's story "Still of Some Use" is a good example (see #9). He tells us about the activities of a modern extended family—a divorced man, his exwife, their two almost grown sons, his exwife's new lover, and a girlfriend of the older son—in ridding an attic of old, unwanted items. In the conclusion, the man responds to the younger son's request that he come with him to the dump; the boy says it's a scary place. " 'O.K.' Foster said, greatly lightened. 'I'll protect you' " (1980, 54). How do readers understand what Updike has implicated here? They assume Foster's statement is somehow related to the title of the story, though not in a straightforward fashion; Updike apparently fails to fulfill the maxim of relation. But he evokes two frames from which readers can infer the relation: throughout the story, Foster has identified with the "forgotten, broken games" they found in the attic—of no use to his exwife and of little use to his sons, who are striving for independence. The "game" frame and the "family" frame both specify roles for players, and together the frames enable the reader to conclude that Foster is trapped in a game and role that no longer allows him to feel useful: exhusband and outgrown father. But the final incident reestablishes him in one role that fathers assume: he can still protect his younger son; he can still be of some use.[17]

A particularly interesting type of implicature in writing comes about through writers using archaic forms or dialect forms. Such forms connote a speaker of a certain time or place or role, and when the writer is not that kind of speaker, he or she fails to fulfill the first quality maxim and may implicate something. Mindess, in the review of *Thy Neighbor's Wife* discussed previously, picks up on the biblical forms *thou,* *thee,* and *thy* to implicate the sinfulness of the delights the book offers (#10): "Since [the erotic passages] are the reason thou mayst covet it, I'll tell thee where to find them. . . . I will insert the page numbers from time to time and thou canst use thy imagination" (1980, 10). MacKenzie in his review of "Grizzly Adams," also discussed previously, uses a backwoods dialect to implicate that the series, though pleasant, is misleading (#11): "Well, sir, it sure would pleasure a feller to settle back and enjoy this easygoing, outdoorsy NBC series, if it wasn't for this question that keeps on a-naggin' me" (1977).

Other aspects of linguistic form may also draw attention to maxim violations. Punctuation marks signal meaning relationships and thus specify that certain clauses should be related. The colon, for example, "indicates that the next clause to come will clarify, expand, or illustrate the idea just mentioned" (Glorfeld, Lauerman, and Stageberg 1977, 31). When the clause following the colon does not seem to be related to the clause preceding the colon, the writer may evoke the maxim of relation. Here's an example (#12) from some examination instructions: "Be as *complete and specific* in your answers as possible: I am not a mind reader." By referring to the "communication" frame (a part of which I am attempting to explicate in this chapter) and to the "examination" frame, readers understand that the writer has implicated that she will not grant credit to implicit propositions in answers to the questions on the exam.

Throughout his novel *Breakfast of Champions*, Kurt Vonnegut uses the past tense to signal an invocation of the second quantity maxim that you not supply more information than is needed (#13). I'll cite just three examples: above a drawing of a revolver, he writes, "This was a tool whose only purpose was to make holes in human beings" (1973, 49); above a representation of Einstein's formula, he writes, "I wrote again on my tabletop, scrawled the symbols for the interrelationship between matter and energy as it was understood in my day" (241); and under a drawing of a handshake, he writes, "This was a symbol of friend-ship between men" (276). Readers in 1973, when this book was pub-lished, need to have none of these things explained. But if they hypothesize a time frame in which Vonnegut's statements are cooperative and do fulfill the second quantity maxim, they can work out what he is impli-cating: that when the present time is past time, these things will need to be explained to readers, and thus that the intended readers for this book are not the readers who are currently reading it—a rather unsettling message.

The use of negation may mark a failure to fulfill the second quantity maxim, because usually to say that something did not happen is to say something more than is required. Labov takes note of the use of negation in narration: "What reason would the narrator have for telling us that something did not happen, since he is in the business of telling us what did happen? . . . The use of negatives in accounts of past events . . . expresses the defeat of an expectation that something would happen" (1972a, 380–81). A current ad for Boise Cascade Corporation (#14) implicates its message in this way. They ask, "Can you find the glue in this tree?" then add, "We at Boise Cascade haven't been able to . . . yet." The glue they're looking for, they explain, is lignin, which could replace the oil-based glues now used to stick plywood together. Why would Boise Cascade want to tell us they have not lived up to their expectations of themselves? We have only to refer to the "corporate image" frame to discover what they are implicating: corporations that aspire to better our lives through research are good corporations.

Advertisers are particularly apt to use implicatures to convey their meanings, since one of the benefits of such indirect communication is that speakers or writers cannot be held accountable for what they im-plicate in the same way they are held accountable for the conventional meaning of their utterances or texts. My final example of an implicature in writing (#15) is found in a current series of ads for Winston cigarettes, which proclaim, "Nobody does it better." Because the referent for the pronoun *it* is not supplied, the statement fails to fulfill the manner maxim that enjoins perspicuity. The advertisers evoke at least three frames on the basis of which an implicature can be worked out. The "product" frame allows the inference that no one produces better cigarettes. The "worker" frame evoked by the photographs of hard-hatted men allows the inference that Winston smokers are good workers. And the "sexual relations" frame, evoked by the allusion to the popular song from which the line comes, allows the inference that Winston smokers are good lovers. The last two inferences are less clearly cases of implicature in that it is doubtful that the advertisers intend readers to make the inferences consciously; the strategy does not have the quality of openness that marks most implicatures.

Certainly writers need much skill and much knowledge of all aspects of the context of their writing to convey their meanings in this indirect way. Many inexperienced writers are misunderstood because their attempted implicatures rely on contextual knowledge that readers do not possess. For example, in a letter to the editor about the language problem in Southern California, David Arthur attempts to ask a rhetorical question: "Is it unrealistic for me to assume a businessman and his employees should be able to communicate in English to their customers?" (1980). Rhetorical questions fail to fulfill the first quality maxim. The writer is not looking for an answer to the question; rather, he is implicating that the answer to his question is obvious—all residents of Southern California should be able to communicate in English. But this implicature depends on his readers sharing his opinion that bilingualism is detrimental to a society. Readers like me who do not share this belief may read his question as a real question, answer it in the affirmative, and infer that the writer is a provincial bigot. All teachers of composition are familiar with students who try, and fail, to be ironic or sarcastic in their writing. They are not yet acquainted with the formal written markers of such intentions, nor with the genre conventions that can signal such intentions, nor are they proficient in ascertaining and exploiting their readers' beliefs. This is the goal of all the exercises in editing, imitating models, and analyzing audiences. For when writers have mastered these special skills, they can then use them to communicate as flexibly, subtly, and economically as they do in speaking. Implicatures represent an especially effective communicative strategy, and because they depend so heavily on mastery of the conventions of writing, as well as on beliefs about the world, and on knowledge of the audience's beliefs, they are among the last strategies writers acquire.

Marilyn M. Cooper

Notes

1. See Grice (1982): "I don't think that meaning is essentially connected with convention" (238). Still, in this essay he equates meaning with the "particular intentions on particular occasions it is proper for [speakers] to have, or optimal for them to have" (239), a move which casts doubt on intention (at least in Grice's usage) as a purely cognitive category.
2. Cf. Steinmann 1982.
3. Three of the lectures have been published separately; see Grice (1969; 1975; 1978).
4. For a more complete discussion of the status and applicability of Grice's maxims, see my *Implicatures in Dramatic Conversations*.
5. Cf. Young, Becker, and Pike: "The writer's goal is to engage in some sort of cooperative activity with the reader" (1970, 171).
6. Michael Hancher (1978) explains that an implicature that involves no maxim violation "simply *invokes a maxim* as a ground of interpretation."
7. Carroll 1976, 71–72. My thanks to Michael Hancher for this example.
8. Pinter 1961, 43. My thanks to Ralph Chapman (1978) for this example.
9. See Searle (1969, 30).
10. Grice calls a situation in which a maxim is violated to avoid violating another maxim a clash (1975, 49). Here I extend the notion of a clash to include situations in which maxims clash with any other belief or convention.
11. As Grice points out, metaphors "characteristically involve categorical falsity" (1975, 53); he says that they convey meaning by flouting the first quality maxim. I would argue that the maxim violation simply marks the presence of a metaphor (and not all metaphors violate the quality maxim); it does not define the nature of metaphor.
12. Numbers key the examples to Table 8–1 (pp. 123–25), where all implicatures are outlined schematically for ease of comparison.
13. Frame theorists assume that the knowledge contained in frames is conventional in the sense that such knowledge relies on perceptions of the world rather than on objective fact. This sense of *convention* is much broader than that assumed by many language theorists and defined by David Lewis (1969).
14. For a more complete discussion of irony and the quality maxim see Robert L. Brown, Jr. (1980).
15. For a parallel example in spoken discourse, see Grice (1975, 53–54).
16. Case grammars, like those proposed by Charles Fillmore and by Wallace Chafe, are a kind of frame analysis of linguistic semantics—they seek to explain how certain beliefs about the world are encoded in language. If these relations are considered to be part of the conventions of the language, the implicatures here are examples of what Grice calls conventional implicatures, implicatures determined by "the conventional meanings of the words used" (Grice 1975, 44).
17. Mary Louise Pratt (1977) explains implicatures in "the literary speech situation" in a significantly different way. I discuss her approach in my *Implicatures in Dramatic Conversations*.

9

The Social Context of Literacy Education

This is an essay about stories. During a break in a workshop for adult basic education teachers, a group of the teachers started trading stories about the home lives of their students. Some of the stories I heard then have found their way into this essay. Actually, I think those stories were the most valuable thing that came out of those workshops. I take that as a demonstration that conferences and workshops should consist as much as possible of breaks, meals, and receptions, when, as everyone knows, the real work gets done.

Stories are ways of organizing experience. Also, to tell a story is to materialize social interactions. As we move from the stories the teachers told that afternoon to the stories their students tell, it is appropriate to note that the stories people tell about one another are also forms of social control and, among other things, ways that communities remain coherent. Stories are often about the tension between the impulse of a community to remain as it has been and that of individuals to change their relationship to the community. This essay is one of those stories.

☐   ☐   ☐

In *Language in the Inner City* (Labov 1972a) William Labov observes that schools exist in a social context and that this context may affect the lives of students—and their decisions regarding education—more strongly than the schools themselves. Those inner city students with whom Labov was concerned who did well in school were not necessarily brighter than those who gravitated to street life and gangs. Often, those who were favorites in the classroom were eager to please their teachers precisely because they were socially maladjusted in their community.

133

Unable to form good supportive networks within their community, they were compelled to weave life-lines in the school. In "Teaching Is Remembering" (p. 226) I refer to a similar phenomenon, that of the intermediate group of students who go to school, but who characteristically spend their time in the back of the classroom, laughing, sleeping, indicating in these and other ways their lack of interest in education or in its forms. Having seen how important Labov's insights are to educational theory within traditional school settings, I was not surprised to find them equally applicable with young adult students in the California Conservation Corps and, more recently, with minority female single parents enrolled in employment skills training programs offered by a national group of community-based organizations funded by the Rockefeller Foundation. The lessons learned in these contexts can be applied in other nontraditional settings and also might be helpful in the schools themselves.

One of the greatest problems for these adult students is the resistance of their children to their efforts to complete their education. The eleven-year-old child of a woman enrolled in a job training program who reacts to her mother's absence from home by staying home herself is realizing the social imperative that the woman's place is in the home, filling that place herself as a demonstration of complex feelings only partially psychological. Startled to find herself in competition with her mother in the area of schooling, unable to compete with her mother's interest in an activity that she feels as the obstruction of desire, the daughter responds by a literal reversal of roles, displacing as she has been displaced. Sometimes she attaches feelings to these actions, expressing resentment or jealousy; often she merely performs them, her dream of a housekeeper, sleepwalking through the gestures of domesticity. These ritualistic actions are the pure manifestation of the socially constituted self inhabiting the body of the girl with the ruthlessness of a biological imperative. The girl dreams a domesticity uniting duty and desire, preparing those meals for herself which she would not otherwise be home to eat, cleaning a house not otherwise inhabited, satisfying her own filial needs evoked by this redundant maternity. She models the life her mother has abandoned. Confronted by those gestures—which are merely one example of many, all of which might be translated by the challenge: "Who do you think you are, girl?"—her mother is forced into a dialogue with her own expectations.

I quote here, selected more or less at random, passages of writing by women in the Rockefeller Foundation Literacy Program. They are not instances of the role switching of mother and daughter, that nearly melodramatic theoretical crux. They simply represent a certain type of life in which that role switching might occur. Both these women are mothers who have sought out employment skills training. The first describes an earlier period in her life:

> I was introduced to bam, it was something new to me. I've never even heard of the drug. I didn't even know the effects it could have on a person, to tell you the truth I didn't even care because I actually enjoyed what I was doing, the high was so good I wanted more and then more. days started going by, months started going by and then years started going by. Before I knew it I was shooting herion and cocain. I started hanging around with that crowd of people. I didn't even realize that I had quit school.

"I didn't even realize that I had quit school." Many of these stories are about sleepwalking, about the absence of decisions. Notice the opposition between "people" and school here: "I started hanging around with that crowd of people." "I didn't even realize that I had quit school." Soon enough the tension between "that crowd of people" and school vanishes as drugs and the prostitution that follows remove school from the realm of possibility.

I think the following statement was copyedited before I received it, but maybe not. This woman has more control over her life than the first:

> About two years ago I gave birth to my son. I am unmarried, and was very scared at the time. My son's father left me, I was three months pregnant with no money and no where to stay. Luckily for me my mother gave me a place to live in her home, but she charged me $200.00 a month. . . . I realized that I really had no skills in what I really wanted to accomplish in my life, for myself and my son. . . .

Those who are successful to any extent in emerging from these circumstances are first successful by a process of individuation resulting from such a dialogue with themselves. This dialogue is made possible by a certain difference, the difference between the socially constituted self and those factors that have formed an individualized ego strong enough to enable her to seek education, job training, literacy. That ego is, in most cases, fragile, a minor quarrel with the world formed by the life around her, a quarrel that is immensely energy consuming. The disruption that it forms is dangerous, a separation from all that makes life possible at the margin: the material and emotional support of friends and family, the internal sense of doing what is right—that is, acceptable. The young woman who linked her drug use to "hanging around with that crowd" soon went back to it. The author of the second statement was luckier:

she found an organization that offered her many kinds of support for her efforts to make a decent life for herself and her son.

In the Bronx and Brooklyn, in Atlanta and Providence, teachers work for school boards that often seem unconcerned with education, in buildings more or less weatherproof, with supervisors who . . . well, who may not be doing their best, and with students who must learn to write and read or they may die much sooner than otherwise necessary. And then there are those teachers who do not work for school boards but for other agencies, for jobs programs—public and private—for unions, in the prisons. Their students, for instance minority women with children, attend classes as part of an elaborate survival plan. The English class will qualify them for the GED class, which will qualify them for the word-processing class, which . . . but wouldn't it be easier just to get pregnant again and qualify for both more welfare money and a form of tacit approval from the neighborhood? Or become a drug addict, or become a prostitute, or do all these things? Not much of this is explicit. But people understand these things, understand their necessity, and see them as the externalization of that desperation that is the consequence of a reasonable analysis of life for those at the margin. To reject all this, to live a life different, no matter how slightly, from those around one, is to reject those around one, to risk being rejected by them.

In a world characterized by forms of domination, the social condition requiring the least energy is that of maximum exploitation. There is no tension between this ideal figure—the whore (of either sex)—and the expectations of the social world, "that crowd of people." Of course this is a negative ideal, the implication of the subculture in its own domination acted out through the bodies of its weakest members. Reduced to the undeniable individuality of the physical, the whore is infinitely exchangeable. Nothing is confusing, everything is clear, each gesture is the expression of pure externality. The drug addict is another such figure of complete domination. In these instances the self is completely reduced to its socially constituted aspect as an organ of the subculture, a function that rejects all mobility and limits all action to sterile reproduction, repetition. Combined, as they usually are, the figures of the drug addict and the prostitute are those of pure authenticity, measures of an absolute zero of self from which we can count the possibilities of the human. And yet even a prostitute addicted to drugs is still part of a community, still draws upon that community for material and emotional support. If she begins to work on a GED, if she does what is not frequently done in the community, she is no longer of the community. WHO DO YOU THINK YOU ARE, GIRL? She must have another community if she is to continue to reach toward a more fully human life. If this is true for her, then it is also true for any one of the majority of people living at this margin who are not prostitutes, not addicts, not yet dropouts. Those who would help them must help them with this also, surely must not deny its presence in the classroom whenever they enter it.

If we are to help people remain in school, if we are to educate those who do, if we are to encourage those who return to some form of schooling after dropping out, we must match the strength of that resistance to schooling. Just as every manifestation of the system of domination is in a sense a replication of the entire system, so every human interaction, insofar as it is human, presents the possibility of human freedom. The point is to make human interactions possible by forming socially beneficial equivalents of gangs, neighborhoods, and street-corner associations that will enable those who are not encouraged by their cultural environment to value schooling to do so. Only in schools are people who fail to decode a text not helped by those around them. ("This is a test.") Is it only in schools that to laugh with friends is a form of aggression? No, probably not, but it sometimes seems so. Lee Leeson, then director of the U.S.C. Writing Project, found teachers spending three-quarters of their communication effort in disciplinary comments and other attempts at getting the attention of their students. Rather than searching for ways to make them be quiet, we should find ways to have their talk—that socially binding talk—work for them, educationally as well as socially. We should find ways to make the schoolroom a reasonable alternative to the street as a survival vehicle, in the short term as well as in the long term.

The resistance to schooling in the inner cities and similar communities is a message. It says that in these cases education is best organized socially, not instrumentally, that it should be centered on the needs of students living in a community rather than on the bureaucratic rationalization of standardized time allocations, curricula, personnel regulations. Our efforts should be directed toward the satisfaction of human needs. They should include at least the following four basic points.

1. *The basic unit of educational organization should be the group of teachers.* If teachers feel alienated from one another and from that which they teach, how are students to feel otherwise? Teachers should be given the opportunity to work together to devise and select curricula and materials. They should have real authority in this as well as adequate support in terms of further education and consultants. Administrators, from department heads to school superintendents, should see themselves as—and should act as—support personnel for teachers. For instance, teachers, rather than counselors or principals, should have authority over scheduling, so that a class can run two hours if necessary, or twenty minutes, if that is enough.

Teachers may model community learning behavior by working together in one another's classrooms, talking with one another, helping one another help students to learn.

2. *Classes should be organized as work groups.* A class, in a school, is all too often the opposite of a group. It is an aggregate of people who, nonetheless, are not individuals. When a classroom is organized in such a way as to be a setting for groups, the people there can work at becoming individuals, using the support they offer one another to take the place of that support from the neighborhood which a commitment to schooling may sacrifice. Those with whom our students are literate may become that group upon which they rely for community support as they attempt to tear themselves out of an unfavorable position on the social network. It is possible to encourage members of a class to be friends with one another, to see one another outside of school hours, to give one another the approval and active help that is necessary if schooling is to be successful under the incredibly difficult conditions that form the day-to-day environment of those who as adults require literacy education, of those who as children live in places where to stay in school seems unimaginable. Some of the teachers of adults I have worked with tell me that they encourage students to have their children join with them in extracurricular literacy activities, jointly authoring family journals, say, or stories for one another, or letters to one another. In the same way, in places where it is appropriate and not yet the case, the friends and lovers and husbands and parents of our students may similarly join them in extracurricular literacy activities. (The Vai, we are told by Scribner and Cole [1981] use literacy for virtually nothing other than these extracurricular family and group activities. Not surprisingly, it may take them only six weeks to become literate in their script.)

3. *We should stop doing harm if we can help it.* In the classroom itself we can begin by simply ceasing to do those things that are most oppressive to teachers and students, that most strictly enforce the literacy system as a device for excluding people. We can stop lecturing about English conjugations. We can stop giving spelling tests to people who will not write sentences for fear of misspelling words. These particular ideas are now commonplaces in many schools and yet in others, particularly in Adult Education centers and GED classes, it is still necessary to point them out.

4. *Student work groups should share the tasks of education and everyday life.* It may be less common, but at least as valuable, to encourage group authorship—the distribution of the writing process among several students or groups of students, so that one drafts a text or part of a text, another edits it, a third checks spelling and format

—as if the writing task in the classroom were as real as it is in the newsroom, say, or in any literate segment of our culture. This may lead to the production of reading texts by the students themselves. Again, working together on literacy skills in the classroom, students may find themselves helping one another in this and other ways outside the classroom. They may form school-based alternatives to traditional neighborhood structures supporting food, housing, transportation, and childcare needs or offering other forms of mutual assistance, such as friendship. If so, they then may be able to bring that community back into the classroom. Laughter may spread from the back rows all around the room, becoming the sign of learning itself. We may wish to work toward the achievement of the noisy classroom. (Foucault [1972] tells us that the silence of groups is the peculiar mark of the modern prison.) The literacy crisis in this country is part of a larger social crisis. Its solution must also be social, must begin with viewing the classroom as a social entity in a context of other, larger, social entities.

Many minority communities support the educational aspirations of their members. Many actively resist the degradation of language promoted by advertising, politics, and segments of the entertainment industry. Any particular school is likely to be at least partially staffed with teachers who are already aware of much of what I have written here. Those good teachers, those concerned communities, will devise other, more specific and better ways than those I have thought of to help shatter the protective and constraining defenses of the functionally illiterate. If these efforts are themselves linked to other, similar efforts and fostered by school boards, schools of education, foundations, and governmental agencies, much can be accomplished.

As I have learned more about people who are not well schooled, I have become convinced of how crucial it is for us to understand the social psychology of individual and community resistance to schooling. Listening to this resistance, we learn about our students, about our society, perhaps about ourselves. We may be able to develop effective classroom practices that use the dynamics of that resistance. But if we merely try to overcome it, we learn nothing and we shall probably fail in our efforts. I believe that this resistance is the internalization—the introjection—of the external forms of domination experienced by marginalized groups in our society. It is not that people simply decide to join gangs, get pregnant at an early age and repeatedly, become prostitutes, become drug addicts. It is not that children simply decide to become school drop-outs. These decisions are the result of the intersection of forces at many levels: psychology, physiology, family, subculture, society. As such, they are in a way rational—a reasonable, or at least logical, reaction to the historical experience of people who belong to the groups most severely oppressed in our society. Resistance to the institutions of the dominant society, of which school is merely one, is a form of group identification, a qualification for that material and emotional support from the community that makes life possible, if barely tolerable, at the margin. Once we realize that these are not random, perverse actions, we will seek to match the real material and social benefits of resistance to education while avoiding its severe cultural and economic drawbacks. We will emphasize group work that promotes a new sense of community rather than isolated study, and we will integrate school life with life outside of school for both our students and ourselves. It is vital to recognize that all too often the organization of literacy education, of schooling in general, in this country is at the service of institutional or bureaucratic rather than human priorities. Failure to recognize this, which amounts to a failure to treat students as human beings rather than as functions in a social system, contributes significantly to the failure of educational and social initiatives. It also contributes significantly to the sum of human misery.

Michael Holzman

10

Women's Ways of Writing

One of the most persistent problems we encounter as writing teachers is the seeming inability of some students to learn to do the kind of writing we want them to do. Even after two quarters or semesters of writing instruction, many first-year students still cannot analyze ideas complexly or argue positions logically; in other words, they do not take well or easily to academic discourse. Two ways of looking at this problem have been proposed. One view is that students who do not do well in writing classes think differently than other students—and they think differently than we do. It might be that these students are at a relatively immature stage of cognitive development (as a reading of William Perry might suggest), or it might be that they have different cognitive styles (as the Myers/Briggs test suggests). The other view is that these students fail to adapt easily to academic discourse because they come from a different community and it is difficult for them to accept the different values and projects of the scholarly community (see Bartholomae 1985; Bizzell 1986).

Assuming one of these views in isolation—either the theory of cognitive deficit or the theory of social difference—will yield radically different classroom practices. In this essay I suggest that the two views might better be considered as complementary. Students—people in general—do think differently and write differently, but these differences are neither immutable nor exclusive; so-called cognitive stages are adaptations to social environments, and as people are exposed to different environments, they develop a repertoire of ways of thinking that are adaptive to (or at least associated with) the variety of intellectual environments they encounter.

The more immediate concern of this essay is how differences in the way women think might motivate different strategies for teaching women to write. In particular, I am interested in how a writing program might help women who have suffered emotional and physical abuse. In planning a program for a shelter for abused women I was led to a recent study of intellectual development in women: *Women's Ways of Knowing: The Development of Self, Voice, and Mind.* The authors' account of their interviews with women in a variety of life situations stimulated my thoughts on both these subjects: how intellectual development and social situation are related and how one might best go about introducing writing activities to abused women. The essay that resulted thus takes the form of a reading of this book.

□   □   □

In a recent review of a history of family violence, Kenneth Keniston concluded, "Contemporary feminist scholarship suggests that even if gender is not the Rosetta stone, it is more than just another variable" (Keniston 1988, 12). The truth of this remark is amply demonstrated in a study by Mary Field Belenky, Blythe McVicker Clinchy, Nancy Rule Goldberger, and Jill Mattuck Tarule, reported in *Women's Ways of Knowing: The Development of Self, Voice, and Mind.* Inspired by the work of William Perry and Carol Gilligan, Belenky and her colleagues set out to investigate how and whether women's intellectual development differs from that of men. The differences they found, however, did not simply complement Perry's developmental scheme, which was based on interviews with male Harvard undergraduates. Instead, bringing in the variable of gender led them to question the status of Perry's scheme and to conclude that it represented not a universal developmental sequence but rather changes in a particular group of people in a very particular situation:

> What we believe Perry heard in his interviews with men and captured so well in his developmental scheme is the way in which a relatively homogeneous group of people are socialized into and make sense of a system of values, standards, and objectives. The linear sequence in development stands out clearly when the context in which development occurs is held constant. (1986, 15)[1]

Interested in general patterns of how women learn, Belenky and her colleagues included in their study not only college women but also women enrolled in programs in parenting. Designed and run by women, these programs and the women whom they serve are not often studied, and their inclusion in this study highlighted the extent to which Perry's results were closely tied to a particular context. Noting the dominant influence of the Harvard environment on Perry's students, they argue: "When the context is allowed to vary, as it did in our study, because we included women of widely different ages, life circumstances, and backgrounds, universal developmental pathways are far less obvious" (15). Similarly, they became "uneasy" with Kohlberg and Mayer's "natural directions" of development, noting that the results of their own study suggest that "directions then assumed to be natural do not come naturally to many women" (228–29).

These observations led them to a more complex view of intellectual development, one that recognizes the effect of social factors both on the ways of thinking that develop and on the trajectory of development. Thus, instead of offering a universal developmental scheme, these authors describe five epistemological perspectives, or positions, that the women they interviewed demonstrate. They claim for these perspectives no more than explanatory usefulness: "these five ways of knowing are not necessarily fixed, exhaustive, or universal categories" (15). Their caution is especially wise in view of the complexity of the picture they paint. For, as they discuss the experiences of the various women, they note that gender interacts with social class, dominant cultural expectations, educational structures, family roles, and patterns of abuse and violence in determining women's ways of knowing.

Partly for methodological reasons—most women were interviewed only once—Belenky and her colleagues for the most part decline to consider these positions as linear stages in development. They criticize Perry's belief "that each position is an advance over the last" (14) and confine themselves to speculating "about different developmental sequences or trajectories" (15). The perspectives are defined predominantly on the basis of the women's attitudes toward the self, toward language, and toward learning or knowledge.

In the position of *silence* women respond to language but do not see it as a means of coming to know the world or themselves. They live in a world of little or no conversation: language directed at them is used to give orders or to vent anger, and they are often punished for speaking. Deprived of talking back and forth, sharing and comparing ideas and viewpoints, they fail to develop representational thought fully. As a result, they do not realize that their babies' cries might have different meanings; they do what they are told to do; they do not know who they are because "No one has told me yet what they thought of me" (31). They become isolated, cut off from their community, their family, and their own selves.

In the position of *received knowledge* women learn by listening to others. They look to authorities to tell them what is true, and they learn by committing these truths to memory. They see the world in terms of either/or: either something is true or it is false; either something is good or it is bad; either I succeed and you fail or you succeed and I fail (and women tend to choose to let others succeed). They define themselves in terms of social expectations and standard roles and occupations, and they see themselves as static, not adaptable and liable to change.

In the position of *subjective knowledge* women learn from first-hand experience. "Truth now resides within the person and can negate answers that the outside world supplies" (54). They listen to their "inner voice" that tells them the truth in terms of feeling. They reject external ideas, logic, analysis, abstraction, and language, all of which belong to men. They reject social expectations and roles and define themselves negatively against these expectations. And, again, they are isolated, "stubbornly committed to their view of things and unwilling to expose themselves to alternative conceptions" (83–84).

In the position of *procedural knowledge* women learn "that the inner voice sometimes lies" (99) and that knowledge depends on correct procedures. The procedures may be the impersonal ones of a discipline (separate knowing) or the general one of empathy (connected knowing), but both allow women to see the world through a different lens. They think for themselves, using these procedures; they do not blindly obey authority, but they do feel obliged to please authorities by using correct procedures for knowing. Their selves, thus, are subordinated to whatever systems that define their thinking: "procedural knowers feel like chameleons" (129).

Finally, in the position of *constructed knowledge* women learn to create their own contextual frames for knowing. They are aware of their own ways of thinking and judging; they are tolerant of contradictions and ambiguities; they demand complexity in the models of experience they construct. Their ways of learning and their self-concepts come together; they are "passionate knowers, knowers who enter into a union with that which is to be known" (141). They value conversation, which is based on reciprocity and cooperation, over debate. They are connected with others and with their community.

Throughout this account of the epistemological perspectives, Belenky and her colleagues use the metaphor of development as a journey: women "move on" (51) or take "another step toward" maturity (55); they are "woman sojourners . . . committed to continuing their developmental journey" (80). But for most of these women, the journey does not take them far. The authors' strongest claim for a developmental sequence comes in their discussion of women in the position of procedural knowledge: "We know from earlier interviews with the women in this [position] or from their own retrospective accounts that most of them once relied on a mixture of received and subjective knowledge, looking to feeling and intuition for some of the answers they needed and to external authorities for others" (87–88). And, though women in other positions also report having acquired different ways of knowing, and though adjacent positions seem logically related, Belenky and her colleagues find no evidence that the different positions represent a continuous developmental path. None of the women they interviewed seem to have moved through all the positions in sequence, and "only a few —usually with the help of supportive friends, neighbors, and excellent schools—were able to move far beyond the epistemological atmospheres depicted in their family histories" (155).

Instead, the authors insist that any developmental sequence must be individual and is highly conditioned by social environment: "The eventual path a woman takes is, in large measure, a function of the familial and educational environments in which she is struggling with these problems" (79). In their chapter on family life they address this question directly. They note a division between the daughters of unhappy families, who for the most part were silent or received knowers, and the daughters of happy families, who were mostly procedural or constructed knowers. Pace Tolstoy, unhappy families are as much alike as happy families, they claim.

The authors characterize the differences between unhappy and happy families by focusing on the way the families talk amongst themselves. In families disrupted by violence and drug and alcohol abuse and unsupported by economic privilege, dialogue is a rarity. Women in the most chaotic families "essentially lived their lives in silence or din" (158); as the people who addressed these women had no expectations of their responding to the content of the language addressed at them, they themselves developed no notion of language as a means of affecting others' behavior or of learning about the world. In families where talk—as opposed to emotionally laden noise—occurred, the conversations were one way: parents telling children (or husbands telling wives) what they needed to know. Talk in these families was a means of imparting information, not of developing understanding. Women in particular suffer from this unequal distribution of access to language; one woman commented, "Women were more or less to be seen and not heard. The men were supposed to be the ones with the voice of the family" (165). Women with such backgrounds not surprisingly come to believe that knowledge is a one-way process too: they can learn what they are told (received knowers), or they can rebel and rely simply on what they know from experience (subjective knowers).

In contrast, talk in happy families is characterized by two-way dialogue in which equality, exchange of perspectives, and understanding of other points of view is valued. And the daughters of happy families develop the perspectives of procedural and constructed knowledge. Belenky and her colleagues point out that "while not all these women came from happy homes, they were much more likely than the women who held other perspectives to describe family relationships characterized by images of connection, care, mutuality, and reciprocity" (176). Families that talk together have no need to rely on violence or abandonment to resolve their differences, and daughters in these families learn to use language as a means of connecting with social structures and of coming to know themselves and their world.

The impact of family situation—and of academic experiences—on development was noted in the discussions of all the epistemological perspectives and particularly in discussions of how transitions from one perspective to another were made. All of the silent women who were interviewed were abused by their husbands and/or parents. It is not surprising that women who have been taught to feel powerless in the home see themselves as incapable of thinking for themselves and dependent on those who have power for their identity and for their very lives. One woman said:

> I didn't think I had a right to think. That probably goes back to my folks. When my father yelled, everybody automatically jumped. Every woman I ever saw, then, the man barked and the woman jumped. I just thought that women were no good and had to be told everything to do. (30)

For those who are outside this perspective, such views may seem irrational, for these women often provide the only stability the family has in terms of income and daily care. But to claim abilities for themselves, people need validation from others; when their families—and many aspects of the culture at large—deny them this, they cannot develop any sense of themselves as effective actors in their own life without sustained support from friends, teachers, or others.

In interviews with women in the position of subjective knowledge, the authors again note a common family environment: "A large number of women we classified as subjectivists or as moving into subjectivism grew up without the protection of a father due to early divorce, neglect, or abandonment" (57). The societally reinforced belief in the male head of the family as the source of security was undermined by their experience, and they often felt angry and betrayed. When this sense of "*failed* male authority" (57) was "coupled with some confirmatory experience that they, too, could know something for sure" (58), these women could move from the perspective of received knowledge, in which all knowledge is seen to derive from authorities, to the perspective of subjective knowledge, in which knowledge derives from the self. Interestingly, this move parallels Perry's shift out of dualism, but as the authors point out, for the women they interviewed, the shift most often preceded their return to educational institutions rather than being stimulated by academic experience.

In contrast, the women they interviewed who were in the position of procedural knowledge noted the presence of "benign authorities" in their lives; the authors argue that "some trust in authority. . . . may be critical to the development of the voice of reason" (90). Again, most of the women who shared this perspective also shared the same social environment: "privileged, bright, white, and young" "attending or . . . recently graduated from prestigious colleges" (85). The systems of family and/or education worked well for them. "They had a lot to lose" (90) in completely rejecting these social structures in favor of the inner voice of subjectivism, and they had a lot to gain and a lot of support in entering into dialogue with the voices of authority they encountered. For these women, the potentially isolating perspective of subjectivism, in which all ideas and opinions from outside sources are rejected, develops into the more public and connected perspective of procedural knowledge by explicit training in the socially accepted procedures of knowing. These women are too well valued by their families and by society to be lost.

But the women themselves may lose something in the process, "particularly if [they] have learned the lesson of 'weeding out the self,' which our academic institutions so often teach" (136). Though women in the position of procedural knowledge are active knowers, unlike women in the position of received knowledge, both perspectives value external sources of truth over the inner voice that emerges so forcefully in the position of subjectivism. To find this inner voice of the self, procedural knowers must get outside the systems of thought that define them "as a woman with a man's mind" (134).

These observations of the correlations between family background and epistemological perspectives directly raise the difficult question of how and why social environments affect development. The authors note that, "given that we have been describing frameworks for meaning-making that evolve and change rather than personality types that are relatively permanent, it is curious that people who share an epistemological position would have so much family history in common" (155–56). They admit that this result might be an artifact of the data, that women speaking from within the same epistemological perspective will be likely to remember and describe their family situations in terms of that perspective. But they also suggest a variety of alternative explanations: that early family experiences limit developmental possibilities, that the interaction between children and parents stimulates development in both, that the economic status of a woman's family shapes her developmental trajectory. The first of these possibilities—that families limit the development of their children—has already been demonstrated, and the impact of children on their mothers' development is noted in the book only in passing, most notably when the authors observe that being responsible for a dependent infant may lead a woman to question the perspective of silence.

The third possibility merits further analysis. Particularly in discussing the differences between unhappy and happy families, the authors emphasize the effect of social class on a woman's path of development: "when poor families fail their children, the society provides precious little help; while children of privilege are more likely to find rich sources of sustenance to promote their development elsewhere" (160). But they seem to ascribe the differences in life chances simply to economic factors, ignoring for the most part the systematic patterns of discrimination against lower classes in our society. The interaction of economic and social factors is apparent in the contrasting stories they tell of two women whose fathers abused them sexually. When the woman in the poor family finally reported the abuse, her father was jailed and she was placed in a series of foster homes and residential schools where she received no effective education or counseling. The woman in the privileged family also reported her abuse, but her father was not jailed, of course, and she was not removed from his care. Though she received little from him that was good for her emotionally, his financial and social status allowed her to receive the benefits of excellent counselors and caring teachers, several of whom served as a "surrogate family" for her. "Having cultivated her capacities as a knower, she could make sense of her experience, put it in perspective, and move on. . . . The daughter from the poor family, having no inkling that hearts and minds could be opened, walks nowhere" (162).

If money cannot buy individual happiness, it certainly can buy conditions that make the development of happy lives more probable. In this regard, the division between unhappy and happy families, and the division between women in the positions of silence or received knowledge and women in the positions of procedural knowledge or constructed knowledge seems to be very closely tied to economic status. For the women in the positions of procedural and constructed knowledge not only come from predominantly happy families, they also come from predominantly privileged families. Families with money send their daughters to prestigious colleges that stimulate the development of these perspectives; parents from these families have also usually attended the same schools and thus have learned ways of thinking and talking that they use to avoid violent solutions to differences.

The patterns of development also bear out this economic class division. Daughters from poor and unhappy families may move from the perspective of silence and received knowledge to the perspective of subjective knowledge, but rarely do they move into the other perspectives. Daughters from privileged and happy families rarely acquire the perspectives of silence or received knowledge, and typically, through the influence of their education and their parents, move quickly out of the perspective of subjective knowledge to the perspective of procedural knowledge, and sometimes to the perspective of constructed knowledge. Inez, from a poor family, was abused by her father as a child and by her husband as an adult. She had by the age of thirty, with the help of an aunt and some therapy, achieved a new perspective on her past and her future, and, when interviewed, she appeared to have moved out of the perspective of silence and into the perspective of subjective knowledge: "I think and feel all at the same time and I know what is right" (53). But despite the immense changes she had made in her life, she commented, "I'm just getting to the point where everybody else starts" (53). Everybody else, of course, means all those "normal" (read "privileged") daughters from happy families.

The difference between the poorer families and the more privileged families is not simply a matter of money. As Shirley Brice Heath has shown in her study of the literacy practices in three communities in the South, differences in income are related to differences in history, employment, ways of thinking, and ways of interacting in words and with words. Indeed, the differences in language interactions Belenky and her colleagues observed between the unhappy and happy families parallel in some ways the differences in literacy practices that Heath observed in two of the three communities she studied. Children in the lower middle-class families of Roadville are taught the perspective of received knowledge by their parents and in Sunday school: they learn the difference between right and wrong and that that difference is absolute, and they learn to always say the right and true thing. Peggy recounts her experience of childhood learning: "They taught us to believe that what they said was right, and we ought to learn what they said" (Heath 1983, 142). As a mother, Peggy trains her son Danny in the same way: "we talk to them kids all the time, like they was grown up or something, 'n we try to tell 'em about things. . . ." (128). Heath notes that Peggy, like the other parents in Roadville, feels "that her guidance is necessary for Danny to learn what to say, how to say it, and what to know" (128). The pattern is very much like the one-way talk Belenky and her colleagues describe as typical of families of received knowers: "These parents assumed that their daughters should and would listen to them, that they would understand them, and that they would obey" (164).

In contrast, the literacy practices of the upper middle-class townspeople are similar to the two-way talk Belenky and her colleagues observe in families of procedural and constructed knowers. Children and parents negotiate intentions and meanings together as equals in conversations; "they are trained to act as conversational partners and information-givers" (Heath 1983, 249). Similarly, procedural and constructed knowers tell stories in which "both parents and daughters were given a voice, each spoke and listened, each had an equal say" (Belenky et al. 1986, 176). Heath's townspeople also train their children to respond to writing in ways that will be valued in school, the ways of procedural knowledge: children are encouraged to relate information from written sources to situations in their daily lives and to hypothesize about what might happen in certain circumstances.

Heath's study makes clear that these differences in literacy practices are not random differences that develop merely because the two communities are separated socially from one another; instead, the practices can be related to such things as the demands of the different jobs held by people in the two communities. The fathers—and some of the mothers—in Roadville families were workers in the textile mills, and their ways of talking and knowing at home replicate patterns adapted to their relatively subservient positions in the mills. Heath notes, "From the old ways, they value church-going, respecting authority, the experience of having to work hard, and knowing how to 'keep a clean nose' [stay out of trouble]" (1983, 42). Their world is coherent and responsive to their assumption that knowledge is something one receives from others. On the job they were told what to do; in church, they were told what to believe; at home, they were told what is true. The townspeople too developed ways of talking and knowing that served them well in their work as executives in the mills: "The mill executive talks with and from written materials, following habitual ways of taking meaning from written sources and linking and extending it to shared background experiences with conversationalists" (1983, 261).[2]

To the townspeople, "these ways of thinking and behaving are natural" (262); they do not perceive them as learned strategies and find it strange that people in other communities—the white and black workers of Roadville and Trackton—do not share them. Conversely, the workers of Roadville and Trackton find the ways of talking in the mainstream community strange and do not understand why their own strategies for success do not work. Belenky and her colleagues similarly point out a "natural" relation between the perspectives of procedural and constructed knowledge and socioeconomic class:

> The perception of multiple perspectives on truth and values is almost unavoidable for advantaged children growing up today, given their opportunities for international travel, discussions and debates with worldly parents and diverse friends, the popular media, and challenging liberal education and educators. (63)

The presumed naturalness of the ways of knowing and using words associated with the privileged classes explains the presumption of a natural intellectual developmental process in which people ascend to "more mature" ways of thinking. These ways of thinking are indeed better adapted to success in a world that is structured and controlled by those who have been trained to think in these ways.

Belenky and her colleagues do not seem aware of the way a pragmatic characterization of certain perspectives as better adapted to present society slips into an idealized characterization of these perspectives as more mature. In discussing the perspective of subjective knowledge, they say "it is also another step toward the kind of maturity that we call connected knowing" (55). But they do explain why certain perspectives handicap a woman. In discussing the perspective of received knowledge, they note that "reliance on authority for a single view of the truth is clearly maladaptive for meeting the requirements of a complex, rapidly changing, pluralistic, egalitarian society and for meeting the requirements of educational institutions, which prepare students for such a world" (43). If received knowledge is not a particularly useful perspective, subjective knowledge is not much better: "Women subjectivists are at a special disadvantage . . . when they go about learning and working in the public domain" (55). In rebellion against authority, they will not consider external ideas as sources of knowledge: "You can't learn things from teachers and books like you can from experience" (74). Only to women in the perspectives of procedural and constructed knowledge does the world seem manageable: "a middle-aged Irish woman said that until recently much of the world had seemed to her 'magic,' beyond comprehension. Now that she had entered college, she was learning things she would not have believed she could learn, and the world had become reasonable" (96).

But developing these more adaptive perspectives has a price: a college education. Only one of the women the authors classified as procedural knowers had not attended college, and she had been trained in procedures of reasoning by a family counselor. The authors distinguish two methods of reasoning that are taught in schools: separate knowing, "based on impersonal procedures for establishing truth," and connected knowing, "in which truth emerges through care" or empathy (102). (They compare the two modes to Peter Elbow's doubting and believing games and Jerome Bruner's paradigmatic and narrative modes of thought.) The two methods are not equally well regarded, and they observe that separate knowing—the preferred method—is associated with attending prestigious colleges: "Teachers at traditional, rigorous, liberal arts colleges are bona fide experts with PhD's in respected disciplines who believe that it is their responsibility to teach their students methods of critical thinking, especially the methods peculiar to their disciplines. . . ." (103). Women in the perspective of constructed knowledge have also all attended college, but in order to claim their own method of knowing, they often find it necessary to get outside this context, to drop out of school and work in a grocery store or as a cook or to change occupations. Both attending college and temporarily interrupting a college education or changing prestigious occupations in mid-career (from musician to counselor, for example) are privileges not equally available to all in our society.

They are not available to the poor, to those who have attended bad schools, to those who must work for a living and support others. Again we see the effect of socioeconomic class structure on the epistemological perspectives an individual is able to develop.

The epistemological perspectives that Belenky and her colleagues describe occurring in the women they interviewed are not steps in some ideal intellectual journey; they are rather ways of thinking developed in response to particular situations, determined by a variety of complex factors, including, dominantly, those of gender and socioeconomic class. All are adaptations to particular circumstances; all are at least in part determined by the particular experiences a woman has had. And moving from one perspective to another is connected with particular experiences and changes in circumstances. As a woman moves through life, she normally encounters different people and different circumstances—she has children, she gets married, she goes to college, she seeks counseling, she gets a job—and all these things may stimulate her to develop different ways of thinking and a different view of herself. If she is lucky and persistent, she encounters people and situations that enable her to develop perspectives that help her to live a happy life, emotionally, intellectually, and economically secure. She does develop in the sense that she changes, and success stories in which women escape unhappy circumstances or move from chaotic and rebellious life-styles into lives better adapted to existing social structures motivate claims that development is good and a social necessity. And as people do not grow younger as they make these changes, development of the better adapted perspectives is often called maturity. But all of these undoubted truths do not allow us to claim that intellectual development is a natural and normal process within individuals, and that women who have not developed certain perspectives are intellectually immature.[3]

Indeed, the ways of thinking elucidated in these epistemological perspectives are perhaps better thought of as a developed repertoire of responses to immediate situations. The authors note that the perspectives are "abstract or 'pure' categories that cannot adequately capture the complexities and uniqueness of an individual woman's thought and life" (15), and that individual women often spoke in more than one "voice." In considering women in the position of constructed knowledge, they point out how a perspective can be contextually triggered:

> Some women told us, in anger and frustration, how frequently they felt unheard and unheeded—both at home and at work. In our society, which values the words of male authority, constructivist women are no more immune to the experience of feeling silenced than any other group of women" (146)

This is certainly something I have felt, and, as I read the book, I often identified with the experiences of women in all the various positions. Sometimes my marginal notes reflected a difference between something I felt in the past and what I feel now, but other times I noted that ways of thinking and feeling that were associated with different perspectives were ways of thinking and feeling I experience in particular circumstances.

Like others who have studied gender differences in development, Belenky and her colleagues argue that women in all perspectives are more strongly oriented than men to the values of caring, connection, and community (45). It is in this context that women struggle with the opposing demands of self and other, and often satisfying the demands of self leads to isolation, a loss of connectedness. On the other hand, caring and satisfying the demands of others often leads to submitting to the voice of authority, and women in our society find it difficult to align themselves with authority: experiencing encounters only with male authorities, "the women in our sample seemed to say 'Authority-right-they' " (44). Isolation characterizes the experience of women in the positions of silence, subjective knowledge, and constructed knowledge, while a feeling of being dominated by authority characterizes the experience of women in the positions of received knowledge and procedural knowledge. Because they are alienated from authority, women have a difficult time finding a role in a community that allows them to satisfy their needs for both connectedness and self-expression and effective action. It was in these experiences of isolation and domination that I noticed most particularly how the various perspectives characterized my own thinking in particular circumstances.

The authors note that subjectivist women from advantaged backgrounds are particularly fearful of the social isolation making their own choices might bring and often feel as if their lives are out of control. Often when I realize that the life I have chosen is different in many ways from that of my parents or my friends, the feeling of power and freedom this gives me is immediately replaced by the fear that I am too self-sufficient, that I will be left alone, that I am not doing the things I should be doing, that I don't know what I am doing. Equally often, however, I feel like the procedural knowers who "treated their mothers and even their friends and lovers, as well as their teachers, as authorities whom they were obliged to please" (126). Sometimes I think I will never stop the process of replacing one authority's idea of who I should be with another's idea, while at the same time fooling myself into believing that pleasing people is a good thing and that even chameleons occasionally make decisions for themselves. But, most of all, I fear that the authors are right when they conclude that "for some constructivist women, particularly those who do not shy away from speaking their minds, enduring, intimate relationships may be hard to establish" (148). I do not know if I can afford to pay the price I know others have paid—of accommodation to the status quo, to a world in which men talk and women listen.

This brings me to the second reason I found this study particularly interesting and useful. By including in their sample not only college women but also women "at the edges of the society," Belenky and her colleagues are able to suggest ways of teaching women in a variety of circumstances. And, as I am in the process of developing a writing program for a shelter for abused women, I will conclude this essay with a discussion of how the results of this study might be applied to create a writing program for women for whom "words were used to separate and diminish people: not to connect and empower them" (24).

Several suggestions for ways of proceeding in designing such a program are immediately apparent. Abused women in particular suffer from experiences of isolation and domination by authority. A writing program must aim to create a community in which women can share experiences equally and can identify with women in a position of authority. As Belenky and her colleagues note, "for women, confirmation and community are prerequisites rather than consequences of development" (194). This suggests an organization of learning around work groups, as is suggested in "The Social Context of Literacy Education" (pp. 138–39), and it suggests that all teachers, aides, and coordinators of the program should be women. Those designing and implementing the program should also be aware of their own difficulties with isolation and domination by authority and alive to their own experiences with the ways of thinking and feeling characteristic of the various perspectives. Just as abused women are found in all social classes, they may be in any of the epistemological positions Belenky and her colleagues have delineated. But their experience of abuse will make them particularly prone to attitudes toward language characteristic of silent women and received knowers.

Women in all perspectives are—and should be—wary of language. Belenky and her colleagues especially note the word phobia of subjective knowers (74–75), but as anyone who has struggled with finding an alternative to the use of 'he' as a generic pronoun knows, our language speaks in the voice of the patriarchy. Nevertheless, it is in language that we develop our sense of self and our connections with others. Silent women and received knowers, who experience mainly one-way talk, are deprived of the essential experience of sharing language:

> In order for reflection to occur, the oral and written forms of language must pass back and forth between persons who both speak and listen or read and write—sharing, expanding, and reflecting on each other's experiences. Such interchanges lead to ways of knowing that enable individuals to enter into the social and intellectual life of their community. (26)

Procedural knowers get this experience in intimate conversations with their mothers or in discussion groups in college where connected knowing is encouraged. In such situations, the meanings that language carries are negotiated among conversationalists, and authority can be seen as resting "not on power or status or certification but on commonality of experience" (118).

Such discussion groups, in which women share common experiences and feelings, can be used in shelters to help abused women develop a sense of connection and personal authority. But often, as is the case in the shelter I am working with, the population of residents is not stable enough to develop ongoing discussion groups. In this situation, I am proposing a mode of written discussion that I have used in college classes—a computer assisted common journal (see "Unhappy Consciousness in First-Year English," p. 31ff.). Women who come to the shelter can read about the experiences and feelings of previous residents and can contribute accounts of their own experiences and feelings. The use of a computer to keep the journals has the added advantage of protecting the identities of the women.

As writing teachers we believe that the activity of writing not only improves people's facility with language but also improves—or at least changes—the way they think. Similarly, Belenky and her colleagues conclude that "the women we interviewed who moved far beyond the epistemological atmospheres depicted in their histories had much in common with" a woman who "learned to immerse herself in at least one symbol system from a very early age" and that "as children these women were producers as well as consumers in the medium that they chose to develop" (162). Whether immersion in writing as an adult will have the same effect is an open question, but certainly the opportunity to share viewpoints in a safe and nurturing context will make some difference in these women's attitudes toward language.

In the final chapters of their book, Belenky and her colleagues suggest that women's ways of knowing require a reorientation of teaching if educational programs are to truly serve women. They argue that given women's dominated and powerless position in our society, education for women must be based not on the doubting game but on the believing game: "every woman, regardless of age, social class, ethnicity, and academic achievement, needs to know that she is capable of intelligent thought, and she needs to know it right away" (193). To replace the banking metaphor that Freire described as characteristic of current educational practices, they suggest the metaphor of the teacher as midwife: "midwife-teachers . . . assist the students in giving birth to their own ideas, in making their own tacit knowledge explicit and elaborating it" (217).

A shift to this mode of teaching is even more imperative in educational programs for abused and otherwise disadvantaged women. Deprived of experiences that would develop their sense of self-worth and confidence in their ability to learn, they have no resources to draw on in facing the fears of isolation and domination that beset even the most privileged women as they struggle to develop successful strategies for dealing with the world. In order to be a midwife to their ideas, a teacher must be a "benign authority," an ally, a confidante, an equal who cares for her students and believes they know something and have a voice. Only then can such women afford to question a situation in which it is all too apparent that men talk and women listen.

Marilyn M. Cooper

NOTES

1. All subsequent quotations from this book will be identified by page number only.
2. For a discussion of the relation between ways with words and social class from another perspective, see "Nominal and Active Literacy," pp. 162–63.
3. I wish to thank my colleague Cynthia Selfe for talking through with me this notion of development.

11

Nominal and Active Literacy

The dichotomy literate/illiterate is one of those oppositions obscuring more than it reveals. As part of the realm of ideology, it is therefore—I argue in the first part of this essay—simply part of our social world rather than an analysis of it. The effort to get beyond that dichotomy has been going on for some time now. Twenty years ago it was common to speak of functional literacy, a term that varied wildly according to the context. I offer here a distinction between literacy that is an integral part of everyday life, *active literacy*, and that which is purely *nominal*.

The essay begins with a discussion of the terms "ideology" and "overdetermination," a discussion that is meant to affect readings of some of our other essays as well. The essay concludes with some specific proposals about the structure of adult education programs and some general reflections about schooling and education.

☐   ☐   ☐

For the past few years I have been working with adult educators concerned with literacy, basic education, and English-as-a-second-language instruction. As historians of politics and literature tell us, there is a truth at the periphery that might not be as evident in the center. The peripheral nature of most adult education is a revealing context for the study of the process by which our society endeavors to reproduce itself. Schools in Westport or Newport, colleges in Madison or Cambridge are evidently educational institutions. But GED classes held at night in a basement in Harlem or in a youth corps barracks in the California Sierra are much more ambiguous situations. Their interpretation—their transformation—is challenging in itself and also has implications for Westport and Madison. This essay presents an outline of an approach to adult basic education that I believe can be widely applied, along with some general comments about education in and out of the schools.

My point of view in this, as in the other essays of this collection, is founded on a certain theory of culture, some aspects of which it might be best to sketch before turning to the specific issues at hand. Without plunging into a discussion of the history of the idea of culture and its place in social theory, I would like here to simply stress the utility of a theory of *ideology* that emphasizes the continuity of the psychological and the social and the advantages of conceiving of economic and su-perstructural influences as resulting in—and from—the *overdetermination* of cultural phenomena. In other words, the way in which people act is continuous with how they feel and think and, in the final analysis, the events of everyday life are rooted in echelons of causes, each contributory, none invariably determinate, but which taken together are wholly ex-planatory. Things happen because they cannot help but happen.

"Ideology" is a word with altogether too many meanings. It is the beliefs of people we do not respect; it is a kind of lie; it is a kind of political theology. But it also refers to the world of ideas itself, and it is this meaning that I find too useful to give up in spite of the confusion. This is, for example, the way that Bakhtin used the word, particularly in his critique of idealist concepts of language.

> All the products of ideological creation—works of art, scientific works, religious symbols and rites, etc.—are material things, part of the practical reality that surrounds man. It is true that these are things of a special nature, having significance, meaning, inner value. But these meanings and values are embodied in material things and actions. They cannot be realized outside some developed material. (Medvedev/Bakhtin 1978, 7)

Bakhtin simultanteously asserts two sides of an argument here. The lan-guages of art and science and, I might add, the commonplace exchanges of everyday life—greetings, farewells, a lover's oath—are significant, meaningful, and valuable. And at the same time they are *things*, not mysterious and detached from life, but part of it, like doorknobs and traffic lights, *like the meaning of traffic lights*, because in Bakhtin's system, meaning is part of the matrix of action, and thus "material." He does not believe in two worlds, one of spirit and one of matter. Following him, we might say, for example, that the neighborhood, the community, is not an "actual" group of streets and buildings, this person and that, opposed to a "spiritual" *community* with a discrete history and unique ways. It is both these things, each completely expressed in the other. A pattern of street repair (or neglect) and a pattern of speech are both "ideology" in this sense.

Bakhtin's use of "ideological" further emphasizes the essentially social nature of human existence.

> Social man is surrounded by ideological phenomena . . . by words in the multifarious forms of their realization (sounds, writing, and the others), by scientific statements, religious symbols and beliefs, works of art, and so on. All of these things in their totality comprise the ideological environment, which forms a solid ring around man. . . . (Medvedev/Bakhtin 1978, 7)

Bakhtin assumes that we live in society surrounded by these "ideological phenomena" as we are surrounded by air. They form a "second nature," as essential to life as the first. Like fish and water, as the cliché has it, we are the last to know about ideology. It is that through which—by means of which—we view the world. It is transparent, invisible. You can't taste ideology either. It just sits there, making the world we think we know.

For Bakhtin this ideological environment not only is a general fact of human existence, it has specific—historical—dynamic inflections.

> The ideological environment is the realized, materialized, externally expressed social consciousness of a given collective. . . . The ideological environment is constantly in the active dialectical process of generation. Contradictions are always present, constantly being overcome and reborn. (Medvedev/Bakhtin 1978, 14)

Just as we all live within the natural world in the widest, most general, sense—on Earth, say—and at the same time in a particular place with its own specific characteristics—Seattle, or Naples—so too we each live in a general ideological environment—perhaps something like "late capitalism"—as well as in the specific, constantly changing, ideological environment of our own nation, region, class, and community. And just as there is no such thing as a truly private language, our psychological reality merges at every point with this constantly changing and flowing ideological stream connecting us with our fellows. (Connecting us most strongly when we are in conflict with them.) Just as there can be no language that is not the manifestation of social relations, so the strong form of this theory claims that without the realm of the social, there can be no thought either.

When we are analyzing social issues, the concept of ideology helps us think about similarities, helps us avoid overemphasis on individual peculiarities. People coming one after another into a welfare office, school, police station seem at first a random collection of stories. Later, they might seem all the same. A theory of ideology, which emphasizes the continuity of the psychological and the social, allows us to realize that they, and we, are each both individual and exemplary. It also helps us to understand that the world of welfare offices, schools, and police stations forms those of us who come in contact with those institutions and is simultaneously formed by us.

Overdetermination is a concept intimately related to that of ideology. The concept arises from attempts by Engels at the end of his life to clarify the notorious assertion of the determining nature of the economic.

> The economic situation is the basis, but the various elements of the superstructure—the political forms of the class struggle and its results: to wit, constitutions established by the victorious class after a successful battle, etc., juridical forms, and then even the reflexes of all these actual struggles in the brains of the participants, political, juristic, philosophical theories, religious views and their further development into systems of dogmas—also exercise their influence upon the course of the historical struggles, *and in many cases preponderate in determining their form.* (Letter from Engels to J. Block, quoted in Althusser 1970, 111–12; emphasis added)

But it was Althusser who brought the concept of overdetermination to the center of our thinking about ideology and society. "History 'asserts itself' through the multiform world of the superstructures, from local tradition to international circumstance," Althusser writes; it is the "*accumulation of effective determinations* (deriving from the superstructures and from special national and international circumstances)" that leads to "overdetermination" (Althusser 1970, 112–13).

Althusser introduces the concept of overdetermination in the context of political history, but its utility is not limited to that field. It can be useful in other contexts, that of education, for example, or what might in general be called "culture" in the anthropologist's meaning of "everyday life," where, as Bakhtin saw, although

> Man the producer is directly oriented in the socioeconomic and natural environment of production . . . every act of his consciousness and all the concrete forms of his conduct outside work (manners, ceremonies, conventional signs of communication, etc.) are immediately oriented in the ideological environment, are determined by it, and in turn determine it, while only obliquely reflecting and refracting socioeconomic and natural existence. (Medvedev/Bakhtin 1978, 14)

This reciprocal determining and determination operates at every level, from that of the most casual individual action to the most deliberate initiatives of nations. And work itself, it seems to me, is also "immediately oriented in the ideological environment." In this, education is a field like any other, in which innumerable decisions and actions accumulate, for example, as education policy at the legislative level, in which legislation influences equally numerous individual decisions and actions. These accumulations occur both within and outside the schools. Each child in a schoolroom is an actor in many dramas, some of which she writes, some of which were written long before she was born. That which she learns—reading and writing, for example—are part of this play of ideology and, in the final determination, economics. But this matter of the final determination is like Keynes's quip about "the long run"—when we are all dead. Although considerations of factors affecting literacy in advanced societies finally must include economics, long before that it is the complexities of ideology that are the vital—overdetermining—factors to be considered.

The illiteracy of adults in this society is a scandal; it is also an entry point for the analysis of a particularly dense area of ideological determinations. It is seemingly characteristic of the way that our society functions now that situations are invisible; only events can be seen. The scandal of adult illiteracy in the United States, thus, usually appears in the form of events, recurrent news stories about people who are unable to decipher much more than traffic signs or their own names.[1] (Or who cannot understand insurance policies or the labels on prescription drug containers—as if anyone could.) These Americans are news because they are largely unknown to the larger society. They are seemingly exotic people who lack what I will here call alphabetic literacy. If we investigate these matters beyond the level of investigatory reporting, we find that the causes of their illiteracy are various, but most frequently those causes involve the relative, or absolute, absence of childhood schooling. Then there is the special case of immigrants from countries without systems of universal education. And there are others: people who grew up in parts of this country where schooling may be restricted due to racism, or in places where overburdened public school systems are willing to graduate talented athletes and quiet children without teaching them to read and write.

What I wish to consider now is a much broader issue than that of alphabetic illiteracy. In addition to the relatively small number of adults who cannot read or write at all, there is a large—and growing—adult population in urgent need of the activation of their purely *nominal literacy* skills. This phenomenon of nominal literacy is even more deeply implicated in the ideological environment of school and community than is alphabetic illiteracy.

In most adult basic education programs the learners are nominally literate. These are people who are not news, whom everyone knows, who can be found everywhere in this country, but who often live in socially distinct communities where nominal literacy is part of their local ideology, the way in which—and a limitation on how—they live and make sense of the world.[2] These are people who have gone to school, who can read and write, for the most part at a level usually described as fifth grade, but who hardly use those skills. For some, reading and writing were always difficult; for others, these skills were simply unimportant. The nominally literate *can* read and write to some extent, if they wish to do so; they do not often wish to do so. In *Ways with Words* Shirley Brice Heath has described the situation of the nominally literate and its effects in two neighborhoods in a small Southern city (Heath 1983). The working-class cultures of her white "Roadville" and black "Trackton," where virtually all literacy skills beyond simple decipherment are superfluous, typify many other communities in this country that have attenuated relationships with literacy.

Heath portrays Roadville as Anytown U.S.A., a neighborhood of pleasant streets and small houses with carefully tended gardens, each with a car in its garage, a boat in the backyard and, perhaps, a recreation vehicle parked out front. People in Roadville identify themselves as middle class on the basis of the way in which they live at home and on weekends, even though during the day and during the work week their jobs involve unskilled or semiskilled factory work.[3] Heath depicts this life in Roadville as comparatively rich in activities reinforcing the nuclear family unit and divided rather sharply in accordance with traditional sex roles. The men work in textile mills all their lives; if the women work there also, it is only insofar as that is compatible with their primary definition in the community as wives and mothers. And yet if most of this picture is formed by ideological factors, eventually the economic world intrudes; there are problems in Roadville, problems that are in part artifacts of its very stability. There is, for instance, growing unemployment. The mills are closing as a result of competition from the Far East, and there are few alternative sources of jobs. Many would judge that education is of increasing importance to the future of this community; unfortunately, literacy itself is not now nor is likely to become an active force within it. The mill jobs do not require it and home life is organized so as to do quite well without it. The future of a community, of Roadville, is a product—a production—of the past, the past a material worked upon by the present. If history moves crabwise—if, for example, it is the ideology of Confucian scholarship in Canton that helps create first-generation Chinese engineers in Massachusetts—the minimal role of education in the ideological world of Roadville is also formative for its economic world in the next generation.

At first sight, Heath's Trackton appears to be a completely contrasting—and unrelated—culture. It is an area on the wrong side of the tracks, where people can have few illusions about being middle class. The black extended family groups of Trackton are less restrictive in many ways than the nuclear families of Roadville, and their methods for obtaining money are more varied. But here too immediate economic survival does not seem to require the active use of literacy skills and the ideology of the community does not emphasize them. In Trackton, as in Roadville, children rarely see adults reading or writing, rarely see any extended texts outside of school. Both communities appear literate, and in a sense they are, but neither would be profoundly changed if literacy were restricted to two or three adults in each. (Nor in fact has the occasional presence of comparatively highly literate individuals in one or the other of the communities changed the role of literacy there.) The point that Heath wishes to make in this already classic ethnographic work is that there are a plurality of literacies, and that in the cases that she studies, those literacies used in Roadville and Trackton, although distinct from one another, are similar in their difference from those used by the "townspeople," the actually middle-class, dominant group, which finds literacy necessary for its bureaucratic labors.

A simple conclusion that can be drawn from Heath's book is that people's ways with words, whether they are actively or only nominally literate, have much to do with their class status. Specifically, the nominally literate are economically vulnerable in a way that the actively literate are not. It could be argued—before the "final determination"— that in some cases economic status is itself determined by literacy practices. We can also see in this example the operations that Althusser calls overdetermination: the jobs that not only do not require the use of literacy, but have no place for it; welfare systems that discourage education; family life practices that are the intimate replication of social restrictions; and looming over all these, the interactions of race and class that reproduce those restrictions.

In fact, in the small Southern city where Heath did her research, white and black working-class literacy practices differ from one another perhaps less markedly than either differs from those of the white middle class. This is significant. This is not a matter of separate but equal communities. Roadville and Trackton are two aspects of a single community—that which does not control the city. And in that city it is black children who know how to read and nevertheless flunk the first grade, black children who burn to death in fires in unheated wooden houses in the winter, black children who have children too early for either to live very long. It is not too much to say that Roadville's chance for comparative prosperity is dependent on the probability of a return to comparative poverty in Trackton.

Racism is the Medusa of America. If we stare at it, we run the risk of becoming paralyzed with hopeless rage. But we cannot avoid racism. The ideologies of our communities and institutions are shot through with it. Thinking about education in this country necessarily involves thinking about racism (sexism, class domination).

One way to read Heath's study is as a depiction of the ideological context of the reproduction of nominal literacy. The white families of Roadville are "placed" in class terms by their literacy practices, practices that go into the schools with their children, practices that, in those schools, are insufficiently challenged by teachers who often enough share much of that community ideology (their husbands work in the mills too). And yes, in black Trackton this limiting of opportunity through community literacy practices is added to the burdens of racism. *Ways with Words* is shaped like a dramatic tragedy. The final act is a failed effort to change the schools, doomed from the start by the way in which school practices are continuous with those of the community and society.

Of course nominal literacy (like racism) is not limited to the South. It can be found throughout the United States, restricting social mobility, impoverishing lives. This is a problem which cannot be entirely traced to—which cannot now be solved by—the public schools alone. The play of overdetermination in this case ranges from legislation through the leisure activities of families to the games of children. Changes in the goals of systems of education are cultural changes, require cultural changes, produce cultural changes; for the cultures of everyday life are a form of education.

Alphabetic illiteracy appears most frequently to be an issue involving individuals—a child becomes seriously ill and misses some months of school, the eldest daughter of a large family has overwhelming childcare responsibilities. And indeed one (black) woman who had been kept at home to take care of her younger brothers and sisters may be an individual issue. But a category of alphabetic illiterates with such histories is not coincidence; it is, among other things, a manifestation of sexism and racism. The restriction of literacy skills to a nominal mode is also sometimes an individual matter; nominal literacy might be a matter of individual choice, *of not liking to read*. But as Heath has shown, in most cases nominal literacy is the result of specific interactions between the school and entire communities. Schools help educate most children (or facilitate their education); but they also administer the education of some so that what is learned is not the curriculum but how to be uneducated, how to define oneself as uneducated.[4] As William Labov, Ray McDermott, and others have pointed out, school is a place where some children learn how *not* to read. One explanation for the way in which this happens is that in certain cases the contrast between the culture of the school and that of the community creates an interference pattern, as it were, more and more successfully blocking the communication, the teaching and learning, of skills and knowledge.

In *Language in the Inner City* Labov shows how in some circumstances the social bonds between children mean more to them than the opportunities presumably presented by school. McDermott has elaborated an aspect of this insight.

> Communicative code differences in a classroom setting can have tremendous effects. A teacher out of phase with his students will undoubtedly fail in the politics of everyday life. Rational interactions with the group will hardly be possible. As a result, the teacher will fall back on his formal authority as a teacher, his so-called "role," to instruct the children in their classroom behavior. The children often reject this authority role and develop an idiosyncratic code, such as the nonstandard peer group code Labov has described. The children's actions make much sense. When rational interaction with a teacher is not possible, that is, when his position of authority makes no sense in terms of his relations with the children, they produce an alternative system and disown the teacher's authority. Reading skills get caught in this battle over which cues are to be attended—peer cues or teacher cues. (1974)

Thus, the children do not learn how to read, or learn that reading is something distasteful, something to be avoided. They are schooled into nominal, or alphabetic, illiteracy. McDermott's work, taken together with that of Labov and Heath, identifies some of the links in the ideological chain that lead from the homogeneous reading group to the welfare office, from the street-corner gang to generations of poverty. Teachers' assumptions about their students, students' attitudes toward the work of learning, interact so that, at best, learning is facilitated for those children most "like" the teachers, made terribly difficult for those most different.[5] These children may learn to read and write, but that is often a nominal accomplishment: they do not learn to use reading and writing for learning. School is seen as the negation of the home (and of the street), its values the negation of their values, its skills hopelessly beside the point in a different—more pressing—context.

Attitudes of passivity toward literacy are cultural artifacts, multigenerational patterns that can be reinforced by the social environment or transformed. Research shows that adults with nominal literacy skills may model literacy education as testing, as punishment, when asked to read to their own children.

What is that word?
Look at the book!
Be quiet!

They are replicating their own experience of schooling. When these patterns are taken together with organizational, economic, and pedagogical factors such as tracking, overcrowding, and an emphasis on correctness over fluency, schooled alphabetic illiteracy becomes possible and the ability of schools to move many students beyond nominal literacy remains limited.[6]

These are some of the ways by which a purely nominal relationship to literacy is reproduced in many communities from generation to generation, paradoxically *via* the experience of schooling.[7]

In a political-economic system increasingly based on information (for communications, command, and control), there are frightening consequences of this fundamental transformation in the labor market for those whose literacy skills are mainly nominal. The small percentage of the population who are truly illiterate and this very large number whose literacy skills are only nominal face increasingly bleak futures economically, politically, culturally. People who do not actively use literacy in their everyday lives are not only likely to have severely limited educational opportunities, they are likely to contribute little to decision making, to the setting of social, political, or business goals, likely to remain dominated by those who do. They and their children are likely to be part of what McDermott (following Weber) calls "pariah castes" and if they are, they have little chance of escaping the limitations that implies. Indeed, this matter of nominal literacy may well be a crucial element in the definition and reproduction of class in modern America. It would not be the first time that class boundaries have been demarcated by literacy practices.

Ethnic, neighborhood, and community pride seem to be beneficial reactions to the economic and ideological domination of the groups in question. If the dominant culture dominates, in part, through the culture industry, then resistance at this level seems as if it would be beneficial for members of those groups. But the work of McDermott and Labov has highlighted the tendency of social networking to enter into a dialectical relationship with other factors, sometimes resulting in a limitation of the educational opportunities of members of groups that have sought to defend themselves from domination through strengthening the ties of community. This research has focused on black communities in the United States. Paul Willis has analyzed nearly identical situations among white English working-class youth who are "learning to labor" while rebelling against the middle-class norms of schooling (1979).[8] There are indications that a similar analysis could apply to the working-class white population of Heath's Roadville. Membership of individuals in particularly disfavored groups is *overdetermined*, in this country the result of a combination of factors often including race, always including poverty, and very frequently including literacy practices, which, with other su-perstructural factors, may perpetuate domination in the name of cultural identity.

One of the claims that I am making here is that schooled nominal literacy is not only the result of individual "learning disabilities," or the sheer randomness of life histories.[9] It is that, and it is also the systematic result of societal and institutional factors integral to the ideological matrix of everyday life in the United States. For this reason its roots in schooling are not an issue to be left in the disciplinary or administrative realms of cognitive or educational psychology in schools of education; it is an institutional problem (McDermott and Hood 1982). Treating it as a "special education" problem restricted to isolated schoolchildren is a method of perpetuating it. Again, the response that teachers should be "sensitized" to the issue is also inadequate. Although social issues are instantiated at the individual level—*this* teacher, *that* student—those moments are merely specifications of a more general level that cannot be reached by discrete activities. In a society characterized by domination, every situation will also be characterized by domination. Changing one or two or a hundred relationships will not change the ideological structure in general. It is for this reason that change must occur at the institutional level in order to be perpetuated at the level of individual action. We live in ideology; the ideological is that which feels natural. Extraordinary demands on or expectations for teachers or others will not result in lasting change. It is among the ordinary teachers of ordinary schools that the struggle for equity must take place. These changes must become the natural way in which schools operate.

If we turn from traditional issues of schooling to those of adult education, Heath's work—focusing as it does on the ideological dynamic of literacy—allows us to see that much of adult education might best be thought of as a process of helping to activate those merely nominal literacy skills inculcated by the schools attended by the children of Trackton and Roadville. If we start from there, we might find a path toward effective methods for adult education, and beyond that, we might discover some ideas useful for the restructuring of schools. And who knows where that might lead?

Many of the learners in adult basic education classes are the same people who, as children, had learned in school that education was not for them and who now seek another chance to negotiate a common language with educational institutions. In spite of the lessons of experience they hope that this situation will be different. And that hope is not entirely futile. It is possible that the bonds of communal ideology may loosen enough on both sides so that learning can take place. Just as, say, the purity of Labov's BEV fades with childhood itself, so adults returning to educational institutions often have already loosened those ties with the ideologies of peer group and community that had influenced their previous efforts. One can become a "lame" at any age. And some teachers of adults are less distant from the values and interests of their students than some teachers of children are from theirs, more willing to negotiate curricula and goals. It helps, also, that adult education in this country is often institutionally marginal. An advantage to teaching in basements and union halls is that few supervisors will venture there.

Nonetheless, many adult basic education classes use school patterns of instruction designed for children, all too often simply repeating those classroom practices by means of which learning had become difficult for their students when those students were children. Further, too much of conventional adult education is based on a deficit model and, being so based, is emotionally punitive. We associate knowledge with pride, ignorance with shame, and all too often begin our work with adult learners by searching out and grading their ignorance. Prospective learners are tested before being "admitted" to classes; lectured at in those classes; given little choice as to content and pacing; treated like children. And then, often enough, like children, they do the only reasonable thing to do under these circumstances—they drop out. And why not? Is this not the pattern of schooling they are used to?

There is no need to perpetuate those patterns. It is not necessary for literacy programs and adult basic education classes to be structured in this way and it is extraordinarily important that they operate more effectively than is often the case: they have an enormous potential as sites for multigenerational change in attitudes toward, and the uses of, education. They can be a site from which nominal literacy practices can be activated. Adult basic education can be an experience that changes the family literacy practices and attitudes of people living in communities with a minimal or only nominal relationship to literacy. The entire family may then tend to identify less with, live less in, the nominal literacy practices of their community. If it does so, the experience of schooling for the children in those families is more likely to be—literally—acceptable.

It might seem that this result would be wholly beneficial. However, as I have pointed out elsewhere, in the short run the effect of such a transformation can be that life may become more difficult for all concerned. Attitudes toward literacy—and what is not at all the same thing, attitudes toward schooling—are central to the ideological core of community. They may be, for instance, a site of resistance to ideological domination. They are often a sign of identity both for the community and for the individuals and families within it. Changing these attitudes is a way of changing that identity, and changes in community identity are a form of internal emigration, an experience that can be sufficiently unpleasant and insufficiently rewarding. Adult education programs should be designed to take these matters into account. They should offer experiences—environments—tantamount to those of an alternative community; they should also offer tangible rewards.

The design of such programs can begin at any of a number of points, but because I am trying to sketch these matters as broadly as possible, I will begin by suggesting that they should include provision for the education of the children of adult learners. The provision of daycare (or evening care) for the children of adult learners while the latter are in class is a sign of commitment by the adult education provider. It also begins to fill part of the gap that may be opening then in the social lives of the adult learners. Daycare in many communities is a reciprocal responsibility: I watch your children when you go to the store or to a movie, and I anticipate that you will do the same for me. But if I go to class every Monday and Wednesday night and you do not, soon enough the exchange will become unequal, the communal ties strained.

Beyond this support function for adult learners, daycare may also include an education program that is integrated with the adult program—adults may share in the task of educating the children. The integration of the educational programs for adults and children is a step potentially more powerful than what might occur in either alone. Linking an adult basic education program with that offered to the young children of learners will model the integration of learning into family relationships, while at the same time, more routinely, provide an early introduction to schooling for the children. Adults who become the teachers of their children are saying something about teaching and learning to those children. Ultimately, adults who are familiar with the schooling of their children can help them with it, can, for example, read to them or listen to them read. If literacy becomes in this way integral also to family life, then the children may see schooling as a continuation of a certain aspect of family life. They may not feel schooling as something wholly divorced from the rest of their activities. It may be less likely that these children will end up with a purely nominal relationship to literacy.

But I have already noted that a program as powerful as this may be disruptive to the preexisting community relationships of learners: *they* now attend school; *their* children are now in preschool or in supplementary programs. These activities may introduce a marked difference into their everyday routines, may break patterns of economic and leisure-time interdependency. This is one example among many, all of which point to the conclusion that it is helpful if activities in an adult education program are deliberately organized to fill these gaps. Even though adult learners may be participating in the education of their children, much effort must also be put into reinforcing the distinction between the assumptions of schooling for children and those of adult education. Each activity in the adult program should be in as much as possible the province of the learners (rather than or in addition to the contributions of staff), learners working together in groups, negating patterns of dependency, and building within the learning community those bonds of reciprocity that characterize the best aspects of organic communities. Induction to the program, placement, evaluation of progress, preparation of some materials—all these tasks that are traditionally reserved for teachers—can be shared by adult learners. Helping one another to learn they will learn more—heal more—quickly.

In some alternative programs, and this is the model endorsed here, the learner's first contact with the program takes the form of an activity resulting in an inventory of that learner's knowledge and skills. Then, in general, each aspect of learning begins with learners, preferentially working in groups, surveying their own knowledge of the subject at hand as a way of laying the foundation for the acquisition of more knowledge. Small work groups are the preferential unit of learning, because in groups, particularly in heterogeneous groups, learners can pool their knowledge and skills with peers, each contributing, none stigmatized as the passive beneficiary of a teacher's wisdom. It is hardly an accident that most productive activities that adults undertake in the world are done as a matter of course in groups: task forces, editorial groups, construction crews, laboratory and surgical teams. This approach works equally well with education.

In adult education, as in the schools, much of the best teaching (and counseling) is collaborative. Just as students learn better when working together, so teachers often find that they, individually, have more to teach when working together than they would if isolated in a conventional classroom. And collaborative teaching is a model for collaborative learning patterns. A teacher who calls on a colleague for knowledge to supplement his or her own is reinforcing the lesson that it is what one knows—rather than what one does not know—that matters, that knowledge is social, that a question is a request for help, not a challenge. Following this model, in a student-centered program, each student is also a teacher: as a member of a group, bringing her knowledge of Central America to the study of a GED lesson; as a native speaker of English, helping interpret a manual in an employment skills program; as a father, working in a daycare center introducing children (not necessarily his own) to literacy. The teaching role of learners brings self-confidence, restores pride, demonstrates that it is possible to accomplish much educationally in spite of inadequate previous preparation. It also frees teachers from unrealistic workloads, responsibilities, and expectations so they can act more effectively as organizers of educational activities.

In addition to the curriculum, other ancillary activities of an adult education program can be organized in the same way. Transportation information, food and clothing exchanges, social activities, preventive health care information and access are opportunities for learning and the practice of problem solving, which leads to more self-confidence and a fuller life. For example, the literal immobility of many of the nominally literate is well-known. In a city like New York many spend decades within sight of buildings they never visit; in a city like Los Angeles many purchase food at premium prices from ghetto supermarkets while there are bargains in Beverly Hills; everywhere the poor live shorter, less healthy lives in a society in which access to health care and information is difficult even for the rich. Facing and solving problems of transportation, health, and other issues of daily life can be an integral part of adult education planning. Everything that prevents learning is an opportunity for analysis, group work, learning. A well-constructed adult education program will see many activities as educational, will use even impediments to access to education as opportunities for it.

Under these circumstances it will soon become clear that basic education is truly the basis for—not the end of—learning. When education is organized as a series of activities, not as a set of barriers; when the knowledge that learners bring to an activity is utilized, activated, and shared rather than disregarded; when goals are expressed and learning plans negotiated rather than assumed and imposed; then the process of skills acquisition truly becomes a basis for education, an education that need not be deferred, but that can proceed at a rapid pace in one area, perhaps, even while things are moving more slowly in another. For example, an adult learner can accomplish much in the acquisition of survival skills, in becoming expert at the techniques of oral history research or consumer education, while still at a relatively lower level in English language acquisition, say, or mathematics (and vice versa). An adult learner's education is, perforce, a matter of such uneven developments. This can be exploited for the benefit of the learner (and her learning group) rather than being ignored or diagnosed. The purpose of an adult basic education class is not solely preparation for the GED class; it is an inadequate GED class that is solely preparatory for the GED examination. Education is—should be—everywhere and always the opportunity to learn and teach, a dynamic process not simply additive, but transforming.

The line of thought I have been following here indicates that for most Americans in need of further education the issue is not the total inability to read or write; the issue is the way in which literacy is lived. Too often it is lived as a nearly useless set of decipherment and inscription skills. For meaningful further education to take place, it must be made an active way of learning. Activating passive literacy skills turns out to be a highly complex process, almost a process of emigration to a new culture. Those programs that wish to facilitate that process may do so best by viewing themselves as committed to engaging learners in every aspect of their lives. Putting this model into practice is not easy. Often, there will be much institutional resistance. And sustaining such practices is perhaps even more difficult. A model program is one thing; humane education as an everyday practice is quite another. However, although we should not delude ourselves about the difficulties involved in change, the alternative is the replication of the present into the future, an alternative that no one concerned with the quality of our society will wish to contemplate.

Michael Holzman

Notes

1. Recent studies indicate that these alphabetically illiterate citizens comprise just one percent of the young adult native speakers of English in this country. See Kirsch and Jungeblut (1986).
2. See "The Social Context of Literacy Education" (pp. 133–40).
3. "Most Americans—in all social classes—believe they are 'middle class' " (Gunnar Myrdal et al. 1944, 670).
4. The literature on this is considerable. See, for example, Friedenberg (1963), Goodman, (1964), Holt (1964), and even Illich (1971) and Kozol (1967).
5. There is also the matter of the force of student attitudes about teaching. In a middle class school, "years of classroom experience allow students to have very specific expectations of how teachers should act in the classroom. Students, for example, expect the teacher to maintain classroom control, enforce rules, and present the curriculum. Students expect teachers to be certain in both their behavior and in their knowledge, and students articulate these expectations if the teacher in any way deviates from this traditional image. In this sense, students do coach their teachers in ways which reinforce school structure and, as such, constitute an immediate source of teacher socialization. So, while teachers are socializing the students, students are socializing teachers" (Britzman 1986, 445–46). In other schools, student expectations are different, but the feedback mechanisms are similar.
6. See Carnoy and Levin (1985) for a broad argument about the position of school in contemporary United States society, particularly in relationship to the "reproduction" of the workforce.
7. Other people from communities with nominal literacy practices do not decide to undertake further education, do not decide to encourage their children to develop active literacy practices, decide, rather, like the residents of Trackton and Roadville, to maintain the values of their community in this as in other matters. It's a free country. Since the Thirties, certain progressives have celebrated this tendency toward cultural isolation of oppressed and marginalized groups, believing that they were observing here something like European working class or folk cultural activities. This is also a significant theme among some adult educators, particularly those teaching in small neighborhood community-based organizations. Oral history projects, for instance, are taken as leading inward rather than outward; the contemplation of the com-

munity replaces the analysis of society; domestic and traditional values are celebrated. However, no matter what virtues such an inward turn had a century ago and thousands of miles away across the ocean, in the United States today the consequences of this move are unfortunate: what at first seems a refuge becomes a prison. Avoiding the mass culture version of ideological domination turns out to be also a way of limiting economic and educational opportunities. The price of cultural independence is pariah status and economic domination.

8. ". . . Paul Willis's study of working-class boys in an English comprehensive school [suggests] that the disdain working-class youth feel for education actually reinforces the school's reproductive function since it hardens into a rejection of all forms of mental labor. In Willis's study, the 'lads' defy the school only to trap themselves in menial jobs. Thus, the school ultimately succeeds in channeling them into class-determined positions, . . ." (Kantor and Lowe 1987, 75).

9. The "randomness" of life histories is only random from the point of view of individuals. Taken together, the lives of the alphabetically illiterate point to societal artifacts grouping around issues of poverty, race, regional disparities, and the like.

The research described in this chapter was made possible by a series of grants from the Equal Opportunity division of The Rockefeller Foundation. The opinions expressed in it are mine, however, and not necessarily shared by The Rockefeller Foundation.

12

Community-Based Organizations as Providers of Education Services

One of my literary theory teachers wrote an influential book entitled *Literature as System* and another professor at the same institution wrote one entitled *System and Structure*. Even now, having moved quite far from the concerns of Guillen and Wilden, I still find it useful to think in their terms, to think about structures and systems in other fields. In education, the idea of system is particularly helpful. This essay and its companion piece on volunteer corps are attempts to examine the boundaries of systems, to seek to understand that which is immediately to hand—community-based organization, for example—and through that to learn more about the system of education in general.

There is much of interest about community-based organizations, their role in our society, their function in contributing to the stability of that society. They are not well understood, but they are very important in education and other related fields. Hence, I have gone beyond the narrower limits of my subject, from time to time, in order to make some more general observations.

There is an astonishing variety of adult education providers. In addition to programs run by the schools, libraries, and community colleges, corporations spend enormous amounts of money on the education of their employees (and characteristically conceive of this as an investment or expense); the government sometimes appears bent on transforming most of the departments of the executive branch into education institutions; and many community-based organizations offer basic skills classes or classes for people wishing to prepare for the GED high school

174

equivalency examination. Among these, community-based organizations appear to be particularly good vehicles for the provision of basic education to groups not well served by more formal institutions and seemingly likely to be sympathetic to the goals and means of the current wave of education reform. However, I argue here that, in general, community-based organizations are not useful sites for education services—that, on the contrary, most community-based organizations are *essentially* unsuitable for this purpose and particularly unsuitable for reforms that privilege the role of teachers. (Although, of course, particular community-based organizations may do superbly well in providing education for those who have difficulty obtaining it elsewhere.)

Community-based organizations—that ill-defined category including churches, ethnic group organizations, settlement houses—are usually characterized, formally, by reference to their nongovernmental status, and yet most are funded by government programs in one way or another. Their classes represent, on the one hand, opportunities for those who wish to achieve a certain measure of education—or certification—so as to have greater economic opportunities and, on the other hand, the extreme reach of what might be called the socialization process. The many types of community-based organizations are increasingly integrated into the official social structure of the United States, occupying positions between institutions that have been criticized as channeling the disadvantaged away from opportunity and those designed to—physically—restrain people who will not passively accept this channeling. The efforts of their employees, for example as educators, to improve opportunities for those not well-served by the schools and related institutions are frequently hampered in ways not unusual in the educational system at large as well as by difficulties peculiar to their own relatively small, poorly funded, ambivalently motivated organizations.

If we are to understand why efforts to reform education practices within community-based organizations are so often—and so surprisingly—frustrated, we must begin with a fundamental appraisal of the nature of community-based organizations themselves, their place and function in society. The requirement for the mediating activities of community-based organizations is a function of the role of governmental institutions—including the schools—in reproducing the structural patterns of society, patterns that are frequently in opposition both to the requirements of a rationalizing economy and to the needs and aspirations of marginalized groups. Many people in the communities served by community-based organizations are unable to interact successfully with potential employers (or, failing that, with welfare agencies). These insufficiently educated or insufficiently socialized people are not fully available as members of a workforce and may create disturbances in a system that has no place for them. When there are institutional requirements to employ them—due either to labor shortages or to political pressures—community-based organizations are useful means for reconnecting them to the economic structure. In the same way, community-based organizations can aid governmental welfare institutions to reach populations too alienated to be reached otherwise, or, perhaps, too ill-educated to negotiate their bureaucracies. These generic services of community-based organizations to social stability and economic growth are recognized and supported by various forms of funding: government grants and contracts and that indirect tax on business that takes the form of charitable contributions to agencies, of which the United Way is the outstanding example.

In addition to their function as extensions of the institutions of the state into the communities of the poor, some community-based organizations may act as support mechanisms for the emergence of a lower middle-class group from those communities. These community-based organizations construct and maintain a welfare and/or educational bureaucracy parallel to those maintained by governmental agencies. The ideal type of such a community-based organization—which could be called the bureaucratic type—would be one that finances corporate-style offices and professional staff by contracting with government agencies, and perhaps the United Way, to provide traditional welfare or educational services to the community. This organization would be particularly characterized by its dependence on and attention to its funding sources. Its officers "look up" or "out" to those funding sources and may be virtually blind to the "view down" to the community which they are ostensibly serving. Among the actual interests served by such an organization are those of its own staff, which at its upper levels benefits in local power and prestige and at its lower levels benefits in status, training, and income preparatory to moves out toward governmental and corporate bureaucracies. Of course it also serves the interests of its funding agencies, their contributors, and local and national business interests. In addition, it may be effective in serving certain members of the community, but often it is not. However, the community is merely instrumental for these interests; therefore, from the bureaucracy's point of view failure to adequately serve the community is not as detrimental to the organization as it might seem to be to outsiders. And as the community is not well-served by any bureaucracy, this lack of responsiveness is acceptable even to it, for a time. At least this one appears to be *its* bureaucracy.

It is consistent with this dynamic that community-based organizations of the bureaucratic type will quite readily use referrals, not only as alternative means of offering services, but, perhaps even more importantly, as ways in which to strengthen their organizational ties with other agencies and with governmental institutions.

Teachers in these organizations may find their attempts to facilitate the education of their students hampered by bureaucratic structures that are dysfunctional for education but rationalized by reference to other organizational priorities: provision of managerial employment, bureaucratic control, and modeling of mainstream institutions as a professional training strategy. In this case, teachers working within the organization but employed by local school districts and therefore not dependent on it may, paradoxically, find themselves freer to experiment with innovative education techniques (such as learner-produced reading materials or oral history projects) than their colleagues who are directly employed by the organization.

An opposite ideal type of community-based organization is one that seeks to utilize funding from government and the private sector in order to further what in its interpretation are the goals of the community of which it considers itself to be an organic part. This could be called the ideological type. Although it may be in the direct line of descent from the settlement house tradition, this type of community-based organization is shifting from traditional philanthropic ideals and methods, where working-class clients are serviced by middle-class social workers, toward a model where teachers and counselors are recruited from the neighborhood community itself. This begins with, and has as its typical mark, peer counseling and calls for the pooling of intellectual and skill resources of the community.

The offices of such a community-based organization will be in a neighborhood house or store front. Procedures will be those of one-to-one social relations rather than bureaucratic screening and processing. There will be strong efforts to minimize perceived differences of status between the staff and those seeking their help. The ideological type of community-based organization will also seek to minimize referrals and will attempt to house most services on-site, utilizing neighborhood people, for example, in childcare activities.

Teachers employed by these organizations are likely to be school district employees, due to the realities of funding, but will nonetheless tend to adopt the organizational culture and identify with it. Certain contemporary innovations in literacy, English as a second language, and basic education will fit well into this culture; others will not. These methods will be evaluated with reference to the goals of the organization rather than to the preferences or learning styles of the students. Managerial staff are frequently highly politicized, distrusting governmental and private sector funders (even while trying to obtain support from them), "looking down" rather than "up" when formulating policies and procedures. Community-based organizations of this type tend to be poorly funded, perhaps in part as a result of their own strongly held egalitarian ideals, which also orient them toward community building activities predicated on European social action models.[1]

An issue demarcating the ideological type is that of the purpose of further education in their characteristically especially deprived neighborhoods. A community-based organization of this type may decide that given the realities of employment and the welfare system, employment skills training might be futile, as there are so few jobs available or few that pay well enough to attract people off the welfare rolls. Educational efforts, then, will be horizontal as much as vertical, intended to enrich and improve existing everyday life rather than to lead, necessarily, to alternative mainstream ambitions. Both organizational types, the bureaucratic and the ideological, are guided by institutional goals that are formulated and carried out with reference to other institutions. Their activities, then, are to be explained in that context, even when it might appear otherwise. For example, the structure and content of writing or English-as-a-second-language classes offered will be determined, in the final analysis, by this institutional context, not by the findings of research or the decisions of teachers and learners.

In addition to this synchronic classification of community-based organizations according to ideal type, a well-developed historicized classification along social psychological lines is also useful. In *The Critique of Dialectical Reason* (Sartre 1976) we find such a theory of society in the form of a historical narrative, which begins during the French Revolution with a crowd drifting toward the Place de Bastille. They are hungry, angry, and afraid. And then an event, perhaps trivial enough in itself, causes each to see his humanity in the other. It is what Sartre calls an *Apocalypse*. " 'By evening,' wrote Monjoye, 'Paris was a new city. Regular cannon shots reminded the people to be on their guard. And added to the noise of the cannon there were bells sounding a continuous alarm. The sixty churches where the residents had gathered were overflowing with people. Everyone was an orator. . . . *The city was a fused group*" (357).

· The "fused group" is Sartre's term for that social formation arising from an *Apocalypse* that is, as it were, a single person, the group as the person, the Other as the self. This condition of wholeness, *Gemeinschaft*, is often part of the original motivating aspiration of community-based organizations. They speak of brotherhood—of sisterhood—of mutual responsibility. Where in what Sartre calls the serial form of collective existence (which is both logically prior to and historically the inevitable result of the development of the fused group), there had been no community, only a collection of third parties each the enemy of the others, the "reality of the praxis of a [fused] group depends on the liquidation . . . of the serial, both in everyone and by everyone, and its replacement by community" (1976, 387). A fused group differs from other, more elaborate, social forms in that it exhibits no trace of what Sartre calls "the practico-inert," that residue of past social practice that forms the basis of and the limits to any contemporary social practice.[2]

To translate the Sartrean narrative and logic into American terms, the "collective" might be represented by the social organization of a place like Harlem or Watts in some normal year, say 1960, with the abstract concept of seriality becoming an all too real and concrete despair in the welfare offices, the schools, the police stations. The fused group appears a few years later, smashing shop windows, starting fires, in revolt against those local and those larger collective organizations that regard and are regarded by people in Harlem, in Watts, as alien, as the Other. Here the dynamism of the historical, actual, fused group represents the result of a breach in the structure of collectives: "the sudden resurrection of freedom" (Sartre 1976, 401). The social fabric is torn and through that gap, according to Sartre, we can catch sight of man's hope, the millenium of social identity. But the ironic nature of history is such that this ideal, in its struggle to free itself from the everyday reality of the collectives, appears nearly always as hatred, and then, of course, as fear, and quickly enough, at least in the case of the paradigmatic development of the French Revolution, as the Terror itself. In a sense, community-based organizations (such as settlement houses) are part of society's defense against this development, just as they are also, as we shall see shortly, the institutionalized successors of the fused group that leads to it.

The Sartrean analysis of society is as much a logical system as a historical narrative. It is explanatory for social formations that actually developed in this way, following the classical development of French institutions, and also for those that developed differently. Organizations that themselves never went through a moment of origin as fused groups nonetheless may bear that moment within them as an ideal prehistory, the narrative of which could be traced, if necessary, in the larger collective—American society. We may take these broken geneologies for granted, but if we do, much that we wish to understand about the possibilities—and the limitations—of community-based organizations will remain inexplicable. The words and gestures of their bureaucrats are, among other things, often enough signifiers of a lost revolutionary signified.

If the fused group could operate in an ideal space free of negation there would never be any internal contradiction, any limitation of freedom. But the fused group arises as the negation of an oppressive collective and therefore develops within itself that first form of inertia, the "pledge." The pledge, in Sartre's lexicon, is the fused group's internalization of the hostility of the collective. It is the inscription of fear, a vow to remain together as a group against that—those—not of the group. Once there, like a seed crystal in a supersaturated solution, it produces structure, rigid bonds, where before all was fluid. Often enough it is literally a pledge, an oath, say, a beginning of the process by which each member of the group is watched by the others, each emerging into the gaze of each— once more—as Other, as potentially an enemy.

The "statutory group" is built on the pledge; at the first moment of its logic this pledge and the existence of the group is an *activity* undertaken by those in the group. The pledge is a freely undertaken limitation of freedom. But for those who join the group after the initial moment of the pledge, the pledge has become a condition that cannot be refused, nor, consequently, can it be freely chosen. Pledging, they join a group that has become reified as something other than a number of people seeking freedom. "The group as permanence is, in effect, an instrument constructed in concrete circumstances, on the basis of a fused group . . . [and] can never be reduced to 'natural', 'spontaneous' or 'immediate' relations" (Sartre 1976, 434). It *was* those who are pledging; it *is* those who have been pledged. The disciples are now, for instance, a Church, and as it can only be joined by those willing to take a pledge created by others, so those who join can be expelled—excommuni-cated—by those others, also. The pledge, which is at first simply an action, then a certain ideal inertia, can now take shape as a concrete inertia: a building, a set of rules, a system of enforcement. The individual is subordinated to the group by a force "which unites the sworn parties . . . as a totalization which threatens to totalize itself without them . . ." (432).

Once the moment of the *Apocalypse* passes, a group is never again able to act outside the historical field, and the historical field is an inertial force that dissipates action. This force, this negation, itself must be opposed if the group is to continue to act. And yet, all too often that which then comes into being through this meeting of force with force is a structural rigidity: reification. We join a fused group by becoming a part of its activity. We join a statutory group by taking a pledge—a pledge, in the final analysis, to act even when alone as if we were always with, always watched by, the rest of the group. But we join an organi-zation by merely agreeing to its rules, which enforce the pledge over time and distance, and the structures that manifest them.

This application of Sartre's theory gives us a second dimension along which to arrange many contemporary American community-based or-ganizations. Some are very close to an origin as fused groups, filled with enthusiasm, barely structured. Others are nearly as bureaucratic, nearly as much a matter of "collectives," as any government agency. Whatever their origins, almost all community-based organizations are truly orga-nizations in the Sartrean sense: they have "apparatuses of mediation, supervision, and inspection, whose essential function is to put the sub-groups into relation either with one another . . . or with the central apparatus . . ." (1976, 543) and, crucially, to connect them with the institutional apparatuses of the state and business. In general, commu-nity-based organizations of every type mediate between the unorganized people in a community—a community defined geographically, ethnically, or economically—and the dominant institutions of collective society: governmental, quasi-governmental, private. This makes them useful—and occasionally essential—for the state and private sectors. Indeed, insofar as they are useful to government and business, they are likely to become virtual extensions of those institutions in their communities. This socioeconomic utility of community-based organizations is found structurally at the level of the pledge. On one side of the barrier formed by the pledge, the community, which may be highly distrustful of other institutions, identifies the community-based organization with that glimpse of freedom once offered by the fused group. On the other side of the pledge, the institutions of the state and business perceive the community-based organization as a bureaucracy, much like any other, one which they find occasionally useful because of its access to disaffected populations in moments of crisis, and, in more normal times, useful because of its relatively low costs as a deliverer of social services.

The economic viability of community-based organizations as providers of support services—such as education—is in large part based on these relatively low costs. Employees of community-based organizations often are not paid as much as people doing similar work for state and local welfare offices or schools. This wage differential, in its turn, necessitates the employment of professional staff not yet qualified for other employment and those who find an ideological compensation for lower salaries in memories, perhaps, of the fused group, the *Apocalypse*, and the promise of a better world. Many community-based organizations are partly staffed by people with memories of the Civil Rights movement or—especially in California of late—memories of messianic unionization efforts.[3]

As well as measuring on at least one dimension congruence with governmental institutions, the bureaucratic and ideological ideal types may be taken to represent differing distances from the fused group: bureaucratic community-based organizations are further from the actuality and the consciousness of an origin as a fused group, closer to the structure and purposes of governmental agencies. There is also a sense in which the ideal types reflect degrees of stability—financial resources, personnel tenure, and so forth being greater in bureaucratic community-based organizations—but in another sense the reverse is true: the ideological type is more likely to have stable goals, more likely to pursue its own interests in spite of outside influences.

The role of education, and hence of teachers, in community-based organizations under this model is complex. In most cases the needs of communities that are served by community-based organizations must be severe and in some sense neglected by governmental agencies as a precondition for the establishment and survival of community-based organizations. (When groups move from poverty and marginalization to mainstream status, their associated institutions—churches, political groups—are no longer spoken of as community-based organizations. The Roman Catholic Church—and its school system—is rarely called a community-based organization.) Under these circumstances the most basic form of the community-based organization is the settlement house, a *place* to which people can go for help in meeting their needs, as those needs arise. Supplemental education is quite often one of those needs. Community-based organizations thus may offer developmental English language skills classes or, more elaborately, adult basic education leading to a GED certificate. Community-based organizations are not alone in offering these educational opportunities, however, and this implies that their offerings will usually be either literally supplemental to those of the schools (public, religious, proprietary), or in competition with them. In either case, community-based organizations will be under pressure to make their educational offerings conform with patterns set elsewhere: GED classes are often determined by the national standardized test and by standardized commercial materials available for learners wishing to pass it; the Test of Adult Basic English similarly influences adult basic education classes; teachers working in community-based organizations are often employees of local school districts, or see their careers as leading to such employment, and have similar expectations in terms of what is taught and how it is taught.

Adult education is not central to the concerns of government and communities for the reproduction of the skills and systems of belief necessary for the perpetuation of society as it is. And yet, seemingly paradoxically, adult education, even as delivered by community-based organizations, is one of the most conservative forms of education. Efforts to introduce progressive, collaborative, or culturally specific models of basic skills, literacy, and English-as-a-second-language education into a community-based organization will almost always be difficult because of a contradiction inherent in the evolution and purpose of community-based organizations. These nontraditional methods of education will be most congruent with the ethos of those community-based organizations that are closest to their moment of origin in the fused group, and these are most commonly of the ideological type. But it is precisely these community-based organizations that are least susceptible to suggestions for changes in their ethos. On the other hand, having relatively undeveloped bureaucratic structures, they may be quite open to suggestions for reorganization and, furthermore, because they are most distant from the institutions of the collective, they are the least well-funded, which will have the effect of motivating them to at least appear to agree to the suggestions of, for example, funders interested in educational reform.

The bureaucratic type of community-based organization, quite distant from any origin in a fused group—itself nearly a form of collective organization—is relatively indifferent to questions of ideology but quite resistant to organizational change, particularly if those changes are not congruent with the goal of developing symmetry with state bureaucracies. Suggesting alternate forms of organization or instruction that differ significantly from those found in the public schools, for instance, may be resisted as potentially interfering with the relationship that the staff and the organization as a whole wish to maintain with the schools. Accreditation may be perceived or presented as an issue, as might referral procedures, but the fundamental problem can be expressed as the organization's commitment to fostering the ability of staff to transfer to the public schools (or similar mainline institutions) and maintaining its own interpenetrability as a collective transparent to the institutional requirements of the state.

A reform in educational practices in community-based organizations parallel to that currently underway in the more progressive school systems—school-based management, team teaching, and the like—would be a return in spirit, as it were, to the earliest stage of the development of community-based organizations in the fused group, by means of a reorganization of the relations of work within the organization itself. The theory presented here would indicate that this reform would be difficult to accomplish in community-based organizations at either end of the spectrum of ideal types. In addition to these theoretical arguments, there is a practical one. The usual practice of delegating educational responsibilities, especially basic education and English-as-a-second-language instruction, to school district employees in community-based organizations is an obvious barrier to institutionalizing an educational model based on participatory management. These teachers are not actually part of the institution in which they are teaching, and they are usually enculturated by the school district rather than by the community-based organization; and the corporate culture of most school districts is inimical to these approaches. This delegation to outside personnel is most likely to take place in organizations that do not find education central to their mission, but it also is done by the ideological type of community-based organization, which does indeed seek (but usually fails) to incorporate these teachers into the pledged group.

Other serious consequences of the typical situation of community-based organizations are high staff turnover, with the subsequent loss of the institutional memory in regard to educational reform efforts, and a continuing adjustment of goals (expressed or implicit, depending on the organization's position on the ideal-type axis) to the requirements of funding agencies. Indeed, the fundamental barrier to the successful institutionalization of progressive models of education in community-based organizations often manifest as funding issues. These organizations usually lack stable funding because they are not a formal part of federal, state, or local governments; they may have ideological commitments at odds with those of significant sectors of funding decision makers; their level of professionalism is not reliably high (this is part of a loop, of course).

Those community-based organizations which are closest to being parts of the institutional structure of their communities, which have few nonconforming ideological commitments, and which have the highest level of professionalism have the best funding records. One conclusion that could be drawn is that the strenuous staff training and organizational effort required for the effecting of fundamental educational reform in the environment of the community-based organization would best be undertaken with these comparatively stable groups. Unfortunately, most community-based organizations (as should be evident from the theoretical framework presented earlier) are not of that type.

I have sought to indicate here that community-based organizations form a continuum from completely unstructured fused groups to collective organizations virtually indistinguishable from government bureaus; they might also be arranged by type from the ideological to the bureaucratic. The services they offer their communities are best conceived of in terms of the central function of mediators between unorganized, marginal groups and the regular institutions of the government. In the long run, very few community-based organizations will be viable providers of other services, whether health care, education, or business counseling. Those that are, in general, will be either delegates of regular governmental service providers (in this sense many sectarian agencies are such delegates, providing services on a contract basis for local or state government) or virtually indistiguishable from private businesses—specialists in providing services to particular communities, funded by government grants, and providing salaries, rather than profits, to their proprietors.

I have been forced to conclude—perhaps not by these arguments, but by the experiences that lay behind them—that a progressive form of education, one liberating rather than restrictive for people who have not been well-served by formal educational institutions, *may* be provided by the few relatively stable and atypical community-based organizations, but may be even better suited for use in more typically stable institutional settings, such as community college, school district, or university programs with well-developed community outreach capabilities and the ability to work with community-based institutions in their more natural role as contact points for the potential learner groups. If the theory set out above has any merit, it is precisely this mediating role that is the proper part for community-based organizations to play in the effort to extend the reformation of educational institutions to those that provide education services to adults.

Michael Holzman

Notes

1. While Gramscian conceptions concerning the development of organic intellectuals might be—or might have been—valid in Europe, in America today it is difficult to argue that individuals who benefit educationally, for instance, from neighborhood community-based organizations of this type will wish to remain in a neighborhood where living is difficult when it is no longer personally necessary for them to do so. And, of course, as they become better educated and find wider opportunities becoming available to them, they will tend to become differentiated from their former community, first economically and then in class outlook.
2. The "practico-inert" constitutes, among other things, the very streets and buildings of the ghetto, what could be described as the *materialization* of prejudice.
3. As has already been noted, community-based organizations that are unable to attract sufficient funding and staff to offer a complete array of institutional functions may still attempt to fulfill the settlement house paradigm by serving as brokers of social and educational services, offering their clients referrals to other institutions and agencies.

13

Educational Aspects of Civilian Volunteer Corps

There is something quite fascinating in the youth corps concept. Many people find the idea of national service ethically compelling; there is also the old progressive idea of providing opportunities to young people who might otherwise be without them. Unfortunately, the reality of the matter, as it plays out in remote camps or inner city centers, has more to do with political expediency and today's everyday world of the ghetto and barrio than with early twentieth-century ideals.

Education is central to this complex of issues. The volunteer corps are not usually thought of as educational institutions, but most of them function as such, often ad hoc. Again, this has little to do with ideals, much to do with the continuity of encounters with educational institutions experienced by those likely to be corpsmembers. As with the educational functions of community-based organizations, those of volunteer corps are part of the larger world of adult education, a world that in addition to having its own vivid reality, serves as a mirror to the structures of the social world of late-twentieth-century America.

□　　□　　□

The success of the California Conservation Corps has encouraged a national trend toward the establishment of similar state volunteer corps and some enthusiasm for a national organization. While bills to set up an American Conservation Corps have not overcome congressional resistance to new domestic initiatives, many cities and states have moved ahead on their own in this direction. These volunteer public service entities, which often have the word "corps" in their title, are frequently thought of by their organizers as idealistic enterprises, domestic equivalents of the original Peace Corps ideal. But there are significant differences between the Peace Corps and these domestic descendents and problems arise when these differences are unrecognized. These problems limit the effectiveness of the new group of volunteer corps.

The Peace Corps developed in a period of full employment and attracted people who could have found other work or educational opportunities, but who sought instead this mode of service. They wished to be useful to those who otherwise would not have been able to afford their services. (Of course, they wanted various other satisfactions also, but this was the basic economic factor.) In a period of structural unemployment for marginalized groups, many of the people whom the domestic volunteer corps attract are those who cannot find an alternative. Their next stop, if they are failed here, may be unemployment or jail. The economic role of the organizations themselves also differs from the Peace Corps model, as the services they offer to local governments are not gratis additions to budgets; increasingly, their services are treated as coming from simply one more vendor in the marketplace, a marketplace in which they must compete by privileging efficiency in project work over other considerations. This trend is fostered by the tendency to assimilate governmental activities to a business model. There is commonly, then, a disjunction between the purposes of the various aspects of the organization and its staff, on the one hand, and the needs of many corpsmembers, on the other, which often serves to minimize the attention paid to those needs, to make it less likely that this, often final, educational opportunity will allow the corpsmembers to move out of marginalization and into a decent life.

In the following pages I will briefly describe the California Conservation Corps, then outline a theoretical framework for the analysis of volunteer corps in general, using the California Conservation Corps as an example. This sketch will use the construction of ideal types—exaggerated models of extreme opposites—to throw some light on actual conditions. The essay will end with a description of the Literacy Program of the California Conservation Corps and an outline of certain aspects of a utopian volunteer corps, by way of providing a context for further work on these issues.

The California Conservation Corps maintains a statewide network of residential and nonresidential centers, each employing between fifty and one hundred corpsmembers of college age. The name of the organization and its slogan—"Hard work, low pay, miserable conditions"— seem typical manifestations of the Peace Corps ethic, designed to attract middle-class youth into self-sacrificing work in the mountains and forests. And that was probably the intention of the C.C.C. organizers. Early in its history there were centers that operated small farms, where some corpsmembers raised goats and chickens. City youth could "return to the land." This *wandervogel* or kibbutz idyll is for the most part long past. The hard work, low pay, and miserable conditions are no longer novelties for the corpsmembers: for many they simply replicate their home environment. In any case, low pay is a relative concept. For the unemployed a steady minimum wage salary is something to aspire to. Thus, for many of the corpsmembers the organization is simply an employer of last resort, equivalent to others offering unskilled work as, say, dishwashers. As a matter of fact, some corpsmembers at nonresidential centers will work during the day for the C.C.C. and at night precisely as dishwashers, or in some similar job, in order to support families, pay debts, save to bring relatives to America from Hong Kong.

These corpsmembers are accustomed to exchanging work in unpleasant surroundings for a minimal wage, when they can get work. For them the "miserable conditions" of the C.C.C. include much the organizers of the C.C.C. must have thought positive: prework physical training, uniforms, hygiene and personal appearance rules, and, finally, the residential centers themselves. Although it may very well be attractive to idealistic middle-class youth to spend a year or so at a remote camp, it is quite a different thing if one is economically compelled to do so. And the residential centers themselves mirror these differences in their design and atmosphere. The spectrum runs from a center that is a cluster of former Air Force officers' apartments on a mountain overlooking the Pacific to one that is a converted cellblock in what was once a California Youth Authority prison. Just as the residential centers offer extremes that can be taken as projections of corpsmember attitudes and illustrative of institutional attitudes toward the corpsmembers, so we can construct other models of the various extremes of orientation among corpsmembers, staff, and supervisory personnel.

Let us, then, construct a model of the C.C.C. from the point of view of corpsmembers who have joined for the minimum wage or as an alternative to incarceration. From the point of view of corpsmembers, the "hard work, low pay, miserable conditions" of the C.C.C. would be regarded as defining a particularly oppressive employment situation, practically a reversion to the workhouse of the early industrial revolution, a life only marginally different from life in a California Youth Authority camp. Housed in former prison cells in isolated areas of the state, uniformed, working side by side with prisoners while fighting forest fires, these corpsmembers understandably view the organization as something less than inspirational.

This point of view would find a reflection—or an origin—in that of C.C.C. staff who are "project oriented" (in their phrase), concerned nearly exclusively with the completion of the assigned work, either as an end in itself or as a state imposed funding requirement. Workcrew supervisors with this orientation may have had experience with the forestry department supervising groups of prisoners constructing roads or fighting fires. In any case, it would be common for them to appear to believe that the corpsmembers are simply another unskilled, undisciplined labor force. Higher ranking staff and managers in this model would sometimes act as if the C.C.C. were an analogue of a business, as if each unit of the organization must contribute to the bottom line, pull its own weight, etc. For them, the value of the work would be monetary, a way of meeting the payroll. It would be as if the Peace Corps had been set up in such a way that the volunteers were paid on a piecework basis by the host governments: so much for each innoculation, reading lesson, village improvement. In the extreme, worst-case model of the C.C.C., these three—the business manager, the foreman, the corpsmember—create among them a dynamic of behavior, attitudes, and mutual internalization of imagery that defines a social structure of domination and oppression forming a self-contained economic world characterized by an artificial scarcity. In the final analysis a corpsmember in this model would know that his labor power is interchangeable with that of the next person in line, his life, then—interchangeable also—reduced to a certain calculation of costs and return. If he rationally calculates it under these conditions, his role in the organization becomes one of minimal effort for the return desired, a continual probing of rules and limits until, inevitably, he goes too far and is fired. As he would have joined the C.C.C. in the first place for the job record as well as for the pay, this may well be the final stage before prison.

The worst-case workcrew supervisor, acting out a scenario in which he believes himself to be the foreman of a military construction crew or prison workcrew, would then interpret the actions of this corpsmember as criminal and find it a simple matter to combine the termination of employment with a recommendation of arrest for petty theft or drug use (ubiquitous in the C.C.C. as in other, similar segments of society). The business-manager type Center Director would regard this philosophically from afar, draw reluctant conclusions about the morals and lack of motivation of minorities or the underclass, and recalculate his labor costs against performance targets. The actions in this model are a familiar ritual, the Sartrean problematic inscribed within a world that elsewhere offers quite different possibilities.

Fortunately, this model does not define the entire society of the C.C.C. or any other volunteer corps. There is at least one other ideal triad, equally extreme, but in this case positive. This typical corpsmember would have joined for the country air, say, and the chance to learn certain skills, enjoy the companionship of other young adults, and, perhaps, to have the opportunity to complete an interrupted public schooling by acquiring a GED. The workcrew supervisor in this model would be himself an ex-corpsmember, or a teacher, or a social worker. The manager would have had experience as a labor organizer or high school counselor. They would all be idealists. For this corpsmember the pay is adequate, the hard work expected—challenging—and the miserable conditions an adventure. Learning to use rip-rap to rebuild a trail in the Sierra or a chainsaw to clear a trout stream of logging debris will be seen not as onerous but as a personal achievement. If a woman, this corpsmember would have the added satisfaction of acquiring nontraditional skills. Not forced into these circumstances, the corpsmember retains personal interests and ambitions, will often take a workcrew supervisor or center director as a role model and seek out educational opportunities. The C.C.C. is a temporary environment for this corpsmember, an occupation between high school and college or a way to finish that interrupted high school education. Some of these corpsmembers grow to like the C.C.C. and are recruited into the ranks of workcrew supervisors or even managerial staff.

The analogous ideal workcrew supervisor, with experience as a teacher or social worker or in the Peace Corps itself, will find interest in helping young people. These supervisors will devote extra hours to corpsmembers, inviting them to their homes, supervising recreational and educational activities, paying attention to the working and living environment, doing what they can to humanize this nearly self-contained world. (I have met many such members of the C.C.C. staff; they are among the finest people I have met in any organization. When the projects are merely funding opportunities, they are unhappy. They take personal responsibility for working against social, economic, and natural entropy, searching for teachable moments—sharing their knowledge with any corpsmembers who happen to be around at such moments.) They look to like-minded managers, people for whom the lives of all young people are of interest, or people seeking social change, or—between these—people who attempt to build protected social environments in which young people might have a chance to repair their lives, to escape marginalization.

In reality, the C.C.C. varies between these models. In any given center the corpsmembers, supervisors, and administrators will cover the entire spectrum between the two extremes sketched above, and life in that center will be as varied. The models allow an analysis of the logic of decisions and structures, which has been illuminating for work in educational matters with the C.C.C. As typical formations, they are useful when considering education in other, similar organizations, when considering these as educational organizations, for education is one of the activities that is negotiated between them.

The best of the education that occurs as a direct consequence of the structure of volunteer corps is experiential, and I have already pointed to it in the description of the second triad of ideal types. Corpsmembers may learn much, may learn employment skills, good work habits, knowledge about the natural world, or—in the case of those at urban centers—the history, structure, and mechanisms of their cities. Corpsmembers, and workcrew supervisors, may even learn about alternative community values in an environment not as desperate as that of inner-city minorities, in nearly utopian communities, protected, paradoxically enough, by a state-supported bureaucracy. Very little of such education is formal. The closest thing to classes, to lessons, might be an evening lecture on local ecology. Formal education under these circumstances takes place extraneously—and here the triads merge—as adult basic education, English as a second language, GED classes organized by the Corps but taught by teachers from local school districts. And all at once even the precarious virtues of the best of the volunteer corps vanish; we are back in the far from ideal world characteristic of all too many of our schools.

The structure of education in volunteer corps mirrors the place of adult basic education in the larger society. Often enough it is the concern of specialists who are not central to the organization. Sometimes they are not employees of the corps, but are related to it only as employees of referral services. Even when this is not the case, there is usually a sharp line between project staff and educational staff. These educational specialists and their work are seen as at once essential and marginal. Most volunteer corps make adult basic education opportunities available, yet none now fully integrate them with their central programs. This is partially due to the fundamental contradiction in their structures referred to at the beginning of this essay. As the conceptual framework of their organizers often contradicts the actualities of their operations, the educational needs of participants are difficult to meet. If an urban volunteer corps, for instance, is founded as a vehicle for allowing idealistic middle-class youth to be of service to their city, then why should it be of service to them? The first considerations for its organizers are the services it will offer to interested segments of the city. As, from this point of view, the California Conservation Corps offers other state departments services not easily obtainable as cheaply from alternative sources—fire fighting crews, flood emergency work, highway embankment weeding—so, too, an urban volunteer corps is constructed with the overriding goal of providing parallel urban services that will not compete with unionized labor or business. Educational services for the participants are thought of, but only as an adjunct, like transit fare. When it is found necessary to provide access to such services, it is often done by referral, as if it were not actually central to the organization's purpose or responsibility to enhance the educational opportunities of its participants.

The typical educational situation for a corpsmember (or "volunteer") is as a student in an adult basic education course—either on a referral basis by the corps or offered seemingly within the organization but actually by a school district employee seconded to it. In the country at large, adult basic education classes are the last resort of those whose education in the schools has been incomplete. Unfortunately, the curriculum and procedures of adult basic education are all too often oriented toward certification, not knowledge, and their teachers are frequently among those least able to resist such institutional pressures. Assigned by school districts, often ad hoc, to venues that offer little support, isolated from other teachers, isolated within, say, volunteer corps, from other staff personnel, they must work with large numbers of adults who have been seemingly carefully trained by the schools to resist education. These teachers often know only the least effective materials and methodologies: workbooks, standardized tests, nearly content-free courses of study. That they are frequently humane and self-sacrificing people only compounds the pity of it.

Before returning to the analysis of education as it takes place specifically in volunteer corps, some general reflections on education, particularly on adult basic education, are in order. The dull, test-oriented curricula of many adult basic education courses replicates those of the schools, which fail to provide so many of their students with satisfactory educational experiences. The lack of true educational content in these courses is experienced as boredom, and it is not going too far to say that this boredom is itself a manifestation of that domination that effectively perpetuates the absence of opportunity for a fully human life for large numbers of our people. This limiting of opportunity is characteristic of contemporary social organization, this boredom experienced as perfectly natural; it feels natural, familiar, to those who design or control institutions as well as to those controlled by them. This differentiation of opportunity is so much second nature for us all that it comes as something of a shock to realize that its perpetuation need not be integral to the operation of institutions. This is still a rich country; it can afford equality of opportunity. It is possible to analyze our institutions and in many cases find instances of "superfluous oppression," that is, structures or activities that limit opportunity, but that are not consciously desired by or necessary for those with the power to change them.

While working through these matters it is useful to remember that Sartre believed that in his country one aspect of the tyranny of the past over the present—which he called the practico-inert—was the petrified hatred of the French middle class for the workers, whose ancestors had been literally murdered by the nineteenth-century bourgeoisie. (He may very well have been right. It is common enough to hate those whom we have given cause to hate or fear us.) Operating in a universe actually characterized by scarcity, Sartre's logic allowed no possible alleviation of domination. But one must modify his theory when applying it to contemporary American life by reference to the unequal development of our regions and a tendency for scarcity to be local within a socio-economic structure also containing great wealth widely distributed.

Late-twentieth-century America is not nineteenth-century France, but even in our society the limiting of opportunity experienced by people appears to vary in inverse proportion to their power to resist it. Heirs of great fortunes, high government officials, world famous scholars—these have great latitude of action. Black teenagers have virtually none. There was once a socio-economic calculus that made this reasonable: the system rested on the work of those at the bottom. It seemed reasonable that they be kept immobile. This is no longer the case, particularly if we restrict our analysis to the area within our national boundaries. Whereas in nineteenth-century Russia or England the bounty of those who had it was derived from the poverty of those who did not, the poverty of the underclasses in the United States today is often economically irrelevant. Although there is a certain potential for violence, as was indicated twenty years ago, the possibility of the prosperity of the underclasses is not now a threat to those currently prosperous.

This would seem to allow a certain margin for the alleviation of the poverty of the underclass within institutional frameworks. Again, the United States is not France, class boundaries are more fluid here (if only due to the effects of racism), and those who control institutions may not have a Sartrean personal interest in the re-instantiation of old crimes. Managers often can be persuaded to alter their organizations in such a way as to minimize particularly onerous burdens on those affected by them. One field in which this can be done is that of education itself as it manifests in institutions not primarily educational. A volunteer corps is such a privileged institutional environment. It is possible within its framework to modify the form of education so as to decrease the tendency to limit opportunity for those most in need of it. I will give two examples of this—one real, large-scale, and well-underway, the other purely ideal.

The Literacy Program developed in the mid-1980s for the California Conservation Corps supplemented the adult basic education and other educational programs that were previously in place. Although some experimental work attempted to modify those structures—notably at the Los Angeles Urban Center and the Del Norte Center—the C.C.C. did not ask, nor did it seem practical, to attempt this on a statewide basis. I believe, however, that the approach used in the Literacy Program could be used for such a systematic change, and indeed that it has already laid the groundwork for such an effort. However, for the moment, the Literacy Program itself involved a tremendous initiative by the C.C.C. and appears to have had a significant effect on the education of some corps-members. The C.C.C. Literacy Program had three phases:

1. Staff training,
2. Literacy "spikes," and
3. Continuing in-service programs.

Staff training for literacy education in the C.C.C. was based on the theory that one of the problems with education in or out of the schools is the isolation of subject areas, teachers, educational opportunities, and the emphasis on noneducational issues, such as assessment and socialization. The first step in making the C.C.C. as a whole an environment in which literacy is widely diffused—not only available but inescapable—was to make it clear that literacy is the responsibility of everyone in the organization. Just as an effective literacy program in a high school would begin with the training of the entire staff as literacy instructors—administrators, physical education teachers, counselors, as well as English teachers—so in the C.C.C. virtually all staff attended literacy workshops.[1]

The form of these workshops become fairly standardized, as did their intention. The procedure was one of detoxification. Previously, literacy, and education in general, was perceived by many in the C.C.C. as having been inflicted upon them as part of the schooling process. We believed that if those who have not identified with this process are to be persuaded that education is of some value, they must first of all be brought to the point where they do not instinctively reject it ("I hate writing"), then given the opportunity to identify it with their own interests. As a consequence, very little traditional teaching went on in the workshops. The C.C.C. staff were brought together under the aegis of "literacy education" to work out among themselves how education was to become a function of programmatic activities within the organization. In order for them to do this, they themselves had to exercise certain skills, acquire and share certain types of knowledge. This process modeled what we believe should occur at the programmatic level.

A workshop might begin with a request that participants consider an education problem they have encountered. They were given some time to write their thoughts down, then placed in random groups of eight to twelve to come up with consolidated lists of such problems. Volunteer recorders from the groups then told the entire workshop what they had found. These findings were summarized and became the task for the remainder of the workshop. Smaller groups were given the assignment of finding solutions to individual problems, then these in turn were consolidated and groups arranged by job or site were asked to make those solutions specific—as plans to change how things were done among, say, fire crews, or at a specific C.C.C. center.

It is probably apparent from this somewhat schematic description that the workshops were notable for a number of things that were not done. No one was judged on the basis of the "quality" of their writing; no pedagogical methodologies were taught in isolation; no one had to work alone. Writing, reading, and learning were not considered apart from their utility for the task at hand. On the other hand, attention was paid to the fact that for many of the C.C.C. staff in the workshops, writing itself and educational concerns in general were more or less unfamiliar. The facilitators discussed, and demonstrated, techniques for individual and collaborative writing and did their best to argue against unproductive common beliefs and assumptions (such as the importance of spelling, handwriting, and strict adherence to distinctions of register). In addition to the materials produced as solutions to the array of problems posed by the workshop participants, the workshops also culminated in newsletters representing the work of as many participants as possible. These formed a record of the proceedings and an initiation into public writing for those participants who did not engage in it.

The California Conservation Corps literacy workshops involved most of the organization's civil service staff in thought and work about literacy and education. This, in itself, achieved the goal of bringing these matters to the fore, of calling into question the exclusive nature of the claims of project-oriented thought in the C.C.C. They also served as a protected environment to work against hostility to education for individual members of the staff, many of whom, like many of the corps-members themselves, had experienced schooling as a process by which education was poisoned for them. The workshops modeled a view of education and activities for replicating this achievement of detoxification in the Corps as a whole and produced plans for further work along this line at the various centers. On the other hand, they did not turn project supervisors into writing teachers and they did not result in a unified educational plan for the C.C.C. Their basic rationale was as a device for reducing resistance to education within the organization. The workshops were successful as measured against this modest goal and were probably successful in other ways also. Some staff were able to think of themselves, perhaps for the first time, as educators. Some began to function as organizers of educational projects of a similar nature. But the C.C.C.—and organizations like it—have powerful structural obstacles to much progress in this direction. The rigidity and hierarchical nature of its personnel practices are not accidental; they reflect the attitudes of the wider society toward the populations from which corpsmembers are drawn and the peculiar lives and career patterns of the staff themselves.

Frequently, the latter has not been particularly successful in competing for a share of the benefits of middle-class life and, having found a secure, comparatively well-paid job, they have internalized the values of the organization that has offered them refuge. Those values are not conducive to education or to the development of opportunities for corpsmembers who are seen as in need of discipline or as threats to property or as in some other way insufficiently socialized. The activities modeled in the workshops were, then, all too frequently thought of as valuable for staff but "unworkable" for corpsmembers.

Another aspect of the California Conservation Corps Literacy Program, the "Literacy Spike," was developed to give corpsmembers an intensive experience of education outside the constraints of the C.C.C.'s own adult basic education classes. ("Spike" is a C.C.C. term for work away from a residential center. A group "on spike" from Los Angeles might, for example, do flood control work at the Colorado River.) We had found that much of the schooling experienced by corpsmembers, both before and after they joined the organization, had been uninteresting for them and, it might be said, an expression of a lack of interest in them. It had been, in effect, a process of steadily reducing the possibilities for learning. The design of the Literacy Spikes was to reverse the structures and goals of school for those who had found school to be an unrewarding experience. There would be no testing, no curriculum, nothing to be learned merely as a requirement. It was to be education for its own sake.

Corpsmembers, many of whom had never been to a college campus, were brought to campuses of the University of California or the California State University and College system in groups of fifty or so, where for a number of weeks they spent a few hours a day with college instructors. The corpsmember to instructor ratio was quite low, about 6 to 1.[2] There was a large variety of resources available, including computers and video equipment, and the projects were often collaborative, frequently designed and carried out by the corpsmembers in small groups. The atmosphere of the Literacy Spikes was that of a research facility, perhaps a laboratory for the development of methods by which people who have been discouraged from seeking access to education would be aided in working out for themselves a way to counteract that experience. The detoxification image might be useful again: learning was to be purified of its poisonous school associations.

Where the experience of corpsmembers in school had frequently been limited to drill in workbooks and simplified readings, on a Literacy Spike they might have read, for example, quite challenging modernist or postmodernist plays. Where in school their relationship to the material studied was passive—they were to learn it—on the Literacy Spike that relationship was active. Working in small groups, they were encouraged to take a critical view of what they read or heard. Where in school they kept silent, or an attempt was made to that end, here they were encouraged to talk. And where in school all too often education was owned by the institution or a culture to which they hardly belonged, the typical relationship of a group of corpsmembers to a play they read was to use that play to enable them to make one of their own—as a text, as a tape, or as a video production. The approach was always one of collaboration, corpsmember initiative, the dissolution of lower-level skills in higher levels. Corpsmembers whose native language was not English were not given paradigm drills; they were asked to edit a newspaper, an instruction manual for computers, a volume of poetry. Those who had difficulty with inscription were given responsibility for composition or editing. Computers were not used as electronic workbooks; they were used as word processors. By the end of a Literacy Spike most of the corpsmembers involved seemed to feel that it had been their time, their experience, not one more thing to be endured, and their attitudes toward education and its possibilities had been changed significantly.

The effect of bringing corpsmembers onto a college campus for education was not altogether positive, nor, when positive, completely unproblematic. We were uncertain how long the novelty of these pleasant, unfamiliar experiences would continue to stimulate corpsmembers, how long this new interest in education by people who had been habituated to living outside the culture of learning would last after they left the campus. As the Literacy Spikes became institutionalized in the C.C.C., they too might have been bracketed by corpsmembers with the adult basic education classes as a mere tiresome necessity, one more demand on their time by an organization that tends to operate in a hierarchical mode—both while using the labor of corpsmembers for ends unrelated to their needs and when engaging in more benevolent activities. And some of the experiences of corpsmembers on campus were quite unpleasant for reasons having more to do with the college environment than with the C.C.C. itself. Black and Hispanic corpsmembers, for example, were shocked to see racist graffiti in the corridors at one campus. They took it to be directed at them, in particular. This is understandable, as they felt acutely that this place was not their place; the graffiti underlined these feelings. The corpsmembers differed from most people on campus in many ways; those differences were emphasized by their uniforms and special status. While the corpsmembers developed easy relationships with the campus maintenance personnel with whom they worked as part of the exchange of labor that financed the Literacy Spikes, they rarely had any informal contacts with students. The college students rarely talked with them, seemed threatened by them, treated them as unwelcome interlopers.

The presence of corpsmembers on college campuses is highly arti-

ficial. It might seem a typical liberal gesture, changing nothing fundamental. The reality of the situation is that few of them, white, black,
Oriental, or Hispanic, will ever go to college as regular students. And
all this takes place as an interlude within their year or less of service in
the C.C.C., as, indeed, only a few hours a day during the Literacy Spike
itself. When they returned to their normal tasks it was not unusual that
they were expected once again to be passive, lacking in and incapable
of initiative, students, perhaps, in an evening GED class intended to
give them a certain certification, not a broad education, or simply members of a workcrew that normally engages in project work as an aggregate
of individuals, individually—and constantly—judged and found wanting. And yet there is some hope that the third phase of the Literacy
Program, that in which the C.C.C. itself undertakes on-going staff training and concern for those matters, will at least influence the C.C.C.'s
own organizational culture toward greater respect for the educational
potential of corpsmembers. This may be the most difficult part of the
program. It seems improbable that a large organization, which conceives
of itself chiefly as having the task of providing the state the services of
young adults who have little employment experience, will change so
fundamentally because of an ancillary activity. But the C.C.C. has committed significant resources for a number of years to this Literacy Program,
has allowed it to function fairly autonomously, and has sought permanent
interagency agreements with the universities and continuing funding for
the program. It is quite possible that many corpsmembers will continue
to find that their experience of the C.C.C. has included an opportunity
to learn how to learn.

The California Conservation Corps is a large governmental institution, part of a continuum of such organizations that form the environment for most of us, from schools through the military, perhaps—or
the prisons, or large corporations—each of which imprints its common
purpose of social control through the effect of its form, as each also fulfills
other purposes through its more often noticed activities: fire fighting,
national defense, education, business. Most large-scale activities within
a society will express the essential characteristics of that society; taken
together, they *are* society. But it is also true that in any complex society
there is room for organized—as well as anarchic—activity that is not,
or attempts not to be, such an expression. Even in a society ultimately
characterized by the differential limiting of opportunities, there are lo-
cales where that character is mitigated by conscious effort or the logic
of social structure itself. The latter case may be illustrated by the comparative freedom of certain privileged groups. The instances of the former
are now fairly rare and usually small and unstable: Communes in the
sixties, alternative schools, religious organizations of one kind or another.
Most of these, too, must have links with the larger society, links that

become points of entry for the dominant structures of society, structures that eventually destroy most of these counter-entropic efforts. Reality intervenes, we become practical, the organization becomes "sounder," more successful, something quite different from what it had been in our naive, idealist period.

Some of the early administrators of the California Conservation Corps have left it to set up local corps, serving individual cities. Or, more accurately, serving young adults in those cities, as much of the impetus for this emigration has apparently derived from a desire to resolve the contradictions in the purposes of the larger organization. I will add to these one that I will call the Xanadu Conservation Corps, a utopian organization with an ideal educational program. The X.C.C. will possess some notable advantages over both the prototypical California Conservation Corps and such seemingly similar organizations as the New York City Volunteer Corps. Primarily, it will not suffer from their contradictory intentions. The X.C.C. will not attempt to find a middle-class group of young adults (and then settle for members of marginalized groups). And it will not be primarily offering itself to governmental agencies as a low-cost source of labor. The X.C.C. will accept middle-class corpsmembers; it will do work similar to the urban projects of the other organizations. However, the X.C.C. will be planned from the point of view of corpsmembers, who will come from marginalized groups as a rule, and the projects will be undertaken for their sake. This unitary orientation will allow the X.C.C. to conceive of all its activities as educational. The split between project staff and educational staff in the C.C.C. and the reliance on referral agencies by the N.Y.C.V.C. will be avoided. All crew supervisors will have the education of corpsmembers as a central responsibility. The minimal framework for this is derived from an analysis of the GED curriculum and examination. As the lack of a GED is an important barrier to opportunity for much of the population from which corpsmembers are drawn, a responsibility to help them with this certification is a given with any such organization. But just as it is, by definition, possible for most high school graduates to pass the GED, it will be possible to so integrate education with all X.C.C. activities that GED tutorials need be no more than an aid with test-taking techniques and other confidence building activities.

The founders of the X.C.C. believe that the schools all too often isolate people from one another, isolate subject areas, discourage responsibility and initiative. People who do not resist this sufficiently to obtain desirable certifications in spite of it often find themselves within organizations that magnify these negative aspects of schooling. As the effective approach to the learning of content for those who have difficulty with rote tasks is not a repetition of those drills but a move to higher level learning, so an effective approach to the form of that learning is to reverse the tendency toward isolation and irresponsibility, in this case to give corpsmembers, collaboratively, as much responsibility as practical. For instance, given a role in the selection of projects, they will naturally seek and acquire that knowledge and those skills required to accomplish the task: reading skills, numeracy skills, knowledge of social structures and historical events. X.C.C. workcrew supervisors will function as facilitators in these activities and as those responsible for the organizational structures that will resist the natural tendency to lapse into behavior and attitudes fostered by schooling in a society elsewhere characterized by domination and artificial scarcity. This will be quite difficult; it is easier to replicate than to replace the ideology of scarcity.

One common manifestation of this phenomenon is our use of the adjective "institutional" to refer to food or shelter: we assume that that food, that shelter, will be minimal, "poor." And it nearly always is. But this is an ideological poverty. Any governmental agency possesses the resources to provide good food, pleasant or even beautiful shelter, if it has the resources to provide these things at all. But it is common for those who manage institutions to ignore this, common for those managed to accept it. Workcrew supervisors in the X.C.C. will have to be carefully trained to resist this. If they are successful, then the rest should follow —if not easily, at least directly. Minimally, corpsmembers will achieve —as a direct consequence of their work—the knowledge and skills necessary to pass the GED.

Beyond that, the educational goals of the X.C.C. are much more ambitious. The link between education and certain ways of making a living is an artifact of economic history. Carpentry, gardening, machine tool operation are things one might do part of the day. There is no reason that one could not also learn—and teach—much during other parts of the day (or simultaneously). The proper organization of work so that it is varied, collaborative, and so that responsibility is widely distributed can foster a community of learning. Too often educational work in nonschool settings is limited to that which is closely linked with mere survival. Everyone should have the opportunity, also, to seek "useless" knowledge.

The educational plans of the Xanadu Conservation Corps are ambitious. One of the advantages it possesses over other, similar, organizations is nonexistence. But there are one or two volunteer corps that have similar goals. It is easy to be hopeful in such cases, easy also to be cynical. Why should success come here when it has failed to appear elsewhere? I, too, have these misgivings. But the organizers of these idealistic local volunteer corps have had much experience and believe it can be done. That belief is also an advantage. People who believe that nothing can be done usually are able to see their belief realized. Those who believe that people who have been failed by educational institutions can, nonetheless, achieve their educational goals might succeed.

The lessons of the literacy program of the California Conservation Corps and those presented as the utopian plans of the Xanadu Conservation Corps are valuable as lessons for those administering and those planning similar organizations. Remedial attention to the educational programs of existing volunteer corps can be similar to that undertaken by the C.C.C. This is already being done in some organizations that have instituted staff training programs in literacy education and attention is being given to the issue by others. As more volunteer corps are begun, corpsmembers' educational needs might well be addressed in the planning stages, so that attention to those needs will be an organic part of their structure. More ambitiously, work toward the organization of an American Conservation Corps may also include such planning. Either nationally or regionally, such possibilities are a positive development. As these efforts mature, attention might be focused on educating the significant population that has been failed by traditional education, so vital to their chances for decent lives.

Michael Holzman

Notes

1. These workshops were designed and facilitated by Lee Leeson, DeDe Gallow, Frank Gaik, and Judith Rodby of the University of Southern California Model Literacy Project.
2. The prototype Literacy Spike was designed and directed by Olga Connolly at the University of Southern California in Spring, 1984. Subsequent Literacy Spikes have been designed, and their staffs trained, by Judith Rodby. The first of these occurred at the University of California, Santa Barbara, directed by Sheridan Blau, the second at San Diego State University, directed by William Covino. More are planned for those and other UC and CSUC campuses.

14

Why Are We Talking About Discourse Communities?
Or, Foundationalism Rears Its Ugly Head Once More

In "Unhappy Consciousness in First-Year English," earlier in this collection, I attempted to use the notion of discourse community to help elucidate what I felt I achieved in a particular first-year writing class. Here I express some doubts about the usefulness of this concept in addressing the problem of how students enter into academic discourse. I believe that often the interest of writing theorists in describing academic discourse communities is an attempt to avoid the task of arguing the values, institutional structures, and language conventions that underlie the theory and practice of composition. Similarly, when in the writing classroom we think of our purpose as that of initiating students into the academic discourse community, we avoid confronting the different values, goals, expectations, and languages our students bring with them from other communities. As stated earlier in this book (see the introduction to "A Post-Freirean Model for Adult Literacy Education," p. 14), a social approach to writing requires always that we ask ourselves, What is it that we are teaching by *how* we teach?

The problem I see with many discussions of the notion of discourse communities is that they are underlaid by an ideology Richard Rorty calls foundational epistemology, an ideology whose primary assumption is that truth is not a judgment made in an immediate social situation but is rather grounded in external standards. In proposing that a hermeneutical perspective will render the notion of discourse communities more useful, I attempt to show how the discussions of discursive formations by Foucault, abnormal discourse by Rorty, and disciplinary matrices by Geertz are related to one another and how they can be used to support our claim that writing is a form of social action.

An additional analysis of the notion of discourse communities is suggested by the discussion of Sartre's theory of society in "Community-Based Organizations as Providers of Education Services" (see pp. 178–80). The established discourse community that is the focus of most research is analogous to what Sartre calls a collective, a group that is not a community but rather a collection of individuals whose actions are regulated by the rules and structures of the group. In contrast, discourse communities at their moment of formation are analogous to what Sartre calls a fused group, a group in which individuals achieve their social identity and act as a single person.

□   □   □

Being cited is a pleasant experience. I suppose it's a sign that one has been accepted into a discourse community. It's also a learning experience of sorts: you learn all kinds of things about what you wrote. From a recent citation I learned that in "The Ecology of Writing" I attempted "to describe a discourse community and the dialectic involved as discoursers and community each act upon the other and change each other" (Freed and Broadhead 1987, 155). I didn't know I had done that. I certainly hadn't been thinking about discourse communities, but, of course, I still could have been writing about them unwittingly. I decided this was a useful reading of my essay: it construed my ideas in a way I don't completely agree with, and it therefore gave me something to think about.

Within the last five years, the notion of discourse community has become the focus of much research among rhetoricians. It is an attractive notion. Raymond Williams observed that "community" is a "warmly persuasive word," one that "seems never to be used unfavorably" (1983, 76). Unlike "society," community is not usually thought of as being opposed to the needs of individuals. For all of us in the interdisciplinary field of rhetoric who have felt the frustration of being excluded from a discourse community, the pain of not being a member, of not being one of those in the know, it is also a comforting notion. Freed and Broadhead suggest that one reason we have begun to study discourse communities is "our profession's desire to establish itself *as* a discourse community," and they cite the benefits such a move would entail: standardization, autonomy, historicity, vitality (1987, 155). Furthermore, it offers us a familiar metaphor to describe a complex phenomenon, building as it does on the study of speech communities and of interpretive communities. In fact, it is such a familiar metaphor that it no longer seems to be a metaphor; it seems, instead, to be a natural, unavoidable way to think about discourse in social contexts.

How exactly to define a discourse community is a matter of some debate; it is a term that has been described as "either misleadingly vague or intriguingly rich" (Herndl, Fennell, and Miller forthcoming). In the broadest terms, most scholars who use the term agree that a discourse community is characterized by certain underlying assumptions, knowledge, values, and interests that its members hold in common and by the the use of certain language conventions—types of argument, genres, vocabulary. James Porter states these conditions concisely: "A 'discourse community' is a group of individuals bound by a common interest who communicate through approved channels and whose discourse is regulated" (1986, 38). Some—but not all—scholars also discriminate discourse communities from speech communities on the basis that discourse communities are defined by the use of written language. Academic disciplines seem to be the prototypical discourse communities, but professions, corporations, and hobby groups also seem to qualify.

I have referred to discourse communities, as I believe many of us do, as a rough and ready way of signaling an interest in the collaborative activities that lie at the heart of discourse, as a substitute for talking about "intertextuality," which encouraged us to see discourse as an artifact rather than as social activity. When I think of a discourse community, I think of very particular situations in which people come together in discourse and negotiate what they want to do and what matters to them. It is a community in the sense that it is concerned about each of its members, their goals, their needs, and what they have to offer. At least that is the ideal type of discourse community. But I am also aware that other people have rather a different sense of what a discourse community is and how it operates. And I am concerned that the concept is easily co-opted to serve purposes that are directly opposed to what I feel to be the most productive way of thinking about discourse.

A discourse community need not be thought of as an ongoing project, as something continually being made by its members. It can just as easily be thought of as an accomplished fact, a social structure that exists separately from the individuals who are its members. When it is thought of in this way, features such as shared values, conventions of language, and norms of behavior, which I think of as continually in flux, determined in an ongoing way by people who are in the discourse community, instead become static standards that are used to determine who is and who is not a member of the community. Thought of in this way, a discourse community is a way of labeling individuals as insiders or outsiders, as people who either have the requisite values, knowledge, and skills to belong, or lack these necessary qualifications. Everyone inside is all alike and significantly different from those who are outside. In this sense a discourse community is a way of regulating who has access to resources, power, even to discourse itself, and it creates gatekeepers to make sure that the right people get in and all others are excluded.

The argument I am making in this essay is that thinking about discourse communities in this way is a repressive political move, an exercise in arrogation of power to an elite. The concept of discourse community is like the concepts of Standard English and cultural literacy, which despite their descriptive potential and the often liberal intentions of those who use them are concepts that serve extremely well to exclude certain sorts of people from positions of power. Both Foucault and Rorty, whose ideas are often cited in rhetoricians' discussions of discourse communities, trace the ideology that lies behind these exclusionary concepts and emphasize the repressive uses of discursive formations and normal discourse, concepts that are often explicitly aligned with the concepts of discourse communities. After taking a brief look at their arguments and at Geertz's discussion of disciplinary matrices, I will demonstrate how looking at a discourse community in a hermeneutic rather than a foundational way (to borrow a distinction from Rorty), or as a way of life rather than simply as an intellectual commitment (as does Geertz), helps us understand better what happens in a real discourse situation— a meeting of the board of an environmental coalition.

Finally, I will suggest that what happens in the writing classroom is not best thought of in terms of joining a discourse community, that this perspective focuses our attention on what changes must be made in students in order to "socialize" them into the community. Like Patricia Bizzell (1986) and Diana George (1988), I am concerned about the way in which the particular values and particular languages of academic discourse exclude students who come from backgrounds other than young, white, middle-class America. But I do not think we will make much progress in helping these students until we refuse to see their situation as the inevitable consequence of the social fact of the academic discourse community and instead use other ways of thinking about discourse communities, ways that will allow us to ask questions such as what students can contribute to the discourse or what changes must be made in our institutions in order to allow students to participate.

Foucault, in his essay entitled "The Discourse on Language," and Rorty, in *Philosophy and the Mirror of Nature*, tell similar stories of the dominant tradition in Western thought, a tradition marked by an attempt to control what Foucault calls "the specific reality of discourse in general" (1972, 227). Foucault offers a taxonomy of mechanisms for the control of discourse, among which he lists disciplines and fellowships of discourse. In the beginning of his lecture he speaks compellingly of the fears an individual has of discourse and the assurance offered by institutions—

social groups; his description reminded me of Shaughnessy's basic writers, individuals for whom "academic writing is a trap, not a way of saying something to someone" (1977, 7):

> Inclination speaks out, "I don't want to have to enter this risky world of discourse; I want nothing to do with it insofar as it is decisive and final; I would like to feel it all around me, calm and transparent, profound, infinitely open, with others responding to my expectations, and truth emerging, one by one. All I want is to allow myself to be borne along, within it, and by it, a happy wreck." Institutions reply: "But you have nothing to fear from launching out; we're here to show you discourse is within the established order of things, that we've waited a long time for its arrival, that a place has been set aside for it—a place which both honors and disarms it; and if it should happen to have a certain power, then it is we, and we alone, who give it that power." (Foucault 1972, 215–16)

It is the disarming and perversion of discourse by social institutions that Foucault discusses in this lecture and in his other "archaelogical" works, and the most powerful of the "systems of exclusion" he discusses is the "will to truth."

He traces the origin of the will to truth to fifth century Greece, when, he says, the Sophists were routed: truth came to be a matter not of the socially situated discourse event but of a regulated way of speaking. Foucault says,

> the day dawned when truth moved over from the ritualized act— potent and just—of enunciation to settle on what was enunciated itself: its meaning, its form, its object and its relation to what it referred to. (218)

This is the moment of foundationalism, the move in which a ground for truth outside of the ongoing event of discourse was made to seem necessary. The move owed its success, in large part, to its principled denial of its own origins: if truth is located not in the particular social milieu but rather in the universal logic of categories of thought and/or language forms, one need not consider the motivating factors for arguments and theories, for they are assumed to be accessible to and unchanged by all who seek after truth. To the Sophists' conception of the reality of discourse, Foucault opposes the new category of true discourse, which is blind to its infrastructure:

> True discourse, liberated by the nature of its form from desire and power, is incapable of recognizing the will to truth which pervades

it; and the will to truth, having imposed itself upon us for so long, is such that the truth it seeks to reveal cannot fail to mask it.

Thus, only one truth appears before our eyes: wealth, fertility, and sweet strength in all its insidious universality. In contrast, we are unaware of the prodigious machinery of the will to truth, with its vocation of exclusion. (219–20)

The self-validating nature of the will to truth—its imperviousness to challenges from particular individuals or groups—makes it difficult to disrupt, or even perceive. By now, twenty-five centuries later, the process of measuring reality against a set of external, unchanging, and therefore valid standards and excluding as false or imaginary any perceptions that cannot be explained by these standards seems simply to be the natural way of proceeding, and any suggestion that truth is a matter of particular actual situations seems dangerously relativistic.

Still, the actual, ongoing, socially situated event of discourse remains a threat to the will to truth, an arena in which the outcome seems to be determined more by practical than by theoretical considerations. And so the event of discourse must be elided:

Western thought has seen to it that discourse be permitted as little room as possible between thought and words. It would appear to have ensured that *to discourse* should appear merely as a certain interjection between speaking and thinking. (227)

The passage between signs and meanings, between signifier and signified, is made to seem automatic, determined once and for all by such notions as that of the founding subject who "grasps intuitively the meanings lying within" the language (228), or that of originating experience, in which "things murmur meanings our language has merely to extract" (228). Truth is simply a matter of finding the right word to match one's inner feelings or to match the evident meanings of the real world; the activities of discourse "never involve anything but signs" (228). Again, the focus is not on the act of enunciation but on what is enunciated.

Foucault's purpose in his "archaeological" studies is to question the will to truth, to restore to discourse its character as an event, to abolish the sovereignty of the signifier. The result, he emphasizes, is not some ideal "world of uninterrupted discourse" (229). The reality of discourse is characterized by its *discontinuity*, which is to say that it is not grounded in any "original," "true" language; by its *specificity*, which is to say that it is not grounded in some prediscursive reality; and by its *exteriority*, which is to say that it is not self-determined or determined by some interior standard of coherence, but rather determined by "its external

conditions of existence" (229). The result is Rorty's version of hermeneutics.

In his arguments against foundational epistemology, Rorty offers
hermeneutics not as " 'successor subject' to epistemology" but as "an
expression of hope that the cultural space left by the demise of epistemology will not be filled—that our culture should become one in which
the demand for constraint and confrontation is no longer felt" (Rorty
1979, 315). Hermeneutics is an attempt to reconceive what it means to
understand something, what it means to be rational, and what it means
to participate in discourse:

> For hermeneutics, to be rational is to be willing to refrain from
> epistemology—from thinking that there is a special set of terms in
> which all contributions to the conversation should be put—and to
> be willing to pick up the jargon of the interlocutor rather than
> translating it into one's own. For epistemology, to be rational is to
> find the proper set of terms into which all contributions should be
> translated if agreement is to become possible. For epistemology,
> conversation is implicit inquiry. For hermeneutics, inquiry is routine
> conversation. Epistemology views the participants as united in what
> Oakeshott calls an *universitas*—a group united by mutual interests
> in achieving a common end. Hermeneutics views them as united
> in what he calls a *societas*—persons whose paths through life have
> fallen together, united by civility rather than by a common goal,
> much less by a common ground. (318)

It is in this context that he introduces the distinction between normal
and abnormal discourse. In a much-quoted passage he explains,

> normal discourse is that which is conducted within an agreed-upon
> set of conventions about what counts as a relevant contribution,
> what counts as answering a question, what counts as having a good
> argument for that answer or a good criticism of it. Abnormal dis-
> course is what happens when someone joins in the discourse who
> is ignorant of these conventions or who sets them aside. (320)

From the point of view of epistemology, abnormal discourse is at best
an accident, something not to be explained but rather to be eliminated
as quickly as possible by either socializing or excluding the ignorant
person. From the point of view of hermeneutics, abnormal discourse is
an important object of study, for though abnormal discourse produces
nonsense, it also produces intellectual revolution.

As Rorty takes care to point out, the difference between epistemology and hermeneutics is not that one is rational and the other ir-

rational. Both are rational on their own terms; both are ways of trying to make sense of the world. Our choice of which way is appropriate or useful depends on how familiar we are with the phenomenon being observed:

> We will be epistemological where we understand perfectly well what is happening but want to codify it in order to extend, or strengthen, or teach, or "ground" it. We must be hermeneutical where we do not understand what is happening but are honest enough to admit it, rather than being *blatantly* "Whiggish" about it. (Rorty 1979, 321)

Epistemology is possible when cultures, or areas of culture, are so stable that the accepted standards are well known and easy to isolate. But when cultures are in transition, when, as Geertz puts it, the genres of discourse blur, hermeneutics becomes necessary, for the well-established standards that epistemology relies upon disappear.

Geertz agrees with Rorty in seeing the current situation in intellectual life as unstable: "the lines grouping scholars together into intellectual communities, or (what is the same thing) sorting them out into different ones, are these days running at some highly eccentric angles" (1983, 23–24). Geertz also emphasizes the cultural impact of ways of thinking:

> the various disciplines (or disciplinary matrices), humanistic, natural scientific, social scientific alike, that make up the scattered discourse of modern scholarship are more than just intellectual coigns of vantage but are ways of being in the world. . . . to set out to deconstruct Yeats's imagery, absorb oneself in black holes, or measure the effect of schooling on economic achievement is not just to take up a technical task but to take on a cultural frame that defines a great part of one's life . . . (155)

Geertz raises here a most worrisome question for those who think of the teaching of writing as the initiation of students into the academic discourse community: is it ethical, or reasonable, or possible to require such fundamental changes in people in return for what we offer them?

His way of framing the question is particularly useful, for he sees intellectual communities not merely as a matter of intellectual beliefs and discourse conventions but rather "in terms of the [cultural] activities that sustain them" (Geertz 1983, 152). Thus, Geertz advocates ethnography as an effective way to study such communities, a methodology that leads one to investigate such things as the relations among community members, which are "not merely intellectual, but political, moral, and broadly personal (these days, increasingly, marital) as well," the career patterns of members, and the different maturation cycles in different communities (157–59). When we see discourse within groups in this way, we are able to discern how participation is limited or otherwise affected by social factors such as patterns of relationship, economic and class structure, and institutional arrangements. Geertz thus offers a useful correction to Rorty's idealistic portrayal of the discourse of hermeneutics, for even if the epistemological assumption of external standards of knowledge is dispensed with, not everyone has equal access to the discourse. What Geertz does, like Foucault, is direct attention to the external conditions of the existence of discourse, so that the source of power within a discourse can be seen to arise not from the meaning, form, and objects of one's discourse, but rather from one's position in the structures of society.

The ideology of the will to truth, or foundationalism, infects many notions we might otherwise find useful in discussing writing as social action. In the February 1988 issue of *College English*, Patricia Bizzell and James Sledd separately explain how, within the context of foundationalism, both the "classless and unchanging grapholect" of Standard English and the canon that is the object of cultural literacy appear as accomplishments, undeniable facts of social life that we must somehow learn to live with. Sociolinguists often define Standard English as simply the dialect, out of many equally valuable dialects, that assures upward mobility in the mainstream culture; socially responsible literary scholars argue for the inclusion of the knowledge and texts of so-called minority cultures within the canon. But the foundational belief that true knowledge and right action must be grounded in standards external to the immediate situation directs attention away from the question of how these standards are used by particular interests in the immediate situation. The requirement for Standard English is set up as a barrier against those whom the dominant classes wish to exclude from economic and social equality; the requirement for knowledge of the canon (especially if it includes a few texts by minority authors) insures the dominance of a uniform culture, protecting it against the "anarchy" of multicultural perspectives. As Bizzell points out, "this view of the monolithic power of academic literacy is . . . itself politically oppressive" (1988, 141).

The notion of discourse communities has been offered as a corrective to foundational notions. What it is possible to say and what language is appropriate to say it in is determined not by some set of universal truths but rather by conventions that serve the purposes of distinct communities of people who are drawn together by common interests and goals. A discourse community, like a speech community, a dialect, an interpretive community, or, in fact, like any social group that can develop into a discourse community, has compelling social functions. As it standardizes rules and expectations and begins to establish traditions, it makes discourse both possible and necessary. But at the same time and in the same way it establishes a mechanism of exclusion: standards for the type of discourse that will be—and will not be—accepted by the community. As Freed and Broadhead describe it:

> The paradigms reign like prelates and governments reign: they set an agenda and attempt to guarantee its meeting, often rewarding those who do and discouraging those who don't. They legislate conduct and behavior, establishing the eminently kosher as well as the unseemly and untoward. (1987, 156)

Discourse communities, like Standard English and cultural literacy, can function as a set of external standards that are used to control and constrain the immediate discourse, legitimating the discourse of those who are members—Orazio Grassi, Antonio Salieri, students who are white and middle-class—and silencing those who are not—Galileo, Mozart, students who are black, Hispanic, native American, foreign, or lower-class. From the perspective of foundationalism, discourse communities are distinguished by features of "what is enunciated" (Foucault 1972, 218)—what language, values, genres, and media of communication are appropriate and required of those who wish to enter the discourse. From the perspective of foundationalism, entering a discourse community means finding "the proper set of terms into which all contributions should be translated" (Rorty 1979, 318). From the perspective of foundationalism, a discourse community is "an *universitas*—a group united by mutual interests in achieving a common end" (Rorty 1979, 318).

Tradition, as Saussure noted, is essential to language and, by extension, to discourse. But there is a difference between seeing it as somehow prior to and impervious to discourse and seeing it as a force within discourse. Bakhtin argues that the centripetal force of the unitary language is always in tension with the centrifugal force of the socially and historically located individual utterance (1981). Sledd, too, emphasizes the importance of this dynamic when he argues that "English will remain a world language only if its users everywhere can feel that in some sense English is their own, so that diversity and individual identity will be served as well as tradition and wide intelligibility" (Sledd 1988, 174). Norms and conventions are always being established in a discourse, but at the same time they are always being disrupted by voices speaking out of the multiple discourses of our pluralistic society. It is this dialectical dynamic of discourse, its essential heteroglossia, that I was attempting to spell out in "The Ecology of Writing"; it is the recurrent eruption of foundationalist assumptions in discussions of the notion of discourse communities that makes me reluctant to adopt it as a model for the operation of discourse as a whole.

One of the most explicit foundationalist definitions of discourse community was offered by John Swales at the 1987 Conference on College Composition and Communication. In order to demonstrate what such a definition excludes, I would like now to apply his definition and his criteria to a particular instance of group discourse—a board meeting of an environmental coalition. I was present at this meeting as a new member of the board, representing one of the seventeen groups that make up the coalition. We met in the staff house of a state forest headquarters, a log building constructed in the 1930s by the Civilian Conservation Corps; coincidentally, I had once lived there when it was a conservation post. The meeting lasted for two days, with occasional breaks for canoeing, botanizing, and bird watching.

As a discourse community, the board members obviously exhibit what Swales calls "a communality of interest": besides personal interests in outdoor activities, members agree on a common goal—careful resource management and preservation of natural environments. At this meeting, the board made the group's common goal explicit by adopting a long-term policy statement: "[The environmental coalition] wants to bring about a basic change to strict enforcement of our environmental and resource management laws." Issues subsequently discussed at the meeting included sand dune protection, pesticide bans, low-level radioactive waste facility siting, bottle deposits, solid waste management, and water management. But the moment at which I recognized the group as a discourse community came at the beginning of the first session, when a board member climbed on a chair to unscrew most of the twenty 100-watt light bulbs in the rustic baroque chandelier overhead. All he said was, "We don't need all of these."

Swales emphasizes that discourse communities share "common public goals," a criterion that allows for the disparate and private goals of individual members, but I think that the cohesiveness of discourse communities relies more fundamentally on such tacit shared values as the valuing of resource conservation that underlies this board member's comment. In fact, it is difficult to enunciate the common public goals of this group in any terms other than the very general ones of the long-term policy statement, for the member groups differ in their positions on many particular issues, in their priorities, and in their preferred strategies for bringing about change. Swales also recognized this difficulty in posing the example of the discourse community of legislators, aides, lobbyists, and political journalists whose common public goal could only be the extremely general one of "manufacturing legislation." The generality and often deliberate ambiguity of stated goals of groups serves a real function: it creates the illusion of agreement by allowing members to interpret the stated goals in their own way.

Swales also points out that "the common public goal may be not that apparent on the *surface* level." But what this means is that the intelligibility of the so-called public goals of a discourse community relies on shared values that are rarely made explicit and thus are inaccessible to analysis or debate. As Stanley Fish said about interpretive communities, "you will agree with me (that is, understand) only if you already agree with me" (1980, 173). Certainly, these values are not as stable as they appear from this perspective; underlying values are in fact what is being negotiated whenever a group argues over its goals. Nor are the values as mysterious as they appear in Fish's formulation: they originate in the perceived needs and experiences of the group's members, and they change along with changes in these perceived needs and experiences. The appearance of such stable, transcendent values is the result of defining a discourse community as a foundational concept; from this perspective the discourse of the community must be grounded in something outside of itself, something more permanent, some preferably inexplicit but well-known values and conventions.

This is not to say that the notion of shared values plays no part in discourse in groups. The assertion of tacit shared values can be used to try to exclude people who are deemed to be undesirable members of the group, as Fish demonstrates so often and so persuasively. Furthermore, challenging or reinterpreting what are assumed to be shared values is a means of asserting power within a group. The initiator of the light bulb incident at the environmental coalition meeting represented a group from one of the remoter areas of the state who, though he was very active in his own group, was unable to attend the board meetings regularly because he could not afford the time and expense of traveling to the normal meeting place in the state capital. Later that morning, he raised the issue of whether the coalition overemphasized the concerns of the groups located in the more populated areas closer to the capital; the next day, he was one of the board members who insisted that meeting times and places be restructured to enable more of the member groups to participate more completely. Reinterpreting the light bulb incident in this context, I would guess that this board member was playing a game of one-upsmanship in his action, attempting to establish the power of the group he represented and of other groups like his. What he meant by unscrewing the light bulbs and saying "we don't need all of these" was something like this: those of us who live closer to the land live our environmental commitments rather than just talking about them as you do in the cities. He drew attention to the question of resource conservation not to align himself with the shared values of the group but to demonstrate a schism in the group and to claim, implicitly, that his group's values were central to the purpose of the coalition.

The second criterion for discourse communities Swales lists is participatory mechanisms: there must be "a forum" in which group members can interact. This criterion seems unquestionable, for if there is no means of interaction, there can be no discourse. But from the perspective Geertz offers on discourse communities, it is clear that participatory mechanisms keep some people from participating at the same time as they enable others to participate. The principal forum of the environmental coalition is the monthly board meetings. At this meeting, the structure of the board meetings was under attack because it effectively disenfranchised some member groups and placed some severe restrictions on people who could serve as board members. The problem might be thought of as purely one of logistics: the state is a large one, and it is always difficult to fit twenty people's schedules together and come up with a meeting time. But economics and class structure are also clearly involved. Environmental groups are not notably well-funded and thus cannot or do not wish to use their limited resources for air travel to meetings or protracted conference calls. Those board members who are paid employees of member groups thus want to meet on workdays, and those board members who are unpaid volunteers can meet on workdays only if they have occupations that allow them flexible use of their time. Though all board members are college educated, many with advanced degrees, the careers of those board members who are not paid staff of the group they represent vary from that of running a bed and breakfast hotel in a resort town to bookstore clerk to lawyer to college professor, with the result that board members have quite different competing demands on their time and energy. Finally, one should recognize that the fact that environmental groups face such difficulties in finding an effective participatory mechanism is no accident given the priorities of our economic system.

A third criterion Swales lists is that a "discourse community has developed and continues to develop discoursal expectations . . . genres that articulate the operations of the discourse community." He allows that "discourse communities will vary in the extent to which they are norm-developed, or have their set and settled ways. Some will be extremely conservative ('This is the way we do things here') while others may be constantly evolving." As he suggests, the attitude a group takes toward discoursal expectations is fundamentally a political one, a fact that is obscured when they are thought of as transparent means of facilitating the work of a group. A particularly interesting norm of the environmental coalition is the veto provision, which codifies the expectation that all positions taken by the coalition must be supported by every member group. Needless to say, this provision makes it extremely difficult for the coalition to formulate positions, and on some issues of significant environmental concern, it has been impossible for the coalition to take a position. When the question of whether the provision could be abolished was discussed, it quickly became apparent that the function of the provision was not simply to assure the successful prom-

ulgation of postions that would come with unanimity within the coalition. The relevant fact is that those member groups who are local chapters
of national organizations cannot take positions that conflict with positions taken by their national organization, and, thus, they would not be
able to maintain membership if the veto provision were abolished. Since
these five groups are the best-funded and most well-known members of
the coalition, contributing 40 percent of the dues, their participation is
clearly essential, and the veto provision tacitly recognizes their political
power. That the provision is intended to serve only this function was
made clear in the discussion that followed the decision to retain it: as
the minutes of the meeting report, "It was agreed that the veto should
be discussed and explained in meetings on a regular basis in order to
avoid misuse of this provision."

A fourth criterion Swales lists is perhaps the one most noticeable
to those outside a particular group: a discourse community "possesses an
inbuilt dynamic towards an increasingly shared and specialized terminology." He notes as especially diagnostic the development of "com-
munity-specific acronyms and abbreviations." This was the first board
meeting I had attended, and many of the board members introduced
themselves using the acronyms of the groups they represented: "feet,"
"cack," "youpeck." Though I recognized that most of the acronyms
included an E for "environmental" I had no idea what most of the groups
were or where they were located, and, thus, not being one of those in
the know, I saw the group as a discourse community. Discourse communities seem to exist most clearly in these moments of exclusion, and
the impenetrability of acronyms and abbreviations may explain why they
in particular create such frustration and bad feeling in those whom they
exclude. But as Labov and other sociolinguists have shown, a person's
use of specialized language is a reliable index of his or her acceptance of
the values of the group. Thus, specialized language is used within the
discourse of a group expressively, to indicate a person's current orientation to the group's values and purposes, and rhetorically, to persuade
other members of the necessity of group solidarity. One of the founding
members of the environmental coalition who always used acronyms in
referring to member groups also expressed impatience with member groups
like mine who found it difficult to attend board meetings consistently.
And specialized language can be used to withhold power from new group
members or marginal group members by effectively excluding them from
the discourse.

The final criterion Swales lists is that a discourse community "has
a critical mass of members with a suitable degree of relevant discoursal
and content expertize." People come and go in discourse communities,
entering as "apprentices" and leaving by death or by choice, but the
"survival of the community depends on a reasonable ratio of experts and

novices." The language Swales uses here indicates most clearly the foundational ideology that underlies his notion of a discourse community. New members are characterized by what they lack—they are "apprentices," "novices"—while the essential members of the group are characterized by what they have—they are the "experts." The only way into a discourse community is seen to be the acquisition of the expertise that somehow exists prior to and apart from the members and that defines the community. Again, at some level, the criterion of expertise could be said to apply to the environmental coalition: most members understand what's at stake in environmental issues and often know quite a bit about the scientific and technical principles involved in waste disposal, pollution, and the ecology of natural populations; they understand legislative agendas and keep track of legislators' positions; they know the regulations that govern nonprofit organizations. Sometimes, people volunteer to represent their group on the board of the coalition so that they can learn more about these things. But more often new members already have this expertise and join the board because they perceive that they have something to offer the group and because they have goals that they think the group can help them achieve. Nor is this, I think, a peculiarity of this particular group. New PhD's and new employees are typically much better read and more knowledgeable about recent scholarship and findings than longer-term members of academic disciplines or professions; even many new members of hobby groups already have a great deal of expertise and join only to avail themselves of the social benefits of interacting with people who have similar interests. New members of groups, in fact, often are a dominant influence in reformulating the values, goals, participatory mechanisms, discoursal expectations, and language of a group and in bringing new knowledge and expertise to the group.

When defined within the perspective of foundational epistemology, a discourse community seems to exist prior to discourse; it serves as the "ground" of all "rational" discourse. Thus, knowledge, power, success are seen to flow from the community automatically to those who before their apprenticeship lacked any relevant cognitive or social abilities. Despite what Fish would have us think, hermeneutics differs from epistemology on just this point: it insists that the reality of discourse need not be grounded in something outside it or prior to it, that it exists in the real world in actual social practices. Within the epistemological domain, assumptions are foundational; they must be accepted in order for discourse to be possible. Within the hermeneutical domain, assumptions are positions within discourse, often changed or modified. Thus, from the hermeneutical perspective, power in discourse flows not from acquaintanceship with the common interests and conventions of communities but from an interplay of social systems and relationships.

Finally, if we turn to the particular situation of discourse within the writing classroom, we find that political activity is not just a professional responsibility, as Bizzell argues (1986), but rather inescapable: consciously or not, what we do both in our teaching and in our theory affects who has the power to engage in academic discourse and who does not. What we choose to do is determined by many complicated and often conflicting factors. We are concerned about defining and establishing composition as an academic discipline. We are concerned about the status of writing teachers, many of whom are graduate students or part-time faculty. We are concerned about the status of writing classes within our universities. We are concerned about governmental pressure to establish standards for the evaluation of writing and of writing teachers. Because we are not in powerful positions within our universities or our society, we may wish to see the writing classroom in a foundational way, as a stable discourse community, one that validates our interests, our values, our status, our way of life, automatically. But we are also concerned that our students—all of our students—become effective writers, learn how to enter into discourses, which may not be the same thing as the foundational notion of joining a discourse community as a neophyte.

Our students' purposes in coming to college are various. They want to get a better job, they want to be certified for a particular career, they need some more time to grow up before taking on real world responsibilities—some even just like school. Their teachers have equally varied purposes. Some of us want our students to learn to think critically and be able to handle language so that they will be able to cope with an increasingly literate and complex world. Others want them to assimilate the central ideas and texts of the dominant culture. Still others offer training in particular techniques and procedures. Except at an extremely general level, it is hard to discern a shared purpose and shared values of what is sometimes called the academic discourse community. Even within disciplines, as Geertz has shown, governing metaphors and conventions of discourse are much less stable than they once were considered to be. Under these conditions, claiming that a foundational notion of discourse communities should guide our teaching of writing can only be seen as cynical and self-serving. And it is far from clear that students want to—or should want to—join any of these communities we are creating for ourselves.

Geertz points out that membership in a discourse community is not a superficial intellectual commitment, that engaging in the activities of a community means taking on "a cultural frame that defines a great part of one's life" (1983, 155). In this respect, drawing an analogy between students in writing classes and doctoral students in English literature or new members of the Detroit Audubon Society may be misleading; academic discourse may be like other discourse communities in some ways, but with regard to the nature of the commitment required of members it is not. In general, when people enter a profession or join a group they do so because people in the profession or group seem to have values and goals similar to their own. As my collegue John Flynn remarked, there are no American Legion members in the Peace Alliance. Geertz cites the example of an associate professor who decided that, despite his successful career, he could no longer tolerate membership in the discipline of mathematics:

> Precisely because there is no "maybe" in mathematics, and because pure mathematics has become so relentlessly detached from reality, I have decided that I cannot afford any more such victories. This fall I will enroll in medical school. (1983, 162)

In these examples, the decision about whether or not to be a member is a relatively free one: no one compels people to join the Peace Alliance or the Audubon Society, and the successful mathematician will undoubtedly become an equally successful doctor. Students entering writing classes are not quite so free. The course must be successfully completed if one is to receive the degree that is the ticket to middle-class security and respectability. Students who discover that the values of this community are not for them face much more serious consequences if they decide to opt out of the community than did the associate professor of mathematics. And the values they are asked to accept may not, at least to them, seem related to what their purpose was in enrolling in college.

This is an agonizing dilemma for writing teachers, for we believe that becoming educated necessarily involves changing at least some values. Earlier in this collection, in "Unhappy Consciousness in First-Year English," I argued that one thing our academic community values is the ability to adopt different perspectives, for the negative viewpoint enables us to disrupt the omnipresent technological rationality of our society. I also noted that one student in my class, whom I called Bartleby, when asked to set out an academic project in this way, said, in essence, I should prefer not to. I wanted Bartleby to come to understand the value of this kind of critical thinking, and I wanted him to do this by demonstrating critical thinking in his papers. But despite considerable encouragement (pressure) from me and from his classmates, Bartleby refused, clinging instead to what I surmised to be his home community's trust in our society and distrust of "socialist" ideas. To do what I asked involved changing values that he would not—or could not—change. Should I conclude that because he refused to change his values, he remained uneducated in some ways, that he deserved the C he got in the course? I think it would be very difficult for most of us to assent to this conclusion, but then how are we to assess satisfactory participation in the writing class?

This apparent conflict between respecting students' values and educating them illustrates how difficult it is to avoid slipping into foundationalist assumptions. Though education does involve changing values,
this does not mean that students must simply adopt their teachers' values,
nor is it clear in general that writers need to assimilate what someone
defines as the constraints of a community before they can participate
within that community. A hermeneutical perspective enables us to realize
that the simple fact of engaging in discourse with people whose values
and beliefs differ from theirs will change our students' values, though
they might not come to value exactly what we value; it also suggests
that our goal in the writing class should be to enable all students to
participate in whatever way they can, that their education depends on
their participation. In requiring Bartleby to demonstrate a certain kind
of critical thinking in his work in the course I acted on the assumption
that valid evaluation must rely on standards that are prior to and external
to the discourse of the class itself. Instead of responding to Bartleby, I
tacitly excluded him from the legitimate discourse of the class by ignoring
the comments he made in the common computer file that I felt to be
irrelevant or inappropriate. I might better have asked Bartleby to explain
why he responded to Marcuse's ideas as he did and evaluated his work
on the basis of what it contributed to the discourse of the class. His
comments might have helped other students understand better their own
resistance to Marcuse's ideas, and validating the usefulness of Bartleby's
contributions in this way certainly would have moved Bartleby closer to
an appreciation of the social value of writing.

If we insist that students adopt what we see as the values of our
community (our values), we will effectively withhold power within academic discourse from all students who come from a different generation,
a different ethnic background, a different race, a different sex, a different
economic class. If we insist on participation in the set forum for academic
discourse—the classroom—we will effectively withhold power within
academic discourse from all students who must hold full-time jobs or who
have children and no daycare or who are handicapped. If we insist on
the use of specified genres and terminology, we will effectively withhold
power within academic discourse from those students who wish to criticize
or explore. If we insist on the acquisition of the narrow range of expertise
relevant to our community, we will effectively withhold power within
academic discourse from those students whose educational goals do not
fit within established disciplines.

Alternatively, we can explain why we value what we do, and listen
to our students' explanations for theirs; we can adopt alternative participatory mechanisms—computer classes? night classes? family classes?;
we can discuss the functions genres and terminology serve and the functions of foregrounding and parodying these conventions; we can dem-

onstrate how new genres and terminology develop by translating our discourse into their language as often as we force them to translate their discourse into our language; we can encourage students to take from the expertise of our community that which is most relevant to their own educational goals, and we can take advantage of their expertise in areas relevant to our own goals. In short, we can treat students as people who do know something about how to engage in discourse and who want to talk and write with us in order that we may all learn something, whether we agree in the end or not.

Marilyn M. Cooper

15

Teaching Is Remembering

In a sense, this essay should come first, as it marks the social turn of our thought, at least as something more than intellectual tradition. It narrates what was quite literally a move out from the university into the world, a move prompted and impelled by the wonderful energy of Olga Connolly, a remarkable woman while throwing the discus in the Olympics or dancing all night barefoot at a Kremlin reception, but most of all remarkable while trying to even out the playing field of life in Watts and El Barrio.

We have decided to conclude with this essay. We are, after all, teachers.

☐   ☐   ☐

The intercom buzzed.

"Yes?"

"Olga Something on line one."

"Thanks."

It was a few days before the spring final examination for Composition 101. I was in my normal condition for the occasion: exhausted, nervous, and bored. It's hard to maintain all three of these at the same time, but I understand that night nurses and soldiers on guard duty are familiar with the required techniques. Olga Something was a CETA clerk with the County—I thought that was what she said—and wanted me to help with writing there. Oh yes, happy to, but a little busy right now, could you call back in ten days?

The intercom buzzed.

"Yes?"

"That Olga person on line one."

"Really?"

People in Los Angeles don't usually call back when they say they will; it must be the Hollywood influence. Yet here was Olga, right on schedule, calling back on the tenth day. It turned out that she was not a CETA clerk. She was working with the California Conservation Corps, Jerry Brown's reincarnation of the Depression era Civilian Conservation Corps. Could she talk with me about teaching the corpsmembers to write? Sure, the grades were in and I had nearly forgotten about being exhausted, nervous, and bored. I found Irene and Betty and told them that Olga Something would be talking with us the next day, about basic writing, I thought. (Irene Clark is Director of our Writing Center, Betty Bamberg is Director of the USC/California Writing Project—they are among the usual suspects for meetings like this.)

Olga told us that the new CCC employs people between the ages of eighteen and twenty-three at the minimum wage on one-year contracts. They clear brush, fight fires, work at emergency sites, are kept to fairly severe work discipline. There are sixty at the Los Angeles Urban Center of the CCC, which happens to be just across the street from USC. Bruce Saito, the Director there, had agreed to include a literacy component in his daily schedule. Half the corpsmembers were without high school diplomas, one third were Hispanic, ten or so were recent immigrants from South East Asia. Would we teach them how to read and write better?

Oh, sure, nothing better to do, have Mr. Saito send me an official letter. We bureaucrats always want official letters.

After the meeting, Betty said: "Do you know who that was?"

"Ah, didn't she say her name was Olga Connolly?"

"She's that Czech athlete who eloped with an American at the 1956 Olympics."

I later learned that Olga had stopped competing in the Olympics after her fifth participation in the Games. And she hadn't really eloped. Anyway, she had worked on projects for inner-city youth, worked (indeed) with CETA, and was now a consultant to the California Conservation Corps.

The next morning, at 7:30, we went over to the CCC operation, which is housed in an old National Guard Armory. We all admired the high ceilings. Then Bruce found us and took us into the room where the corpsmembers were. They wore khaki uniforms, sat with their arms folded, stared at us. Olga helped a lot. She said: "This is Michael Holzman." They all stared at me. I'm not used to this sort of thing. Mostly I write memoranda and make speeches to teachers. The People is a nice concept, but hard to face at 7:30 a.m. in the form of dozens of very strong black and brown young adults. The uniforms also did not help. Were they prisoners, soldiers, cops? There was nothing to be done. I talked about how important it is to know how to read and write. Then I asked for questions. Three corpsmembers asked the same question: "When do we start?" I could deal with that. We would form small groups and begin writing. Betty gave me a "You could have warned me" look, shrugged, and took eight corpsmembers off in search of a room with a table. Mr. Saito's letter arrived the following Monday; classes started Tuesday.

Wednesday morning I met Steve Krashen in the park between the Hall of Humanities and the Administration building (this is my usual locale, symbolically). I told him about the CCC. He said: "You're in over your head."

"I know."

"What are you going to do?"

"Round up some good teachers, use small groups—individual tutorials if any of the CCC people turn out to be actually illiterate."

"Let me know how it goes."

"Sure."

We found ten instructors for the sixty CCC people. We put those corpsmembers who could not speak English into one group (they named themselves "The Internationals"; ESL apparently has a pejorative meaning) and grouped the others at random. During the second meeting we found one person who could only read his own name and the word "the." At the next meeting we found three more. We put two of these students with Irene, two with another instructor, improvised materials. (We actually had some good things on hand that had been developed to help the athletics department.) In the second week of the collaboration between the CCC and our writing instructors something rather odd happened. I didn't understand it at first. It began when twenty of the CCC people had been sent to the Colorado River to sandbag resorts and houses there. That left some of our groups with six students, some with one or two. When I tried to rearrange people, to even out the groups at four, the students resisted. They wanted to stay with their particular instructors. "Wanted" is a mild way of putting it. They refused to be regrouped. I found this a bit annoying, but when the instructors sided with the students there was nothing that I could do about it, no matter how strong my drive toward organizational symmetry. I decided to make the best of a bad deal and went off to think about the meaning of this resistance. Just calling it "resistance" made me feel better; it sounded vaguely clinical, made me feel in intellectual if not bureaucratic control of the matter.

The next day I was talking to a secondary-school teacher who specializes in teaching basic reading to students at a high school just off campus, that is, near Watts. I told her about our CCC class and asked how it happened that so many of these young people had been through the public schools but, like her students, had learned little.

"You know," she said, "the classes are so large and the school must do so many different things. And you can't isolate the children from the community. Truancy is such a big problem."

Truancy. Absenteeism. If the students are not in school, they can hardly be taught much.

"At my school the attrition rate is 135 percent a year. And you hardly ever have more than four or five students in the class three days running. The others come and go."

And, in spite of the best efforts of the teachers, they are forgotten. The teachers, naturally enough (with five classes of thirty or forty students each day), concentrate on the students who are there, not those who are absent. When does this start? At the beginning. We like to believe that in the United States every six-year-old is free to go to school. This is true for students from Watts and for students from Beverly Hills. All have equal opportunities. Some have home environments that encourage schooling; some have home environments that are indifferent to it. In some neighborhoods unemployment among young adult males is over 50 percent, violence is endemic, twelve-year-old girls become prostitutes, gangs recruit in the junior high school corridors. By fourth grade matters are sufficiently advanced for the less fortunate children; tracking will take care of the rest. Students who have missed a crucial week or two of work on reading or writing are relegated to less intensively supervised parts of the educational system. They grow bored. They learn little after that. They are forgotten.

Which brought me back to my stubborn CCC students. Their reluctance to be separated from their instructors was not whimsical or arbitrary. They had been forgotten before; they did not wish to be forgotten again. The seemingly arbitrary nature of their identification with instructors whom they had barely met simply testified to the intensity of their feelings. If Doug Cazort or Judith Rodby knew their names, seemed interested in their lives and education, that was sufficient—it was practically unique in their experience. No wonder that they were unwilling to risk a new organization, risk exposure to a new representative of middle-class society. The evidence of their own experience was that such a new person would not care about them. Why take risks?

It is not necessary to analyze the consequences of neglect from an ethical or humanitarian angle. The economic context will suffice. The most advanced sectors of the industrialized world now are those that produce and distribute not goods but information. In the United States, where these changes are not cushioned or concealed by traditional social structures or consistent state intervention, the result is the obsolescence of entire industries, and, in a movement parallel to that in the beginning of the nineteenth century, of entire categories of workers. Whereas the development of mass production eliminated the need for skilled craftspersons (weavers, for instance) in favor of unskilled workers and machines, now it is the unskilled and semi-skilled workers who are becoming superfluous. The bottom steps of the social ladder have been sawn off.

Let me give a very recent example of this. A common path for social advancement in the middle part of the twentieth century was through clerical work, the most basic type of which might be taken as that of a bank teller. Even a recent emigrant with basic English skills could stand at a bank counter eight hours a day, accepting deposits, certifying withdrawals. Eventually this might lead to the possibility of the acquisition of other, more complex skills, of other, more highly paid work. In just the last two years many of these positions have been eliminated by the introduction of machines to perform those basic tasks. Very soon, for all practical purposes, there will be no entry level positions for unskilled white collar workers in banking. One can see that similar changes will occur in other service industries. (At one time it was thought that the service industries would employ those "freed" by the disappearance of heavy manufacturing and extraction industries, but this is less and less likely.) From one point of view this is a very good thing indeed. Gradually the white collar equivalent of ditch digging will be eliminated. There will be no need to employ hundreds of thousands of people to spend their days in mindless, repetitive tasks. As heavy earth moving equipment has freed men (for the most part) from one type of physical drudgery, so automated bank tellers, that is, the application of computing to the service aspects of information transfer, will free women and men from a type of mental drudgery.

The problem here, for a society like ours, is that those menial white collar jobs were a form of education, a preparation for the slightly more interesting work to be encountered elsewhere in the bank, say. As we will probably not be willing to consider one of those north European solutions (such as the early retirement offered to the entire last generation of Belgian coal miners, without regard to age), we have two alternatives: permanent unemployment for those population groups not educationally equipped to find work in the new economy, or more investment in education. The former choice is much more costly than the latter. It involves extensive construction of prisons, epidemic control, unemployment benefits, welfare payments, higher taxes, higher crime rates, shorter lives. There is not much that need be said about the prospect of condemning a large part of the population to marginalization, except perhaps to comment on the word itself. What sort of margin is it that contains so much of the human "text" of society? We are talking about a margin only in the sense that these are people at the margins of the attention of those who plan society.

One significant problem that Olga has told me about is the disincentives from education for traditionally educationally disadvantaged groups. There are already many educational institutions available for those interested in basic education. There are, for instance, high schools, both regular and adult, continuation and trade. There are community colleges. If Rex Johnson or Nguyen duc Tuan wishes to improve his employment opportunities by learning to read and write in English, or by improving those skills from fourth-grade level to a point where they are useful in the emerging information society, all that Johnson or Nguyen need do is enroll in a free or nearly free course. That is all, but, as with elementary education, in some cases it is too much.

Let us think about Johnson for a minute. He was born in Los Angeles nearly twenty years ago. He is black. He grew up in an extended household composed of his mother, grandmother, and a number of brothers, sisters, half-brothers, cousins. (You have heard this story before.) No one he knows has a college degree. There are virtually no books in his house, virtually no reading materials of any kind. None of his friends has a job that requires anything more than fourth-grade literacy skills (of course, not many people he knows have jobs at all). In fourth grade he missed his week or two of school (a younger sister was ill and had to be looked after, his mother was beat up by the man who had been living with them, there was a gang war in the neighborhood and it was unsafe to go to school). That left him a bit behind on his reading and writing skills, so he was bored for the rest of the year, not understanding the lessons. The teacher tried to help, but there were those thirty-eight other children in the class, many of whom were more in need of personal attention than Rex. Rex never learned much more in school, attended irregularly, became more and more involved with gangs, or simply began drinking and taking drugs. One of his stepfathers had him sent to jail as an incorrigible ("It will do him good"). After that it was hard for him to get jobs, with no skills and a jail record and the habit of not showing up places when he felt like doing something else. How likely is it that Rex, at nineteen, will suddenly decide to go to night school? And if he goes, what is it that he will want to be taught? He already knows how to read and write—ask him.

Olga says that people like Rex live in a world that is at once magical and violent. The violence is real. They get shot or stabbed as frequently as middle-class people get in automobile accidents. Some of them do the shooting and stabbing, as some of us, perhaps, are at fault in automobile accidents. Women in Rex's world get beat up frequently, get pregnant and abandoned, have trouble holding jobs or finishing school. The view that Rex and his friends have of the world that they do not live in, the world they see on television and in the movies, is magical in a pernicious way. In that magical world things are not connected. One day you are a typical high-school student, the next you have a contract from a professional football team. There is a link between this television magic and street violence, a link that makes the magic in a sense believable.

It is that in Rex's everyday world the transitions are television-sudden, if always negative. One day you are a typical high-school student, the next you are dead. Rex and his friends live in a domestic Third World, one that appears to have been designed by Gabriel Garcia Marquez but has actually been designed by those of us who work in the consciousness industries. If life itself is actually so precarious, it is not unreasonable to believe that positive changes also (if they can occur) will be characterized by sudden and inexplicable transformations. If Rex goes to night school, it is more likely that he will wish to study computers than reading. Computers are magic. The problem for those who would intervene in this world, benevolently, is to remove the magic, and not just from computers, to reveal the causal links between events. This must be done before any technical education can be accomplished (and I am counting literacy here as a technique, although not invidiously, as I have elsewhere). General knowledge, Olga told us, must precede literacy. If it does not, the acquisition of literacy literally makes no sense. Why read if you believe that it is sheer chance that will either kill you or make you rich?

I think that the very relentlessness of the negatively magical vision of everyday life that possesses Rex and his friends might serve to justify some intervention in the process by which they make their choices. If they are frequently told by television and motion pictures that success in life happens by means of a gun or through a gratuitous gesture by benevolent millionaires or through the recognition of physical characteristics (not achievements), and they are told by their own senses that failure occurs also without their willing it, by means of random gunfire, arrests, drug impurities, then it is probably not improper for them also to be informed that there are other alternatives. That in return for relinquishing the magical explanation of success (or survival), they may find some possibility of survival (or success) through the decidedly nonmagical means of education. They have been forgotten by our society, a process of forgetting that is a mode of exclusion. If they are to re-enter that society—and not be parasites on it—they must learn that it exists; it must be made nonmagical, real.

This is the purpose of the literacy preparation program that Olga had devised for the CCC. It consists of two areas of education: she (and her friends) tell Rex (and his friends) about that society which is not Hollywood and not Watts—how the water system works; how the stock market works; how a bank works; how the athletic system works (exactly, really, not magically, how one becomes an Olympic or professional athlete); how these matters are connected. And then she has Rex and his friends take an inventory of their own skills, where they can fit into these systems. She asks: "Would you like to be an athlete? What diet do you follow?" And then she teaches them about nutrition. They seem not to have heard about it before, or about simple anatomy, or about the complexities of reproduction. Olga says that "they know nothing about the human body under its skin." This is fairly worrisome, as some already have children, many of whom were born to undernourished mothers (living on widely advertised processed foods: Hostess Ding Dongs for breakfast). Gradually they learn that only part of the world is magical, caught between random violence and fantasy; that the part of the world (our world) that is the source of theirs is not magical at all; there, everything is connected, and, from the point of view of the individual, all these connections begin with literacy.

Olga's approach to the problem of adult illiteracy and semi-literacy showed me that I had been looking in the wrong place for solutions to these problems. I had thought that it was a technical problem, that I would find some procedure that would be applicable. It is not only a procedural problem. Literacy is not a felt need in a magical world. Before we as teachers could apply to them as students the procedures of our professional expertise, they had to become students, and accept us as teachers. The first step is the demystification of the world. The second is our willingness to give up the protection of our roles as teachers, to remember each of them as individuals, to agree that our relationships are personal. When I had failed to rebalance the groups, I had learned that in this situation, at the limit of education, teachers are only allowed to be teachers if they are Doug and Betty and the students are Rex and Tran. Relationships between individuals must replace relationships between roles. With such relationships in place, the corpsmembers *were* learning basic literacy skills, often quite rapidly. Irene reported that after three class sessions her illiterate student had progressed from his name and "the" to all three letter words with the vowels "i," "e," and "a." The Internationals were talking among themselves in English, which they had denied knowing at the beginning of the course. Enrique Valasquez, a recent emigrant from Mexico, had become something of a cross between an ethnographer and a native informant, giving me weekly written reports on the progress of the corpsmembers. Some of the black corpsmembers were pointing out black dialect features in their writing and asking their instructors how standard English differs. Literacy among unschooled young adults is not entirely a technical problem. It is also, one might say, a motivational problem. One might say that, as one might say that the Civil War was a policy disagreement. They must acquire the motivation to live. Then they can be taught to write better, to read.

We did learn some technical-pedagogical things. About half way through the experimental summer program, Doug Cazort started having his students tape-record narratives, then write them down from their own recorded "dictation." I thought this was fairly strange at first; our usual procedure with freshmen had been to have them record essays they had already written. Doug explained to me that this reversal was a solution to another problem that we had been worrying about: most of the corpsmembers, when asked to write an essay, would write perhaps three words and erase two. It is difficult to finish a composition with this technique. They were apparently operating in accordance with a theory that "correctness" and the avoidance of error is the primary aim of writing. Expression and communication were reserved for speech. We had begun by simply telling them that this is not a correct theory, that Derrida, for instance, would point out that it is a typical instance of logocentricism in Western culture, but this had not made much of an impression. Doug (following Steve Krashen's theoretical lead in this) had found a way to smuggle expression and communication, and thus interest, into writing. The corpsmembers liked to use the tape recorders, liked to *tell* stories, and did not view the inscription of their own dictation as "writing," in the negatively charged sense that the word had for them. Soon people who had difficulty filling half a page with direct composition were filling two or three pages in an hour class session from their own dictation. Fortunately, we had readily available a tape laboratory normally used for foreign language instruction. Many of our students began living there during their hours with us. The more advanced, more verbal students were particularly attracted to, and helped by, this device.

After a few weeks of our summer job, working with the CCC personnel on what was often, and necessarily, a mutual education project (I now know a bit too much about the phenomenology of prison culture), Bruce Saito asked us to continue literacy education for his corpsmembers during the academic year. I asked if the corpsmembers themselves wanted this. They did. That left two more questions: Why should a private university do this? And who would pay?

When the question of money comes up, it is my custom to write a letter to the Vice President of the College, Irwin C. Lieb. The letter got me a meeting with Dr. Lieb. He said that although it was clearly a worthwhile project he did not find in my letter any compelling argument that it was a suitable task for a university. I advanced the claim that if one is aware of a task that should be done that is not being done, and if one is capable of doing it, one should do it. He responded that budgets are limited, and a university is an institution for higher education and research. I offered the information that there are many CCC centers, that if we developed a significant model for literacy work it could be adapted for work with the CCC and similar groups, that little research had been done in this area. He said he would see our development people for the money and that I should see Steve Krashen about the research.

By the time I met with Dr. Lieb, I felt that we had already accomplished something more than a one-shot effort at improving literacy skills for a random group of educationally handicapped young adults. The observation about the rapidity of small group bonding could be attributed to the origins of the disability itself and to a method for overcoming that disability. These poorly educated young people were poorly educated not by chance, but because they had been forgotten by the educational system. Their literacy could be improved if they were remembered, if particular educators cared about them. I believe that here, as with so many matters, psychological and sociological phenomena form a continuum. If Freire was successful in teaching peasants to read and write by presenting the achievement of literacy in a political context, he did so by persuading them that literacy is one component of a task involving the transformation of their lives as individuals and as individual representatives of a class. Literacy, in the Third World, can become the locus of hope itself. It is highly unlikely that this particular contextualization of literacy can be widely applied in the United States. (There are exceptions—farm workers, for instance.) The relevant application of Freire's technique is to show individuals that their personal welfare can be enhanced by improvements in their literacy. Since this is a personal matter, direct personal involvement is crucial. The pedagogical instantiation of this theory is that of small group tutorials, not classes, and a degree of stability in instructor/student relations. The connection with the CCC gave us a stable student population, and we had learned to emphasize the stability of our instructor/student groups.

The use of tape recordings of verbal texts by the students themselves as the basis for composition is probably not novel, nor is it an answer in itself to the technical questions of adult semi-literacy. It is, though, a demonstration of the richness of the teaching environment as the source for technical and theoretical innovation. In our ESL group Judith was able to achieve significant results by helping her students express that which they wished to express—not, "This is a table" but, "The CCC makes us work hard." Why learn to say, to write, words that do not matter? As Steve Krashen tells me at least once a week, only university students will put up with the material in most traditional textbooks. Working with young adults who were certainly living in the real world and who, we learned quickly enough, intensely desired to improve their literacy skills, we spent little time with techniques that satisfied us but not them. We asked the students to help us design the "curriculum"; we asked them to evaluate the program. We might as well ask; if we do not, they will tell us anyway. It happens to matter to them whether they acquire more survival opportunities.

There are certain skills and resources present in the university not present among the corpsmembers. These are being assembled by Steve Krashen and others as a research area within our Linguistics Department. Some of the instructors in what has become the USC Model Literacy

Project will be graduate students working with Steve on this research. The researchers will learn from the project; the project will benefit from the research; and the results, if significant, will be promulgated in the usual ways, particularly by means of the National Writing Project.

In a way the CCC connection came as a gift. The more general problem, the more difficult problem, is that of reaching similar young people without an institutional affiliation. Yet if our project was to be more than the literacy component of the California Conservation Corps, if it were indeed to contribute to what I have romantically called "an epidemic of literacy," we have to find a way to go beyond the corps-members to their brothers and sisters. It seemed an insoluble problem to me. I could think of no organization similar to the CCC. What were we to do—recruit on street corners? I had forgotten about Olga. One morning she said, "I've been walking around the neighborhood talking to people about our project."

"What happened?"

"It was interesting. I'm thinking."

The next day she said, "I'm going to ask the corpsmembers."

Stupid of me—who else was an expert on the matter?

They were ahead of us. They had already told their sisters and brothers and cousins and lovers about the project. Many were eager to attend our classes. The problem had two parts: letting people know about the project and selecting those appropriate to join. Both these matters had been taken care of by the corpsmembers themselves. They had told the community about the project, and they would select new students. They were proud of what they—we—had done together. They would be responsible in choosing their fellow students. (An unworthy thought about the need for expert recruiting personnel enters here and is quickly assisted to a nearby exit. This is not an employment project for professionals.)

This is what is now in place: Persons new to the project, whether in the CCC component or the open program, first join us in the enterprise of examining the world as a real, nonmagical entity where they have a place directly connected to the rest. Then, often simultaneously, they become part of a literacy group of half a dozen or so, including a literacy teacher from the University. The groups meet three times a week for eight weeks, an hour at a time. If they wish they can enroll in additional eight-week terms. The instructors study with the students, learning what is needed to be learned and taught, learning about the world in which the students live. Then they work together with other researchers to perfect techniques of literacy instruction. A student-teacher ratio of six or eight to one is fairly expensive. However, the context is that of welfare payments of four or five thousand dollars a month for a group that size if they are unemployable because of deficient literacy skills. I believe that is a fairly good cost/benefit ratio, if one wants to talk about cost/benefit ratios. I do not. It is a mark of barbarism when a society treats people as if they were things. Things may be forgotten. People must be remembered.

Michael Holzman

Works Cited

Aelgh, Hugo. 1978. "Conversation as Paranoia." *Lingua Pranca*. Ed. T. Ernst and E. Smith. Bloomington: Indiana University Linguistics Club. Mimeo.

Althusser, Louis. 1970. "Contradiction and Overdetermination." *For Marx*. Trans. Ben Brewster. New York: Random House. 87–128.

Arthur, David. 1980. "Letter to the Editor." *Los Angeles Times* (25 Oct.) 2:5.

Ashbery, John. 1976. *Self-Portrait in a Convex Mirror*. Harmondsworth, Eng.: Penguin.

Bach, Kent, and Robert M. Harnish. 1979. *Linguistic Communication and Speech Acts*. Cambridge: M.I.T.P.

Bakhtin, M. M. 1981. *The Dialogic Imagination*. Ed. Michael Holquist. Trans. Caryl Emerson and Michael Holquist. Austin: U. of Texas P.

Bamberg, Betty. 1984. "Conditions for Global Coherence." Conference on College Composition and Communication. New York.

Banta, Martha. 1980. "Anxiety of Influence in the Classroom, or, The Will to Ignorance." *College English* 42:109–20.

Barthes, Roland. 1974. S/Z. Trans. Richard Miller. New York: Hill.

Bartholomae, David. 1985. "Inventing the University." *When a Writer Can't Write: Studies in Writer's Block and Other Composing-Process Problems*. Ed. Mike Rose. New York: Guilford. 134–65.

Belenky, Mary Field, Blythe McVicker Clinchy, Nancy Rule Goldberger, and Jill Mattuck Tarule. 1986. *Women's Ways of Knowing: The Development of Self, Voice, and Mind*. New York: Basic.

Berkenkotter, Carol. 1984. "Student Writers and Their Sense of Authority over Texts." *College Composition and Communication* 35: 312–19.

Berlin, James. 1982. "Contemporary Composition: The Major Pedagogical Theories." *College English* 44:765–77.

Bernstein, Basil. 1971. *Classes, Codes, and Control.* London: Routledge.

Berthoff, Ann E., and Warner B. Berthoff. 1980. "Staying Viable." *College Composition and Communication* 31:84–86.

Bhola, H. S. 1984. *Campaigning for Literacy: A Critical Analysis of Some Selected Literacy Campaigns of the Twentieth Century with a Memorandum for Decision-makers.* New York: UNESCO

Bitzer, Lloyd F. 1968. "The Rhetorical Situation." *Philosophy and Rhetoric* 1:1–14.

Bizzell, Patricia. 1982. "Cognition, Convention, and Certainty: What We Need to Know About Writing." *Pre/Text* 3:213–43.

———. 1984. "William Perry and Liberal Education." *College English* 46:447–54.

———. 1986. "Foundationalism and Anti-Foundationalism in Composition Studies." *Pre/Text* 7:37–56.

———. 1988. "Arguing About Literacy." *College English* 50:141–53.

Black, John B., Deanna Wilkes-Gibbs, and Raymond W. Gibbs, Jr. 1982. "What Writers Need To Know that They Don't Know They Need To Know." *What Writers Know: The Language, Process, and Structure of Written Discourse.* Ed. Martin Nystrand. New York: Academic. 325–43.

Bleich, David. 1978. *Subjective Criticism.* Baltimore: Johns Hopkins UP.

Bok, Sissela. 1979. *Lying: Moral Choice in Public and Private Life.* New York: Vintage.

Braudel, Fernand. 1981–85. *Civilization and Capitalism.* 3 vols. New York: Harper.

Britton, James. 1970. *Language and Learning.* Harmondsworth, Eng.: Penguin.

Britzman, Deborah P. 1986. "Cultural Myths in the Making of a Teacher: Biography and Social Structure." *Harvard Educational Review* 56:442–56.

Brodkey, Linda. 1987. "Modernism and the Scene(s) of Writing." *College English* 49:396–418.

Brooke, Robert. 1987. " 'Underlife' and Writing Instruction." *College Composition and Communication* 38:141–53.

Brown, Gillian, and George Yule. 1983. *Discourse Analysis.* Cambridge: Cambridge UP.

Brown, Penelope, and Stephen Levinson. 1978. "Universals in Language Usage: Politeness Phenomena." *Questions and Politeness: Strategies in Social Interaction.* Ed. Esther N. Goody. Cambridge: Cambridge UP. 56–289.

Brown, Robert L., Jr. 1980. "The Pragmatics of Verbal Irony." *Language Use and the Uses of Language.* Ed. Ralph W. Fasold and Roger W. Shuy. Washington, DC: Georgetown UP.

Brown, Roger, and Albert Gilman. 1960. "The Pronouns of Power and Solidarity." *Style in Language*. Ed. Thomas A. Sebeok. Cambridge: M.I.T.P. 253–76.

Bruffee, Kenneth A. 1972. "The Way Out: A Critical Survey of Innovations in College Teaching, with Special Reference to the December, 1971, Issue of *College English*." *College English*, 33:457–70.

———. 1981. "Collaborative Learning." *College English* 43:745–47.

———. 1984. "Collaborative Learning and the 'Conversation of Mankind.' " *College English* 46:635–52.

Burke, Kenneth. 1969. *A Grammar of Motives*. Berkeley: U of California P.

Carnoy, Martin, and Henry M. Levin. 1985. *Schooling and Work in the Democratic State*. Stanford: Stanford UP.

Carrell, Patricia L. 1982. *Cohesion Is Not Coherence*. TESOL *Quarterly*, 479–88.

Carroll, Lewis. 1976. *The Complete Works*. New York: Vintage.

Chapman, Ralph. 1978. "Power and Politeness: The Logic of Conversations in Pinter's *The Collection*." Ms.

Charnley, A. H., and H. A. Jones. 1979. *The Concept of Success in Adult Literacy*. London: ALBSU.

Chomsky, Noam. 1980. *Rules and Representations*. New York: Columbia UP.

Cipolla, C. M. 1969. *Literacy and Development in the West*. London: Penguin.

Cole, Michael, Lois Hood, and Ray McDermott. n.d. *Ecological Niche Picking: Ecological Invalidity as an Axiom of Experimental Cognitive Psychology*. Laboratory of Comparative Human Cognition and Institute for Comparative Human Development, The Rockefeller University. New York. Mimeo.

Cooper, Marilyn M. 1980. *Implicatures in Dramatic Conversations*. U of Minnesota. Diss.

Culler, Jonathan. 1975. *Structuralist Poetics: Structuralism, Linguistics, and the Study of Literature*. Ithaca, NY: Cornell UP.

Dijk, Teun. A. van. 1977. "Semantic Macro-Structures and Knowledge Frames in Discourse Comprehension." *Cognitive Processes in Comprehension*. Ed. Marcel Adam Just and Patricia A. Carpenter. Hillsdale, NJ: Lawrence Erlbaum. 3–32.

Dillon, George L. 1981. *Constructing Texts: Elements of a Theory of Composition and Style*. Bloomington: Indiana UP.

Dobrin, David N. 1986. "Protocols Once More." *College English* 48:713–25.

Dyson, Anne Haas. 1985. "Second Graders Sharing Writing." *Written Communication* 2:189–215.

Eco, Umberto. 1980. *The Name of the Rose.* Trans. William Weaver. New York: Harcourt.

Ede, Lisa, and Andrea Lunsford. 1984. "Audience Addressed/Audience Invoked: The Role of Audience in Composition Theory and Pedagogy." *College Composition and Communication* 35:155–71.

Elbow, Peter. 1981. *Writing with Power: Techniques for Mastering the Writing Process.* Oxford: Oxford UP.

Enkvist, Nils E. 1978. "Coherence, Pseudo-Coherence, and Non-Coherence." *Cohesion and Semantics.* Ed. J-O. Ostman. Abo, Finland: Abo Akademi Foundation.

Ericsson, K. Anders, and Herbert A. Simon. 1980. "Verbal Reports as Data." *Psychological Review* 87:215–51.

Fahnestock, Jeanne. 1983. "Semantic and Lexical Coherence." *College Composition and Communication* 34:400–16.

Faigley, Lester. 1985. "Nonacademic Writing: The Social Perspective." *Writing in Nonacademic Settings.* Ed. Lee Odell and Dixie Goswami. New York: Guilford. 231–48.

———, and Stephen Witte. 1981. "Analyzing Revision." *College Composition and Communication* 32:400–14.

Faulkner, William. 1964. *As I Lay Dying.* New York: Vintage.

Fish, Stanley. 1980. *Is There a Text in This Class? The Authority of Interpretive Communities.* Cambridge: Harvard UP.

Flower, Linda. 1981. *Problem-Solving Strategies for Writing.* New York: Harcourt.

Flower, Linda, and John R. Hayes. 1981a. "The Cognition of Discovery: Defining a Rhetorical Problem." *College Composition and Communication* 31:21–32.

———. 1981b. "A Cognitive Process Theory of Writing." *College Composition and Communication* 32:365–87.

———. 1981c. "The Pregnant Pause: An Inquiry into the Nature of Planning." *Research in the Teaching of English* 15:229–43.

———. 1984. "Images, Plans and Prose: The Representation of Meaning in Writing." *Written Communication* 1:120–60.

———. 1985. "Response to Marilyn Cooper and Michael Holzman, 'Talking About Protocols.'" *College Composition and Communication* 36:94–97.

Foucault, Michel. 1972. *The Archaeology of Knowledge and The Discourse on Language.* Trans. A. M. Sheridan Smith. New York: Pantheon.

Freed, Richard C., and Glenn J. Broadhead. 1987. "Discourse Communities, Sacred Texts, and Institutional Norms." *College Composition and Communication* 38:154–65.

Freire, Paulo. 1972. *Pedagogy of the Oppressed.* London: Penguin.

Friedenberg, Edgar Z. 1963. *Coming of Age in America.* New York: Random House.

Fulton, C. 1980. "Letter to the Editor." *Los Angeles Times* (29 May) 2:6.

Gebhardt, Richard. 1980. "Teamwork and Feedback: Broadening the Base of Collaborative Writing." *College English* 42:69–74.

Geertz, Clifford. 1980. *Negara: The Theatre State in Nineteenth-Century Bali*. Princeton: Princeton UP.

———. 1983. *Local Knowledge: Further Essays in Interpretive Anthropology*. New York: Basic.

George, Diana. 1988. "Constructing the Language of Interpretation in the Writing Class." Conference on College Composition and Communication. St. Louis.

Gilligan, Carol. 1982. *In a Different Voice: Psychological Theory and Women's Development*. Cambridge: Harvard UP.

Glorfeld, L. E., D. A. Lauerman, and N. C. Stageberg. 1977. *A Concise Guide for Writers*. 4th ed. New York: Holt.

Goffman, Erving. 1981. *Forms of Talk*. Oxford: Blackwell.

Goodman, Paul. 1964. *Compulsory Mis-Education*. New York: Horizon.

Goody, Jack. 1968. *Literacy in Traditional Societies*. Cambridge: Cambridge UP.

Grice, H. P. 1967. *Logic and Conversation*. William James Lectures, Harvard. Mimeo.

———. 1969. "Utterer's Meaning and Intention." *Philosophical Review* 68:147–77.

———. 1975. "Logic and Conversation." *Speech Acts*. Vol. 3 of *Syntax and Semantics*. Ed. Peter Cole and Jerry L. Morgan. New York: Academic. 41–58.

———. 1978. "Further Notes on Logic and Conversation." *Pragmatics*. Vol. 9 of *Syntax and Semantics*. Ed. Peter Cole. New York: Academic. 113–27.

———. 1982. "Meaning Revisited." *Mutual Knowledge*. Ed. N. V. Smith. New York: Academic. 223–43.

Gumperz, John J. 1982. *Discourse Strategies*. Cambridge: Cambridge UP.

Hake, Rose L., and Joseph M. Williams. 1981. "Style and Its Consequences: Do as I Do, Not as I Say." *College English* 43:433–51.

Hairston, Maxine. 1982. "The Winds of Change: Thomas Kuhn and the Revolution in the Teaching of Writing." *College Composition and Communication* 33:76–88.

Halliday, M. A. K. 1978. *Language as Social Semiotic: The Social Interpretation of Language and Meaning*. London: Edward Arnold.

———, and Ruqaiya Hasan. 1976. *Cohesion in English*. London: Longman.

Hancher, Michael. 1978. "Grice's 'Implicature' and Literary Interpretation: Background and Preface." Meeting of the Midwest Modern Language Association. Minneapolis.

Hayes, John R., and Linda S. Flower. 1980. "Identifying the Organization of Writing Processes." *Cognitive Processes in Writing.* Ed. Lee W. Gregg and Erwin R. Steinberg. Hillsdale, NJ: Lawrence Erlbaum.

Heath, Shirley Brice. 1983. *Ways with Words: Language, Life, and Work in Communities and Classrooms.* New York: Cambridge UP.

Hegel, G. W. F. 1977. *Phenomenology of Spirit.* Trans. A. V. Miller. Oxford: Oxford UP.

Herndl, Carl G., Barbara A. Fennell, and Carolyn R. Miller. Forthcoming. "Understanding Failures in Organizational Discourse: The Accidents at Three Mile Island and the Shuttle Challenger." In *Text in the Professions.* Ed. Charles Bazerman and James Paradis. Madison: U of Wisconsin P.

Holt, John. 1964. *How Children Fail.* New York: Pitman.

Hope, Ann, and Sally Timmel. 1984. *Training for Transformation: A Handbook for Community Workers.* Gweru, Zimbabwe: Mambo.

Humboldt, Wilhelm von. 1971. *Linguistic Variability and Intellectual Development.* Trans. George C. Buck and Frithjof A. Raven. Philadelphia: U of Pennsylvania P.

Hunter, Carman St. John, and David Harman. 1979. *Adult Illiteracy in the United States.* New York: McGraw-Hill.

Hymes, Dell. 1972. "Models of the Interaction of Language and Social Life." *Directions in Sociolinguistics.* Ed. John J. Gumperz and Dell Hymes. New York: Holt. 35–71.

Illich, Ivan. 1971. *De-Schooling Society.* Garden City, NY: Doubleday.

Jameson, Fredric. 1981. *The Political Unconscious: Narrative as a Socially Symbolic Act.* Ithaca, NY: Cornell UP.

Johnston, O. 1980. "No Deal Has Been Made To Free Hostages, Muskie Says." *Los Angeles Times* (2 Nov.) 1:1, 12.

Kantor, Harvey, and Robert Lowe. 1987. "Empty Promises." *Harvard Educational Review* 57:1, 75.

Kantor, Kenneth, Dan R. Kirby, and Judith Goetz. 1981. "Research in Context: Ethnographic Studies in English Education." *Research in the Teaching of English* 15:293–309.

Keenan, Elinor O. 1977. "The Universality of Conversational Implicatures." *Studies in Language Variation: Semantics, Syntax, Phonology, Pragmatics, Social Situations, Ethnographic Approaches.* Ed. Ralph W. Fasold and Roger W. Shuy. Washington, DC: Georgetown UP. 255–68.

Kempson, Ruth M. 1975. *Presupposition and the Delimitation of Semantics.* Cambridge: Cambridge UP.

Keniston, Kenneth. 1988. "Wife Beating and the Rule of Thumb." *The New York Times Book Review* (8 May) 12.

Kinneavy, James. 1971. *A Theory of Discourse.* Englewood Cliffs, NJ: Prentice-Hall.

Kirsch, Irwin S., and Ann Jungeblut. 1986. *Literacy: Profiles of America's Young Adults.* Princeton: National Assessment of Educational Progress.

Knoblauch, C. H., and Lil Brannon. 1983. "Writing as Learning Through the Curriculum." *College English* 45:465–74.

Kozol, Jonathan. 1967. *Death at an Early Age.* Boston: Houghton-Mifflin.

———. 1978. *Children of the Revolution: A Yankee Teacher in the Cuban Schools.* New York: Delacorte.

Kroll, Barry M. 1984. "Writing for Readers: Three Perspectives on Audience." *College Composition and Communication* 35:172–85.

———. 1985. "Social-Cognitive Ability and Writing Performance: How Are They Related?" *Written Communication* 2:293–305.

Labov, William. 1972a. *Language in the Inner City: Studies in the Black English Vernacular.* Philadelphia: U of Pennsylvania P.

———. 1972b. *Sociolinguistic Patterns.* Philadelphia: U of Pennsylvania P.

Laubach, Frank C. 1947. *Teaching the World to Read.* New York: Friendship.

Lauer, Janice M. 1982. "Writing as Inquiry: Some Questions for Teachers." *College Composition and Communication* 33:89–93.

"Laying Golden Eggs." 1980. *Los Angeles Times* (11 Feb.) 2:6.

Lewis, David K. 1969. *Convention: A Philosophical Analysis.* Cambridge: Harvard UP.

Lewontin, R. C., Steven Rose, and Leon J. Kamin. 1984. *Not in Our Genes: Biology, Ideology, and Human Nature.* New York: Pantheon.

Lunsford, Andrea, and Lisa Ede. 1986. "Why Write . . . Together: A Research Update." *Rhetoric Review* 5:71–81.

McCarthy, Lucille Parkinson. 1987. "A Stranger in Strange Lands: A College Student Writing Across the Curriculum. *Research in the Teaching of English* 21:233–65.

McCulley, George A. 1985. "Writing Quality, Coherence, and Cohesion." *Research in the Teaching of English* 19:269–82.

McDermott, Ray P. 1974. "Achieving School Failure: An Anthropological Approach to Illiteracy and Social Stratification." *Education and Cultural Process.* Ed. George D. Spindler. New York: Holt.

———, and Lois Hood. 1982. "Institutionalized Psychology and the Ethnography of Schooling." *Children in and out of School: Ethnography and Education.* Ed. P. Gilmore and A. Glathorn. Center for Applied Linguistics. Washington, D.C.

MacKenzie, Robert. 1977. Review of "The Life and Times of Grizzly Adams." *TV Guide* (28 May) 34.

MacKillop, Jane. "Open Houses: An Alternative Intake Procedure for Adult Education Programs." Ms.

Marcuse, Herbert. 1964. *One-Dimensional Man: Studies in the Ideology of Advanced Industrial Society.* Boston: Beacon.

Markels, Robin B. 1983. "Cohesion Paradigms in Paragraphs." *College English* 45:450–64.

Mason, Edwin. 1972. *Collaborative Learning.* New York: Agathon.

Medvedev, P. N./Bakhtin, M. M. 1978. *The Formal Method in Literary Scholarship: A Critical Introduction to Sociological Poetics.* Trans. Albert J. Wehrle. Baltimore: Johns Hopkins UP.

Miller, George M., Eugene Galanter, and Karl H. Pribram. 1960. *Plans and the Structure of Behavior.* New York: Holt.

Miller, Valerie. 1985. *Between Struggle and Hope: The Nicaraguan Literacy Crusade.* Boulder: Westview.

Mindess, Harvey. 1980. "In Terms of Love and Letting Go, Talese Treads a Delicate Terrain." *Los Angeles Times Book Review* (27 Apr.) 1,10.

Mitchell, Ruth, and Mary Taylor. 1979. "The Integrating Perspective: An Audience-Response Model for Writing." *College English* 41:247–71.

Morgan, J. L., and M. B. Sellner. 1980. "Discourse and Linguistic Theory." *Theoretical Issues in Reading Comprehension: Perspectives from Cognitive Psychology, Linguistics, Artificial Intelligence, and Education.* Ed. R. J. Spiro, et al. Hillsdale, NJ: Erlbaum.

Morrow, Lance. 1980. "The Temptations of Revenge." *Time* (12 May) 84.

Moskovit, Leonard. 1983. "When is Broad Reference Clear?" *College Composition and Communication* 34:454–69.

Murray, Donald. 1978. "Write Before Writing." *College Composition and Communication,* 29:375–81.

Myers, Greg. 1985. "The Social Construction of Two Biologists' Proposals." *Written Communication* 2:219–45.

———. 1986. "The Writing Seminar: Broadening Peer Collaboration in Freshman English." *The Writing Instructor* 6:48–56.

Myrdal, Gunnar, et al. 1944. *An American Dilemma: The Negro Problem and Modern Democracy.* New York: Harper.

Odell, Lee, Dixie Goswami, and Doris Quick. 1983. "Writing Outside the English Composition Class: Implications for Teaching and for Learning." *Literacy for Life: The Demand for Reading and Writing.* Ed. Richard W. Bailey and Robin Melanie Fosheim. New York: MLA. 175–94.

Park, Douglas B. 1982. "The Meanings of 'Audience.' " *College English* 44:247–57.

Perry, William G. 1970. *Forms of Intellectual and Ethical Development in the College Years.* New York: Holt.

Pfister, Fred R., and Joanne F. Petrick. 1980. "A Heuristic Model for Creating a Writer's Audience." *College Composition and Communication* 31:213–20.

Pinter, Harold. 1961. *Three Plays.* New York: Grove.

Porter, James E. 1986. "Intertextuality and the Discourse Community." *Rhetoric Review* 5:34–47.

Pratt, Mary Louise. 1977. *Towards a Speech Act Theory of Literary Discourse.* Bloomington: Indiana UP.

Purves, Alan C., and William C. Purves. 1986. "Viewpoints: Cultures, Text Models, and the Activity of Writing." *Research in the Teaching of English* 20:174–97.

Reddy, Michael J. 1979. "The Conduit Metaphor—A Case of Frame Conflict in Our Language About Language." *Metaphor and Thought.* Ed. Andrew Ortony. Cambridge: Cambridge UP. 284–324.

Reither, James A. 1985. "Writing and Knowing: Toward Redefining the Writing Process." *College English* 47:620–28.

Resnick, Daniel P., and Lauren B. Resnick. 1977. "The Nature of Literacy: An Historical Exploration." *Harvard Educational Review* 47, 3:370–85.

Richards, I.A. 1929. *Practical Criticism.* New York: Harcourt.

Rodney, Walter. 1981. *How Europe Underdeveloped Africa.* Washington, DC: Howard UP.

Rorty, Richard. 1979. *Philosophy and the Mirror of Nature.* Princeton: Princeton UP.

Rosenblatt, Roger. 1980. "The People's Analyst." *Time* (29 Sept.) 92.

Sartre, Jean-Paul. 1976. *The Critique of Dialectical Reason: I. Theory of Practical Ensembles.* Trans. Alan Sheridan-Smith. London: NLB. (Originally published as *Critique de la Raison Dialectique.* Paris, 1960.)

Saussure, Ferdinand de. 1966. *Course in General Linguistics.* Ed. Charles Bally and Albert Sechehaye in collaboration with Albert Riedlinger. Trans. Wade Baskin. New York: McGraw-Hill.

Schank, Roger C., and Robert P. Abelson. 1977. *Scripts, Plans, Goals, and Understanding: An Inquiry into Human Knowledge Structures.* Hillsdale, NJ: Erlbaum.

Schleusener, Jay. 1980. "Convention and the Context of Reading." *Critical Inquiry* 6:669–80.

Schwartz, J. L., and E. F. Taylor. 1978. "Valid Assessment of Complex Behavior: The Torque Approach." *The Quarterly Newsletter of the Institute of Comparative Human Development* 2.

Scribner, Sylvia, and Michael Cole. 1981. *The Psychology of Literacy.* Cambridge: Harvard UP.

Searle, John R. 1969. *Speech Acts: An Essay in the Philosophy of Language.* Cambridge: Cambridge UP.

Shaughnessy, Mina. 1977. *Errors and Expectations: A Guide for the Teacher of Basic Writing.* New York: Oxford UP.

Sledd, James. 1988. "Product in Process: From Ambiguities of Standard English to Issues that Divide Us." *College English* 50:168–76.

Smith, Rochelle. 1984. "Paragraphing for Coherence." *College English* 46:8–21.

[Spaulding, Seth, and Arthur Gillette]. 1976. *The Experimental World Literacy Programme: A Critical Assessment.* Paris: UNESCO Press, UNDP.

Spitzer, Michael. 1986. "Writing Style in Computer Conferences." *IEEE Transactions on Professional Communications* 29:19–22.

Steinberg, Erwin R. 1986. "Protocols, Retrospective Reports, and the Stream of Consciousness." *College English* 48:697–712.

Steinmann, Martin, Jr. 1982. "Speech-Act Theory and Writing." *What Writers Know: The Language, Process, and Structure of Written Discourse.* Ed. Martin Nystrand. New York: Academic. 291–323.

Sternglass, Marilyn S. 1986. "Commitment to Writing and Complexity of Thinking." *Journal of Basic Writing.* 5:77–86.

Sticht, Thomas G., William B. Armstrong, Daniel T. Hickey, John S. Taylor. 1986. *Cast-Off Youth: Policy and Training Methods from the Military Experience.* New York: Ford Foundation.

Stotsky, Sandra. 1983. "Types of Lexical Cohesion in Expository Writing: Implications for Developing the Vocabulary of Academic Discourse." *College Composition and Communication* 34:430–46.

Street, Brian V. 1984. *Literacy in Theory and Practice.* Cambridge: Cambridge UP.

Swales, John. 1987. "Approaching the Concept of Discourse Community." Conference on College Composition and Communication. St. Louis.

Swarts, Heidi, Linda Flower, and John R. Hayes. 1984. "Designing Protocol Studies of the Writing Process: An Introduction." *New Directions in Composition Research.* Ed. Richard Beach and Lillian S. Bridwell. New York: Guilford. 53–71.

Tannen, Deborah. 1979. "What's in a Frame? Surface Evidence for Underlying Expectations." *New Directions in Discourse Processing.* Ed. Roy O. Freedle. Norwood, NJ: Ablex. 137–81.

Tierney, Robert J., and James H. Mosenthal. 1983. "Cohesion and Textual Coherence." *Research in the Teaching of English* 17:215–29.

Trimbur, John. 1985. "Collaborative Learning and Teaching Writing." *Perspectives on Research and Scholarship in Composition.* Ed. Ben W. McClelland and Timothy Donovan. New York: MLA. 87–109.

Tryzna, Thomas. 1983. "Approaches to Research Writing: A Review of Handbooks with Some Suggestions." *College Composition and Communication* 34:202–07.

———. 1986. "Research Outside the Library: Learning a Field." *College Composition and Communication* 37:217–23.

Updike, John. 1980. "Still of Some Use." *The New Yorker* (6 Oct.) 52–54.

Vonnegut, Kurt. 1973. *Breakfast of Champions.* New York: Dell.

Wallerstein, Immanuel. 1974. *The Modern World-System: Capitalist Agriculture and the Origins of the European World-Economy in the Sixteenth Century.* New York: Academic.

Watson, Robert I. 1963. *The Great Psychologists.* 4th ed. New York: Lippincott.

Widdowson, H. G. 1978. *Teaching Language as Communication.* Oxford: Oxford UP.

Williams, Joseph. 1981. *Style: Ten Lessons in Clarity and Grace.* Glenview. IL: Scott.

Williams, Raymond. 1983. *Keywords: A Vocabulary of Culture and Society.* Rev. ed. New York: Oxford UP.

Willis, Paul. 1979. *Learning To Labour.* New York: Columbia UP.

Witte, Stephen P., and Lester Faigley. 1981. "Coherence, Cohesion and Writing Quality." *College Composition and Communication* 32:189–204.

Woolf, Virginia. 1977. "Herman Melville." *Books and Portraits.* New York: Harcourt.

Young, Richard, Alton Becker, and Kenneth Pike. 1970. *Rhetoric: Discovery and Change.* New York: Harcourt.